THE UNITED STATES OF AMERICA

THE UNITED STATES OF AMERICA

A HINDU'S IMPRESSIONS AND A STUDY

BY

LAJPAT RAI

GYAN

Published by

GYAN

Gyan Publishing House
5, Ansari Road
Daryaganj, New Delhi-110002
Phone: 011-47034999, 9811692060
E-mail: books@gyanbooks.com

Distribution Network
gyanbooks.com
India, USA, Canada, UK, Australia, France

ISBN: 978-81-212-7991-8 (PB)
First Published, 1916

2nd Impression 2023

Printed at: Gyan Press, Delhi.

THE UNITED STATES OF AMERICA
Author: LAJPAT RAI

LALA LAJ PAT RAI
(From an oil painting in possession of Mrs. C. H. Rieber, Berkeley, California.)

THE UNITED STATES OF AMERICA

A HINDU'S IMPRESSIONS AND A STUDY

BY

LAJPAT RAI,

AUTHOR OF "THE ARYA SAMAJ,"
"THE STORY OF MY DEPORTATION," &c.

ILLLUSTRATED

CALCUTTA
R. CHATTERJEE
210-3-1, CORNWALLIS STREET
1916

PREFACE

My first trip to the United States was made in 1905, but it was a very short one, as I could not spare more than three weeks for a stay in the country. This time, however, I have travelled almost all over the country, from Boston in the North to New Orleans in the South, thence to Chicago and then to the West. It is needless to say that the trip has been extremely interesting as well as instructive. The country is beautiful, grand, and up-to-date, according to the best standards of modern life. The buildings are magnificent and everything else, too, is on the grandest possible scale. In several respects the country is much more interesting than any in Europe. But it is not the purpose of this volume to describe either the natural or man-created beauty of the land, but to embody the results of my studies in certain of its problems. My selection of subjects for particular study has been made with an eye to their practical usefulness for our own development. In several respects, the problems of the United States are very similar to those that face us in India, and I have thought that an account of them and of the manner in which they have been dealt within the United States might be of some help to us in India. The manuscript was completed, with the exception of two chapters on the history of the United States and the woman movement, in June, 1915. At the time of writing this preface I have not the manuscript before me and do not propose to say anything more on the subject matter of the book.

My chief duty now remains to express my indebtedness to those good friends and acquaintances who made my path easy. It was quite suddenly that I left England (in November 1914); consequently I could not obtain very many letters of introduction for the United States from friends there. But the few letters given to me by my valued friend, Mr. Sidney Webb, proved of incalculable value, for which I am very grateful to him. One of these letters was addressed to Professor Seligman of the Columbia University, New York. Professor Seligman introduced me not only to the members of the University Faculty, but also to many other ladies and gentlemen, prominent in the various departments of life in New York, in the study of which I was particularly interested. Throughout my stay in New York he was my main stay. Through him I came to know Professor H. R. Mussey, whose friendship I consider to be one of the valuable fruits of my visit to the United States. Similarly my acknowledgments are due to Professor Felix Adler of the Ethical Union; to Mr. John Quinn, attorney-at-law; to Mr. & Mrs. J. Keir Hardie, Jr.; and to Mr. Walter Lippmann of the New Republic, for their hospitality and help. In the study of the charity organizations I was particularly helped by Dr. Hart of the Russel Sage Foundation. At Boston I received much help and kindness from Professor J. Woods of the Harvard University and

Rev. Charles Wendte of the Unitarian Association; at Washington from Mr. W. L. Stoddard of the *Boston Transcript*; at Chicago from Miss Edith Phelps of the John Creinen Library. In the study of the conditions and problems of the coloured people in the United States, I was materially helped with letters of introduction, from Dr. Dubois of the *Crisis* and Miss Mary Ovington of New York. At Atlanta, President Hope of the Morehouse College and his wife showed us (I had a friend travelling with me) great courtesy and kindness and rendered material help in the study of the Negro problem in its different phases, and so did Mr. & Mrs. Booker T. Washington at Tuskegee. My best acknowledgments are also due to the heads of the various departments of State in Washington and other places for having smoothed my way to see everything I wanted to see. Amongst these I may specially mention Secretary Lane of the Interior Department, General Macintyre of the Insular Office, Assistant Secretary Mr. Smith of the State Department, Mr. F. Lewis Post of the Labour Department, Miss Julia Throp of the Children's Welfare Bureau, the Commissioner of Indian Affairs, the Commissioner General of Education, and also the Director of the Smithsonian Institute. Nowhere in the world have I found officials of State so courteous and obliging and so easily accessible to the public and the traveler as in the United States. At Chicago our stay was made pleasant by Mr. John Arnold of the First National Bank of Chicago, and in California by Prof. and Mrs. Rieber and Prof. and Mrs. Pope of the University of California and by Prof. Morse Stephens, who introduced me to President Wheeler. I cannot speak sufficiently warmly of the friendship and kindness of the Riebers and the Popes. I must not omit to mention the help and courtesy which I received from my own countrymen and country-women everywhere I went, particularly from the different chapters of the Hindusthanee Students' Association and their American sympathisers. In the end I have to acknowledge my thanks to Miss Frieda Hauswirth, a graduate of the University of Stanford, for having written for me the chapters on the history of the United States and the woman movement, and also for having generally helped me in preparing the manuscript for the press. But my greatest thanks are due to Babu Ramananda Chatterjee, Editor of the *Modern Review*, Calcutta, for reading all the proofs and seeing the book through. But for him, perhaps the publication of the book might have been delayed indefinitely.

BERKELEY, CALIFORNIA, U. S. A.
March 25, 1916.

CONTENTS

ILLUSTRATIONS

DR. W. E. BURGHARDT DU BOIS,
Editor, *The Crisis*.

OUTLINE OF THE HISTORY OF THE UNITED STATES OF AMERICA

When in the 14th century, the Osmanly Turks began to blockade the Mediterranean path of the occidental traders to the East, European nations had to discover new paths to what was then vaguely called "the Indies," or give up all thought of the coveted treasures of the East. In 1492, Christoforo Colombo, in the service of the court of Spain, undertook to discover a westward route to "the Indies,"—China, Japan, India and the Far East. After a most daring journey into the unknown wastes of the Atlantic, he discovered the islands now known as the West Indies, and took possession of them in the name of Spain. The natives he met were savages of a reddish skin and long, straight, black hair, living the tribal life of hunters. He called them "Indians," firmly believing that he had discovered "the Indies." From this and two succeeding journeys he failed to bring back the expected treasures from the fabled cities of gold and ivory of the East, fell into disgrace at court, and died in misery, never knowing that he was the discoverer of a new world. Amerigo Vespucci, another Italian in Portuguese service, discovered the large southern continent, named after him America, a name that was soon extended to the northern continent likewise.

Meanwhile the real Indies had been reached by another sailor, a Portuguese, by way of the Cape of Good Hope, who brought back the wealth Europe coveted. This route took too long, however, and the other European nations began to send their navigators to the New World, still hoping to find a strait that would furnish them a shorter route to Asia. They were after the fabulous wealth of Asia, not after the wild tracts and tribes of America. These early discoverers were fortune-hunters. While engaged in this pursuit Spain conquered a confederacy of Indian tribes in what is known as Mexico. These Aztecs lived in communal houses and it is said that they offered human sacrifices to their gods. In Mexico, Peru, and in the islands of the Gulf of Mexico, the Spaniards built up a great empire by the aid of slave labor. They captured and brought tens of thousands of negro slaves from Africa, and forced them to work under the lash in the fields and in the silver and gold mines which they discovered. For some time fabulous wealth flowed into the treasury of Spain.

Up to the beginning of the 17th century, America north of the Gulf of Mexico was still completely in the hands of the Indians. When the nature of this land became better known, it became evident that it would have to be settled for agricultural purposes mainly. This put an end to adventurous exploration and a new type of men began to stream into America ; men willing to meet the hardship of turning wilderness into cultivated and settled homes ; men of a more democratic, hardier type. Most sea-faring European nations were eager to colonize. They fairly tumbled over each other to grab land in the West. These powers never dreamt of the possible right of the native Indian to the land of his birth. Wherever the white men had first come into contact with the red man, he had been received with great friendliness, but the treachery and cruel treatment with which he treated the red man, soon turned the latter into his bitter enemy. The Indian was far inferior to the white man in warfare and culture, and existed for him only to be brushed out of the way. The invaders took no notice of the native except when their advance forced them to meet and crush him in bloody and unequal battles, or when they could use him as a tool against rival nations. These powers never scrupled to make alliances with him and to break them according to their interest, and it is an undisputed fact that they whipped up rivalry and hatred between the different tribes for the sole purpose of having them fight and exterminate each other to make the work of advance easier for the white man.

Sweden settled posts on the banks of the Dalaware ; the Dutch settled on the shores of the Hudson River, building the town of New Amsterdam ; France took possession of the St. Lawrence in the North and of the Ohio and the Mississippi valleys further south ; Spain was master in Central America, Florida and Peru ; England settled on the eastern coast of North America.

The English king gave charters to different companies, granting them specified lands to settle on. The London Company formed the "Virginia Colony" ; the Plymouth Company and the Massachusetts Companies settled farther north, in the region called "New England." Fearful hardships were encountered by these early colonists. For instance, in Virginia, the earliest English colony, the "starving time" of 1609-1610 reduced a total of 600 men in October to only 60 in the following June. In 1619 this colony received a shipload of maidens from the Home Company in England, to be sold to the settlers as wives in exchange for tobacco. This marked the foundation of the first English homes in America. Two other important events marked this same year: the first ship-load of negro slaves arrived in the colony, and the first representative assembly convened on American soil,—the foundation of slavery and of democratic government.

The English Colonies.

On the coast settled by the Plymouth Company, there landed in 1620 the "Pilgrims", men and women who had separated from the Church of England because they objected to its empty formalism and its corruption. They fled from strong persecution in England to seek freedom of worship in the New World. They arrived without a charter and without a right to the soil, pledged themselves to self-government, and exercised a tremendous moral influence on later American history through their bravery and love of liberty.

The Massachusetts Company consisted of "Puritans", who likewise objected to the corruption of the Church of England, but intended to purify it from within. These Puritans, the "aristocracy of righteousness", admitted only "free men" (members of the Puritan churches) to a share in the Government and to the vote. A curious British trait began to manifest itself early: those who shortly before had contended for their own freedom from religious domination, began to deprive other colonists, who did not conform to their demands, of their franchise and their liberty. This naturally caused strong protests from the more liberal spirits and a new emigration of dissenters started, this time away from the parts first colonized. These separatists formed new settlements, and became remarkable for their spirit of democracy and religious freedom. Government was "held by free and voluntary consent of all the free inhabitants." The Massachusetts colony, however, continued its reign of despotism and fanatic cruelty against all dissenters, hanging Quakers and women for witchcraft. In matters of government, this colony, when king Charles I. entered on the despotic period of his reign, quietly removed its charter to America, and later refused to surrender it. The colony disregarded the laws of the king, at one time drove out his governor, ignored the collectors of revenue, and by so doing finally lost its charter and became a Royal Province.

The various colonies had little community of interest and no concerted action. Thirteen colonies altogether were formed under three different forms of grant from the government: (1) Virginia and Massachusetts were corporate (later royal) colonies,—charters given to companies of men under royally appointed governors; (2) Self-governing colonies,—the offshoots of Massachusetts colony, such as Rhode

Island and Connecticut; (3) Proprietorships,—land granted to single men or small groups of men. In the royal provinces the king himself, through his Privy Council, appointed governors, established courts, collected taxes and carried on the executive government. In the self-governing colonies the people elected their own governors and other officers, both civil and military, controlling them through the democratic legislatures. In the proprietary provinces the proprietors appointed the governors, established the courts, collected taxes, but remained always subject to the limitations imposed on them by their charters.

The king's interference with and control over the colonies steadily tended to increase until all were on the verge of being turned into royal provinces. Only two colonies escaped such control. England held the firm belief that the colonies existed for the advantage of the mother country. It forced Navigation Acts upon them, which seriously restricted their trade by forbidding them to sell or buy directly in the markets of Europe, and hampered their manufacture by forbidding competition with the mother country.

Learning was early and carefully fostered in New England and the public school system was made compulsory. Harvard University was established as early as 1726 and before 1754 seven colleges were founded. In 1690 the first newspaper appeared and was immediately suppressed by the government, but in 1734 the freedom of the press was guaranteed by court decision. In 1710 the British postal service was introduced into the colonies. It was not likely that a liberty-loving people, enjoying such advantages and feeling independent because of the great distance separating them from the mother country, would submit to much unfair treatment without opposition.

As the colonies became more settled, social life sprang up. In this, a marked contrast early developed between the southern and the northern colonies. The southern colonies, remarkably adapted to cotton growing, had almost from the very start followed the Spanish example, in that African slaves worked on large estates managed by the white master. This condition, where neighbors lived far apart, created a feudal order of society in which the few white owners lived sumptuous, aristocratic, indifferent lives. The South did not bother much about intellectual pursuits and did not establish a public school system until the latter part of the 18th century. The North, however, settled by men who tilled their own soil and started their manufacture and trade by the toil of their own hands, tended to be frugal, bigoted and sturdy. These manufacturing New England sections became much more closely settled, a fact which tended to foster the democratic spirit and intense interest in public matters and politics.

Conflicting Interests.

Early, therefore, it became apparent, that there were great conflicting interests developing through the settlement of the New World. (1) A struggle for possession was certain between the different European nations; (2) the interests of the colonies were clashing with the demands of the mother country; (3) the northern and southern colonies were developing antagonistic types of civilization; (4) a never-ceasing warfare with the native inhabitants was on.

Clash between European Powers.

The greed and aggressiveness of the European powers soon broke loose. The Spaniards in the South early incited the Indians to attack the English colonies. First, the Dutch forced the Swedish settlements out of existence, and in 1664 the Duke of York appeared in the Hudson with his fleet and forced the surrender of the Dutch colony, whose main town New Amsterdam, was re-named New York. France made strong alliances with some of the Indian tribes and established a chain of army posts extending from the St. Lawrence River to the Gulf of Mexico. France and England were the two greatest rival powers for the possession of America. The two powers were evenly matched for the coming conflict. In 1689 the struggle broke out between them, a struggle that was to last through seven wars occupying 60 years, fought in Europe, in India, and in America. The French in Canada incited the Indians to raids of English settlements, and frightful Indian massacres resulted. In the treaty of Utrecht, Louis XIV was forced to cede the territory of Nova Scotia, Newfoundland, and Hudson Bay to England. In 1745 the English colonists seized the fortress guarding the mouth of the St. Lawrence. In 1749 both the French and the English moved to occupy the Ohio valley, which became the centre of the struggle. In 1763 peace was concluded in Paris, by

NORTH AMERICA IN 1989 AND 1763

which France ceded to England all of Canada and the region east of the Mississippi, and to Spain New Orleans and the country west of the Mississippi. England restored Havana and Manila to Spain. This left the English colonies in power in North America and strengthened their position in the impending struggle with England.

The War of Independence.

Two main reasons led up to this struggle : (1) the trade relations, in which the colonies were slighted and severely hampered ; (2) the question of representative government, or the supremacy of Parliament over the colonies. Parliament, steadily growing in power, attempted to exercise it over the colonies; the colonies on the other hand had come to look upon their own assemblies as taking the place of Parliament and considered themselves subject only to the king. Roosevelt, a later President, wrote that the American Revolution was "a revolt against the whole mental attitude of Britain in regard to America, rather than against any one special act or set of acts."

As the colonies were not permitted to compete with English manufactures, but sold raw products to England and in turn had to buy the finished products from England and at higher rates, and as their trade with other nations was likewise restricted, only illicit trade could furnish them with the money required to buy English manufactured goods. After the French war was over, in order to help pay the national debt, England decided to strictly enforce the Navigation Acts, making illicit trade impossible. The British Parliament in addition decided to levy a stamp tax on the colonies. This taxation was intended only to defray part of the expenses of a small standing army in America. All the money raised by the tax was to be spent in America; the measure in itself was fair enough. The colonies, however, rose in violent protest, denying the legality of any taxes but such as were levied by their own assemblies. England realized the seriousness of the spirit of revolt and repealed the Stamp Act in less than a year. The next Prime Minister, however, introduced measures which increased English control in the colonies, and gave orders to levy heavy duties on tea, lead, glass, paper, and printer's colors imported into the colonies. Boston answered by a boycott on British goods and the government was forced to spend 200,000 pounds to collect duties amounting to only 16,000 pounds during three years, where it had confidently expected to collect at least 120,000 pounds. The colonies sent a circular letter of protest to the ministry, but were answered by the dispatch of two British regiments to Boston with intent to intimidate. Boston intensely resented this and it came to conflicts between the citizens and the soldiers. The governor was forced to withdraw the troops and Parliament was cowed into repealing these Townshend duties.

King George, however, insisted that a small tax on tea should be kept for the sake of asserting the right of Parliament to control the colonies. In order to render this less objectionable, he allowed the East India Company to sell its tea to America without paying the heavy English duty. This enabled the company to sell the tea, inclusive of the tax, to the colonists at a lower rate than they were paying for tea smuggled from Holland. The colonists, however, refused to pay the tax in any form, standing firmly on their principle of "no taxation without representation." They did not permit the tea-ships to land in Philadelphia and New York, and in Boston a number of prominent citizens disguised themselves as Indians, boarded the ship and dumped the costly tea into the harbor. For this "Boston Tea Party" the king determined to punish the colonies. In 1774 Parliament passed the "Intolerable Acts," as measures of punishment and revenge. The colonies called "The First Continental Congress," which petitioned the king to remedy 13 acts specified as violating their rights. A Committee of Safety started to collect ammunition, and when the Governor of Massachusetts tried to seize these, the first clash between British troops and colonial militia occurred at Lexington.

A second Continental Congress met in 1775, assumed temporary powers of a regular government, and made formal declaration of war. George Washington was made commander of the militia. On July 4, 1776, a Declaration of Independence was adopted and issued. This "declaration by the Representatives of the United States of America in Congress assembled," stated :

"When in the course of human events it becomes necessary for one people to dissolve the political bonds which have connected them with another, and to assume, among the powers of the earth, the separate and equal station to which the laws of nature and of nature's God entitle them, a decent respect to the opinions of mankind requires that they should declare the causes which impel them to the separation. We hold these truths to be self-evident: That all men are created equal; that they are endowed by their Creator with certain inalienable rights; that among these are life, liberty, and the pursuit of happiness. That, to secure these rights, governments are instituted among men, deriving their just powers from the consent of the governed; that, whenever any form of government becomes destructive of these ends, it is the right of the people to alter or to abolish it, and to institute a new government, laying its foundation on such principles, and organising its powers in such form, as to them shall seem most likely to effect their safety and happiness."

This document declared the English government guilty of destroying those ends, enumerated 27 arbitrary and despotic acts against the liberty of the colonies and declared that the colonies were "Free and Independent States."

At first, the fortunes of war turned against the colonists. Then the tables turned. When Britain found herself forced at Saratoga to surrender 6000 men, it sent an embassy to the American Congress conceding all the rights for which the colonies had contended; but these were no longer after concessions, but complete independence. England then attempted to induce the South to secede from the alliance. Great numbers of loyalists enlisted in the British army and the fight in those colonies took on the character of a civil war. France was supplying the colonists with money and men. Volunteers from all over Europe joined the rebels, sympathizing with their struggle for freedom. Washington's army contained eleven foreign major-generals.

On October 19, 1781, Lord Cornwallis surrendered to Washington at Yorktown,—a victory which ended British claims in the colonies. All the territory east of the Mississipi and south of the Great Lakes accrued to the United States, and England acknowledged the independence of the new republic.

The New Republic.

Thirteen years elapsed between the Declaration of of Independence and the inauguration of George Washington as the first President of the United States. During this time, a powerless Congress made an attempt to govern, but between October 1788 to April 1789 there was absolutely no United States government. Anarchy was imminent.

Finally a convention was called in Independence Hall at Philadelphia in May 1787 to devise a government for the United States. Delegates from the different States submitted and discussed plans for a new government, and the question was whether it should be confederate or national, that is, a national federation or a confederacy of States. The struggle between the advocates of the differing views was bitter and even led to rioting. It was finally decided that there were to be three independent departments, the legislative, the executive, and the judicial. The government, therefore, was to be national, deriving its power directly from the people of the nation at large rather than a confederation, depending for its existence on the will of the various state legislatures. Each State, large or small, was to have an equal number of delegates to preserve their equality of representation in the upper House of Congress (the

Senate), while the members of the lower House (the House of Representatives) were to be elected by the people of the States, each State having a number of representatives in proportion to its population. The members of the lower house were to have control of the public purse, with the sole right to raise a revenue and to levy taxes. The President was made the sole executive of the laws framed by Congress. Congress might legislate on the regulation of currency and coinage, the declaration of war and the direction of military and naval forces, the control of territories and public lands, the care of the Indians, etc. Other matters, such as protection of life and property, creation of town, city and county governments, marriage and inheritance, education, punishment, etc., were left to State governments. Every citizen, therefore, was to live under two systems of law, national and state. The constitution drawn up for the new government was submitted to the various states for ratification and accepted with amendments guaranteeing free speech, a free press, immunity from arbitrary arrest and the right to be tried by a jury of one's peers after a public hearing of witness on both sides.

All States that had Western claims surrendered them to the United States, and all the lands between the Alleghany Mountains and the Mississippi River were made national domain. This land was organized into the "Northwest Territory," placed under a governor and three judges, slavery was excluded from it, free public education introduced, political and religious liberty granted, and provision made to carve the land into States as soon as it should be thickly enough populated. This territorial policy was followed out with all territory acquired by the United States in later years.

From the beginning of the new republic, two factions were politically active, the advocates of federal extension of power and the opponents of "federal usurpation." The South was the slave-holding section and opposed to federal power; the North was free and in favor of the extension of federal power. The South favored agriculture; the North manufacture. The North advocated a union under a strong centralized form of government; the South a confederacy of independent states. These two factions, standing for paternalistic and for democratic government, assumed different designations at different times, but the principles for which they contended remained the same. A high protective tariff imposed on foreign goods and intended to pay the debts of the government, helped the North and harmed the South.

After the war, the need for union and a centralized form of government grew imperious and the Federalists came into power and held the reigns of the government until 1801. Since then, the two factions alternately held sway. The Federalists united the lately freed states, ordered the finances at home by establishing national banks, restored the credit abroad which had been lost during the period of anarchy, encouraged domestic manufacture, and stimulated the foreign trade. The tariff brought abundant revenue into the treasury. The large territory of Louisiana, lately transferred by Spain to Napoleon, was bought from him and doubled the size of the United States. All this served to increase enormously the power of the centralized government.

The War of 1812.

European conditions began to affect the new republic. France and England were still at war. No decade of United States history passed without new provocation of some sort on the part of Great Britain. There was a perpetual quarrel over the rights of fishing off the Canadian coast and over boundary disputes between Canada and the United States. This time, England forbade all neutral vessels to trade with any country under Napoleon's control unless such vessels first touched at British ports. She seized all vessels that violated this order. The French on the other hand seized all that touched at British ports. This meant the annihilation of American trade. Congress also found out that the British had been supplying the Indians with ammunition and inciting them to raids on the Americans. Feeling ran high against Britain and war was declared in 1812. Great Britain repealed the Orders in Council interfering with American trade just at the moment when the President signed the declaration of war, but news did not travel fast enough in those days, and war was on, though England was anxious to avoid it. On land the United States first lost, but was signally victorious at sea, capturing some 2000 British vessels before the end of the war. Andrew Jackson, at New Orleans, defeated the British in a battle of only twenty

The United States in:

1783

1803

1848

minutes' duration, in which 2000 Britishers were laid low on the field. In 1814 war ceased between England and France and with this ceased the cause for war between the United States and England.

Expansion.

An "era of good feeling" followed the war. A strong national consciousness was awakening. The sectional spirit lost strength. National authority was asserted over state authority in several Supreme Court decisions. The country entered upon a period of great prosperity. In her new sense of power, she thought of expansion in the South and West. She disputed the claim of Spain to Florida and moved to occupy it. She had no justification for doing so, but desired the advantage of the coast. The seizure of Florida was nothing less than robbery. At this time Spain also lost her South American colonies (1807-1825). The allied powers of Russia, Prussia, Austria and France intended to aid Spain in restoring her sovereignty over these colonies. President Monroe, eager to see the weakening of European powers in America, recognized these republics and incorporated the "Monroe Doctrine" in the annual presidential message to Congress. It declared that the continents of the Western Hemisphere were "henceforth not to be considered as subject for future colonization by any European powers." It announced the intention of the U. S. government to "consider any attempt on their part to extend their system to any part of this hemisphere as dangerous to our peace and safety." The United States thus checked the thought of increasing their hold in America on the part of foreign powers.

At this time (1832) came the first great American business "boom," which was to collapse, as so many have done since then. It was a period of over-confidence in the country's growth. "Wild-cat banks" issued notes far beyond their real capital in gold and silver and the fever of speculation reached its height in the enormous purchase of Western lands. President Jackson issued the "Specie Circular" demanding gold and silver in payment to the Treasury for the sale of public lands. The "wild-cat banks" did not have the gold and silver to pay for the notes they had issued. Land sales dropped tremendously and nine-tenths of the factories were closed in the eastern states in 1837.

The United States, however, continued in her expansion. Texas was a province of the new republic Mexico. Americans were steadily crossing into Texas until by 1830 there were nearly 20,000 of them in the province. The intent of the Mexican government was to stop American influence in Texas; that of the United States to acquire Texas. Texas was incited to revolt, and set up a republic. After nine years it was annexed to the United States. Over this annexation, war broke out with Mexico. The city of Mexico was captured, California was seized, and New Mexico was occupied by the United States troops. Mexico was forced to cede California and New Mexico to the States and to recognize the Rio Grande as the boundary of Texas; an easy triumph over a far weaker nation.

Between 1830-40, the age of steam dawned. Grain reapers, coal mines, iron smelting, screw propellors for ships, steam locomotives came into use in those days and revolutionized every aspect of the industrial, agricultural, and political world. Far distant places were connected by a few days' travel, where formerly months were required. The greatest hindrance to Western development before the war of 1812 was the lack of roads. It had been unprofitable to raise wheat far from the banks of navigable rivers. Now railroad building became imperative. At this time arose the danger and grave import of letting the opportunity of state erection and control of railways and canals slip out of government's hands. The President praised the spirit of New York State in completing the Erie Canal, 1825; and tried to stimulate Congress by this example to the "accomplishment of works important to the whole country, to which neither the authority nor the resources of any one state could be adequate." But the country was too much split up by sectional interests to prevent the control of these public utilities from getting into private control. Private corporations began to build, own and manage the great railroad systems under charters from the state governments.

After the war of 1812 a stream of immigrants began to pour into the country from the countries of northern Europe. They were of a hardy, fine stock. In 1848, gold was discovered in California. The product of these mines and washings was simply fabulous. Five years after the discovery the gold yield was $65,000,000 in a single year. In fifty years over $2,000,000,000 was taken from the mines. The immigration by sea and land raised the population of the state in the single year of 1849 from 6000 to over 85,000. The West was rapidly becoming settled, and the United States grew by leaps and bounds in wealth and territory.

Political Parties.

The two great opposing political powers, termed Democrats (South) and Republicans (North) developed into concise party machines at this time. Between 1830-40, the national conventions for nominating the candidates of each party for President and Vice-president, and for publishing the declaration or "platform" of the principles of the party took place. As a result of this, officers became the tools of parties, and government offices became the prizes of a war that was fought at the polls. "To the victor belong the spoils" became the ruling principle and government offices became desired for what personal returns they might be made to yield. This was known as the "spoils system." At this time, 1833, a Labor Party made its first appearance and formulated demands for higher wages, shorter hours and more sanitary conditions in shops and factories. This marked the beginning of the struggle between capitalism and labor.

Sectional interests.

The manufacturing North, the wool-growing West, and the cotton-raising South had discovered that their interests were quite antagonistic. The "era of good feeling" was rapidly changing into a period of bitter sectional strife. The rich manufacturers and merchants on the Northern Atlantic coast were consolidating power in their hands. These had retained all the inherited European ideas of distinctions of rank socially, though not politically. A New England aristocracy of merchants was opposed to a planter aristocracy of the South, and the West opposed a rugged pioneer democracy to both. There were about 75,000 large planters in the South in 1850 out of a population of about 5,000,000 whites. Their prosperity was that of a ruling class confined to the few, and not diffused through all classes as in the North. These planters were constantly planting and selling more cotton and buying more slaves and more land, while the majority of the white inhabitants lived in poverty and enforced idleness, seeing the labor market daily more filled with slave labor. Of these whites 15% were illiterate, as there was no free public school system. These forms of civilization in the North and South were irreconcilable. In the democratic, industrial and commercial North, population was rapidly increasing through immigration from Europe. In the South it remained more stationary, though the number of slaves steadily increased. Around 1840 the conflict between the North and the South began to overshadow all other problems of the times. The conflict came to a crisis on two issues; extension of slavery into the newly acquired territories, and the tariff. The tariff of 1824 averaged 36% and was purely sectional. Without manufactures or the hope of such, the South saw itself taxed by the tariff to support the industries of the North. The increase in Northern population constantly increased the majority of the North in the House of Representatives. The South, with but one-third of the votes of the house in its hands, paid over two-thirds of the customs duties.

The Question of Slavery.

Agitation against slavery started from the beginning of colonization. The British Crown had vetoed colonial statutes against slavery, and the British merchants and capitalists were primarily responsible for the slave traffic of the 18th century. Great Britain, at the beginning of the 18th century, demanded as one of the terms of peace with France the monopoly of the slave trade between the African coast and the New World. Queen Anne and her courtiers invested large sums of money in the slave trade. At first slavery was legal in all the colonies, but the Northern colonies soon began to restrict it. The Continental Congress of 1774 and 1776 forbade the further importation of slaves into the colonies, and the North-West territory was made free territory. Already in Washington's time petitions began to pour into Congress for the abolition of slavery in the United States. These continued until the close of the Civil War. An attempt was made to re-colonize free Negreos and a settlement, Liberia, was started on the western coast of Africa. Between 1820-1860 this Society spent almost $2,000,000 and colonized but 10,900 Negroes, less than were born in one month in the United States. This was a well-meant, but most ineffectual remedy, and the country was to pay more dearly for the cruel injustices done to the enslaved race.

It was the question of the growth of the West which became most vitally connected with the question of the extension of slavery. The South needed more slave territory. The crisis over the slavery issue arose not so much as a struggle between the North and the South, but as a struggle of the North and the South over the West. In the North, abolitionist societies began to be formed, carrying on an active anti-slavery propaganda. The South tried to muzzle these through denial of free speech, an attitude which increased greatly the number of opponents. Public discussion brought slavery into prominence from the moral aspect, instead of the purely economic one.

For a time a compromise was reached between Republicans and Democrats through the principle of "squatter sovereignty," a plan of compromise: each territory, when the time came for it to apply for statehood, should decide for itself as to whether it wished to come in as a free or slave state. The Free Soilers, a small party, refused to compromise. The struggle was to become local now. The Free Soilers determined to colonize Kansas with abolitionists and thus secure it as a future free state. The slave-holding Missourians, the neighbor state, resented this attempt and "invaded Kansas" at election times, fraudulently securing the election of a pro-slavery legislature. This led to bloody encounters, a massacre of pro-slavery men on the Pottowatomie river by John Brown; in revenge the sacking of Lawrence, the capital of the Free Soilers in Kansas; and the assault of a senator in the senate chamber. These three attacks occurred between May 19—24,1856. A new governor was sent to Kansas with authority to use the U. S. troops; order was restored, and the political parties awaited in an armed truce the next presidential election, which would decide the issue. In 1860, the Republican Convention met, adopting a platform distinctly opposed to slavery, and nominated Abraham Lincoln. The legislature of South Carolina was in session when the election was announced. It decided to secede. Within six weeks the states of Mississippi, Florida, Alabama, Louisiana, Georgia, and Texas severed their connection likewise.

The resources of the North exceeded those of the South. It could furnish 5,000,000 men to only 1,500,000 of the latter. Civil war was on. The battle of Bull Run, July 21, 1865, was the first great battle of the war; the fall of Richmond, April 3, 1865, where the Southern General, Lee, surrendered to the Northern hero, Grant, terminated the war, after the South had been brought to the point of actual destitution. During this war, Great Britain had again provoked ill-feeling by rendering assistance to the South.

On New Year's Day 1863 Lincoln issued the Emancipation Proclamation which liberated all the slaves in the rebellious states. Lincoln's highest desire was the preservation of the Union.

> "If I could save the Union without freeing any slave, I would do it; if I could save the Union by freeing all the slaves, I would do it. . . Whatever I do about slavery and the colored race, I do because I believe it helps save the Union."

He saved the Union and intended to deal most leniently with the South. He planned to recognize the government of any lately seceded state as legal as soon as 10% of the voters of 1860 should form a loyal government and accept the legislation of Congress on the subject of slavery.

Under his lenient and wise care the South would have recovered quickly. But in April 14, 1865, he was assassinated while attending a play and the South lost in him the best friend. Under his successors, Congress deliberately forced Negro suffrage on the South at the point of the bayonet, and permitted unprincipled politicians to bleed and misrule the stricken South in a manner which it has hardly yet forgotten or forgiven.

Further Expansion and Imperialism.

The end of the war saw national supremacy firmly established. In naval strength the United States rose from the 12th to the 5th position among the naval powers. This marked the beginning of her colonizing period. She occupied the Samoan Islands in the Pacific ocean under a tripartite agreement between Great Britain, Germany, and herself. In 1867, Russia asked her to buy Alaska of her. The distant arctic region seemed to have little value except for its seal fisheries, and the United Sates paid $7,200,000, only about two cents an acre for the huge territory. It has proved immensely rich in its coal and gold deposits. In the Hawaiian Islands American residents first came as missionaries, then as planters and merchants to exploit coffee and sugar farms. The United States took advantage of the revolt incited by a native queen, Liliuokalani, to send a detachment of troops and declare the islands a "protectorate" of the United States. Since then Hawaii has been annexed as a fully organized territory with U. S. citizenship (1900). Cuba had belonged to Spain ever since Columbus discovered the island. In 1895-1898 an especially severe insurrection broke out in the island against the Spanish government. The United States had previously made offers to Spain to buy Cuba, but Spain refused. In the Ostend Manifesto the United States had announced the "right" to seize Cuba if Spain would not sell it. Now the United States eagerly expressed sympathy with the Cuban rebels and both houses in 1898 passed resolutions for the recognition of Cuban independence. The battleship Maine in the harbor of Havanna was blown up. After this provocation the United States demanded the immediate withdrawal of Spain from the island. In the ensuing war between Spain and the United States, Admiral Dewey won a victory over the Spanish fleet at Manila and Admiral Sampson destroyed another fleet in Santiago. This brought Spain to sue for terms. She ceded Cuba, Porto Rico, Guam, and the Philippine Islands. Cuba was organized into a republic after the U. S. pattern and Congress established a protectorate over the island. The United States has done a great deal for the sanitation of Cuba, spending over $10,000,000 for this purpose. In the Philippines, the Filipinos had been in revolt against the tyrannical Spanish government at the same time as the Cubans and the Filipino troops had entered Manila with the victorious Americans. Unlike Cuba, they had a strong native leader, Aguinaldo, who refused to be considered merely as the ally of the Americans and organized a Filipino republic with himself at the head. He prepared to defend it against the Americans. For two years a guerilla warfare was carried on to subjugate the Filipinos. The warfare was unspeakably cruel and sickening. Whole villages of natives were butchered, including women and children. The anti-imperialists accused the administration at Washington of having converted a war which began for the liberation of the Cubans, into a despicable struggle for the enslavement of the Filipino. In the Chinese Boxer rising of 1900, the United States troops aided the other powers to capture Peking. There was no doubt but that, in spite of severe opposition from anti-imperialists, the United States too had entered upon the struggle for colonial supremacy and world trade. The Monroe doctrine, warning European powers away for nearly a century from the Western Hemisphere, had been stretched to let the United States seize possessions in the Eastern Hemisphere. The Monroe doctrine has also been extended in the case of Santo Domingo. Its treasury being bankrupt, in order to satisfy European creditors, the President, Roosevelt, appointed a receiver to manage its financial affairs. Between Great Britain and Venezuela existed boundary disputes. Great Britain refused the proffered arbitration of the United States government. Congress then recommended that it take the decision of the boundary between Guiana and Venezuela into its own hands. The Prime Minister gave way and the United States settled the dispute. All this means, that if this policy be followed out further, it must mean the virtual protectorate of the

United States over all the weaker republics of the South. In the present Mexican revolution, the late President Taft interfered by sending troops to the border, and it is very likely that the United States may ultimately interfere in a still more tangible manner.

As regards the Indians, their frontier had disappeared by 1890. The government had taken every means to break up the tribal organization of the Indians. With the stubborn resistance of the Sioux Indians in Dakota in 1890, the Indian wars, which had lasted since the beginning of American colonization, were at an end, and the native race was almost wiped out. Since then, government has tardily tried to atone for this crime by taking care of the remaining Indians on lands reserved for that purpose. How many Indians originally inhabited North America will never be known; at the present time only about 225,000 are left.

Trust and Politics.

As far-seeing men had long before predicted, the war-debt placed the U. S. Government into the power of the moneyed men. The mines, railroads, oil-fields, iron industry, meat-packing houses had become concentrated in the hands of a few powerful capitalists. J. Pierpont Morgan, for instance, controlled railroads, industries, steamship lines and banks capitalized at about $10,000,000,000. A clique of Wall Street bankers practically governed the country during Grant's presidency following the war. Since then, they influenced the legislation through their "coal senators" of West Virginia, their "iron senators" of Alabama, their "lumber senators" of Montana and the West, their "sugar senators" of Louisiana, their "railroad senators," etc., who were sent through the influence of the trusts into Congress to "protect their interests." Their influence kept the tariff high (40@ average in 1913) to shut out European competition. They received favors and immunities from Congress at the expense of the nation at large, which has made them fabulously rich. Their wealth made it possible for them to influence the judiciary and to secure the best legal talent in the form of "corporation lawyers." Altogether it seemed that government was existing primarily for the purpose of protecting the wealth of these trusts and giving it a chance to grow. It was nothing uncommon for Congressmen to accept large amounts of railroad stock as "presents" from the trusts who desired legislative favors for the roads. The importance of the American industries may be judged from the fact that by the end of the 19th century, the United States mined 230,000,000 of the world's 720,000,000 tons of coal, 257,000 of its 470,000 tons of copper, and 25,000,000 of its 79,000,000 tons of iron. By 1900 about 250 trusts had been formed with a capitalization of over one-twentieth of the total wealth of the United States.

The Republican party, in control after the Civil War until 1884, had become absolutely corrupt and was finally overthrown. Meanwhile the wide gulf between the privileged rich of the country and the laboring classes, between capital and labor, increased enormously. While in government circles a wave of reaction against corruption replaced the "spoils system" by the "merit system" in civil service appointments through a system of competitive civil service examinations, a strong movement for organization developed in laboring circles. The Knights of Labor, organized in 1869 in Philadelphia, counted over 700,000 members in 1886. It declared that "the alarming development and aggression of great capitalists and corporations, unless checked, will inevitably lead to the pauperization and hopeless degradation of the toiling masses." Labor objected to the high tariff which enriched the trusts and taxed the poor in the necessaries of life. In 1886 President Cleveland sent to Congress a special message, the first presidential message concerning Labor in the United States history. This Labor Problem had come to the front, and the administration has had to face it ever since. In 1894, the Pullman Palace Car Company discharged a number of employees and cut the wages of the rest though it was paying 7°/₀ dividends at the time, and had accumulated a surplus of $25, 000,000 on a capital of $36,000,000. The employees struck and prevented the trains from leaving the yards in Chicago. Among these were mail trains carrying Pullman cars. An injunction was issued by the federal courts ordering the strikers to cease obstructing the United States Mails. In answer, riots broke out, and for the first time in the history of the States, the federal troops fired upon American citizens to preserve order. This has been repeated since then in other strikes, and has marked the beginning of the open clash between capitalism and labor.

The old party lines between Republicans and Democrats are being obliterated rapidly, but the coming struggle is that between socialism and capitalism.

The past ten or fifteen years have witnessed the awakening of the American public to the immense seriousness of the problem of monopoly and trust control. A very strong movement has started for the purification of politics and the checking of the influence of money power on government. This movement found its climax in the administration of Colonel Roosevelt. Colonel Roosevelt was a determined opponent of the trusts, determined to curb them. He fought for regulation by the government of all trusts which monopolized the people's necessities of life, such as beef, coal, oil, sugar, transportation. He ordered his Attorney-General to commence over forty suits against railroads or industrial corporations during his terms of eight years. The government lost most of these suits, but the moral effect was tremendous. During his presidency, when a severe strike in the coalfields threatened to bring on a famine of coal during winter, he called together representatives of the organized miners and of the owners of the coal fields, and persuaded them to submit to the arbitration of a commission appointed by himself. This started the arbitration of disputes between capital and labour, through government. Roosevelt advocated trust regulation, labour legislation, direct primaries, an income tax, tariff revision, national preservation. This expresses the tendency of the times concerning government control. In his conservation policy, Congress authorized him to withdraw large coalfields in Alaska from public sale, also large timber-lands in the States, to be held as national property. Through irrigation schemes he turned great sandy waste in Arizona into rich farm-land, adding tremendously to the national wealth. He formed an Inter-State Railroad Commission regulating rates for the public, and did a great deal towards furthering government control and government ownership of public utilities.

In his term of office, the building of the Panama Canal came to the front. Roosevelt bought out the French Panama Company which had gone into bankruptcy. Then he tried to negotiate with Colombia concerning the construction of the canal. Colombia, however, rejected the treaty offered. As a result U. S. gun-boats were sent to the isthmus ; a "quiet uprising," induced by the U. S., took place in Panama, and within a week after this the government at Washington recognized the new republic of Panama. From this it bought a ten mile strip of land and went ahead with government construction of the canal, completed in 1914. Its treatment of Colombia in this matter was new proof of the regard of the United States for the rights of the small American republics.

The American government, state as well as national, is growing more and more democratic ; many states have accepted the initiative, the referendum and the recall, and the nation seems determined to drive business-control out of politics.

Next to the Labor problem, the most vital and interesting problem that faces the United States is its immigration problem. Since the beginning an endless stream of immigrants has flowed to its shores. At first they came from Northern Europe. Of late years' they have started to come from Southern and Eastern Europe, and also from China and Japan, and even India. To this latter immigration tremendous opposition has been developing, ending in the exclusion of the Chinese and the Hindoos from the soil. Their competition in the labor market is not desired. In the South the Negroes form about half the population. The South needs the labor of the Negro, but both the South and the North object to Asiatic immigration. Altogether the country is facing a race problem more serious than any other nation in the world, and no solution has been found as yet.

To sum up : the United States stands to-day with the promise (or curse) of imperialism ahead of her, with the tremendous problems of government ownerships of public utilities, with an imminent war between capitalism and labor, with race problems, and with the question of woman suffrage, the last of which is referred to in another chapter. It is truly "the melting pot" of the different nations of the world, of its social, political, and economic problems, and its past and future history is well worth the watching.

EDUCATION IN THE UNITED STATES.

I think one of the elementary tests by which the civilization of a country should be judged is the importance which it attaches to the national care and education of its mothers and children. Most of the modern States of the West, at least all of them which are considered great now, recognise the national value of the child as distinguished from the value attached to it by the family and the parents. Hence most of them are elaborating laws and framing schemes to facilitate the birth of healthy babies and their development on healthy and sound lines after birth. There is nothing modern in the idea that the child is the father of the man and the citizen. The idea is as old as the world. All the ancient civilizations of the world recognised it and the Hindu *Smritis* (Law-codes) attached great importance to the care and education of the child. The modern world is, therefore, in this respect, at least, following the track laid down for it by the older and more ancient nations of the earth. In Europe and America, the idea is of comparatively recent growth, and it cannot be said that it has reached the height of development it is capable of. In ancient civilizations the need of education was based on religious and spiritual grounds. In the modern it is based on economic grounds. In the former case the guiding motive was the care of the soul : in the latter that of the body, individual and politic. In Europe the idea was first materialised by compulsory school attendance laws. The object was to increase the intelligence and efficiency of the units of the body politic in the material and national interests of the latter. Some years ago the President of the British Association of Science, in the course of his annual inaugural address, remarked that national expenditure on education was even more necessary than that on the Army and the Navy. The safety and efficiency of the nation depended as much if not more on the former as on the latter. The school is the manufactory of a nation. A comparison of the expenditure incurred by the great nations of Europe on education and on armaments will disclose that the colossal growth of the latter has been followed by proportionate growth of the former. One competition has led to the other and very properly too. The object of an efficient Army and Navy *is power to acquire new territories* and *to defend those already acquired*. The ultimate object is wealth and glory. Success in the struggle for wealth and glory depends certainly as much on efficient and thorough training of the mind of a nation as on the training of its body and muscles. Hence the great nations of the West have been vying with each other in their provisions for national education. Germany was the first in the field. Its compulsory school attendance laws are more than a century old and at the present moment it is easily first in its educational activities and equipments. In Prussia more than

16.4 per cent of the population attend school. In all important German cities more than 99 per cent of the children (from 99.2 to 99.93) finish the eighth grade course (i.e., eight years' school course). In the United Kingdom, Scotland was the first in the field of compulsory school attendance and it maintains its first position in educational efficiency. Similarly much has been done in England, Wales and Ireland also, to bring them up to the level of Germany in educational efficiency. The United States has followed suit and to me it seems that the facilities for education in America are perhaps even greater than in the United Kingdom. The educational problem in the United States is rather complicated by reason of the unceasing flow of comparatively uneducated and illiterate immigrants into the country. Yet the educational achievements of America are monumental. In 1913 in a total population of about 97 millions, with an estimated school-going population (of persons 5 to 18 years of age) of about 25½ millions, the number actually in schools was a little over 18½ millions. The development within the last 40 years may be judged from the following figures.

1. In 1877 the population of the United States of America was a little over 46 millions and the number of students enrolled was about 9 millions. In 1913, with a population of 97 millions, the number enrolled was 18½.

2. *Complicated problem*: The educational problem in the United States is seriously affected by the constant inflow of immigrants, by the Negro problem and by the problem of the Indians. School at-

tendance is not yet compulsory in some Southern States where the Negro problem is the largest. The Negro publicists complain that the States do not give them sufficient facilities for educating their children ; the schools are few ; the school buildings inadequate ; the teachers underpaid and overworked : the provision for higher and secondary education almost nil. Similarly the percentage of literacy among the Indians is comparatively low, as they do not take to schools kindly and easily. As for immigrants, the number of immigrants admitted into the United States has been never below 500,000 since 1870. In 1914 it reached the colossal figure of 1,400,000. In some schools in Boston (Massachussets), New York, and Chicago the children of the immigrants speak as many as 25 different languages. In certain factories and workshops in these cities the number of languages spoken is even larger. The workmen employed do not understand each other except by signs and signboards hung up in the premises as warnings or for other purposes which are printed in as many characters as the nationalities that are represented in the factory. Consequently the percentage of illiteracy in these big States is higher than in some smaller States which are not so seriously affected by the annual influx of immigrants; although school attendance is compulsory in these States and the amount of money spent by these States on Public School education is enormous. The State of New York alone, for example, maintains 11,642 Elementary Schools for a total population of about nine million souls. The following table gives the number of educational institutions directly administered by the State of New York :

Elementary Schools	11642
High Schools	948
Universities & Colleges	34
Professional Schools	34
Nurses Training Schools	36
Fine Arts Schools	11
Manual Schools	16
Training Schools	136
Indian Schools	7
Schools for Defectives	10
Business Schools	21
Public Libraries	513
Vocational & Agricultural Schools ...	65

3. Higher Education : The Development in higher education in the United States within the last 40 years may be judged from the following figures:

	1877 A. D.	*1913 A. D.*
High Schools		
Institutions	1340	13445
Teachers	6759	67092
Students	98485	1283009
Universities & Colleges		
Institutions	433	596
Professors & Instructors	4865	19858
Students	66737	202231
Schools of Medicine & Theology		
Institutions	249	411
Professors & Instructors	1799	10019
Students	16422	49081

In 1913 altogether 564,460 teachers (not Professors and Instructors in Colleges) were engaged in the work of School education, of which 451,118 were women.

In 1913 the total expenditure incurred on school education was over 534 million dollars, i.e., 1602 million rupees, or say 160 crores of rupees. This is exclusive of expenditure on College education as well as on education imparted in special or professional or Vocational Schools. These figures do not include schools maintained by private agencies.

The exhibit of the United States Bureau of Education at the Panama Pacific International Exposition, San Francisco, puts the figure of expenditure on education which is under the review of the Department at 800 million dollars, i.e., 240 crores of rupees a year.

There are twenty Universities in the country which spend from a little over a million Dollars (i.e., 30 lakhs of rupees) to about 4½ million dollars (i.e., one crore & 35 lakhs of rupees) each. The annual income of Harvard University in round figures is about 4400 thousand dollars and that of Columbia about 3800 thousand dollars. The number of students who receive instruction in these 20 Universities, omitting the minor ones, ranges from 3225 in the Universities of Missouri to 10884 in the Universities of Chicago. Three of these 20 big Universities are situated in the State of Illinois alone claiming between them over 21000 students. Similarly there are three big Universities in the City of New York claiming between them over 17,000 students. The State of New York alone administers 34 Universities and Colleges (exclusive of Columbia and other privately endowed Universities). These 20 big Universities in the country employ a staff of from 242 to 716 Instructors and Professors *each.* The privately endowed University of Harvard provides for 1052 subject courses and the State University of Minnesota for 1622 subject courses. The figures for higher education given above do not necessarily include the Technological Institutes and the other Vocational and Trade and Industrial Schools maintained by private endowments and private agencies which train and educate hundreds and thousands of students besides those receiving education in regular High Schools and Universities, nor do the figures include the numerous proprietary Colleges and Schools maintained by individuals or Associations for profit.

4. *Sources of funds for education :* The funds for educational purposes are derived from the following sources—

(1) Federal Revenues.
(2) State Revenues.
(3) City Funds.
(4) Private Endowments.
(5) Fees.

The income from (4) in some places far exceeds the amount spent by the first three sources. The Americans are most lavish in making gifts and giving donations for educational purposes, and their gifts amount to millions of dollars.

5. *The responsibility of the State*: But what impressed me most was the responsibility assumed by the Government for the education of every child born in the country, male or female. The co-operation of private agencies, individuals and corporations is welcomed, but that does not relieve the Government of its duty and responsibility. The facilities provided by private agencies only supplement what is being done by the various State and City Governments in the performance of their Governmental duty. For example, there are numerous private agencies in the country for child welfare. Their work begins with the care of *expectant* mothers and extends to taking care of the child till it reaches its majority. The State maintains a children's Bureau as an integral part of its Labour Department whose duty is "to investigate and report upon all matters pertaining to the welfare of children and child life," among all classes of the American people, and which specially investigates the questions of infant mortality, the birth rate, orphanage, Juvenile Courts, desertion, dangerous occupations, accidents and diseases of children, employment, and legislation affecting children in the several States and Territories comprised in the U. S. A. "This Department has nothing to do with the Health Department which is separate. It is maintained by the Federal Government as a Federal Establishment and is in close touch with all child welfare agencies, public or private, Governmental or Municipal in the different States and Territories of the U. S. A. The Federal Government maintains complete statistics

of all children in the country wherever born, with particulars as to their "sex, age, race, nationality, parentage and geographical distribution." The child welfare agencies keep a complete record of children born in their respective spheres of activity and follow them from the date of their birth up to the date of their entering life as adults. These agencies provide for visits to expectant mothers, giving advice and help when needed with a view to the welfare of the child when born. Then after birth, these agencies teach the mother how to take care of the child. Lady visitors and nurses visit the homes and give advice to mothers free, where the family is not in a position to pay. In cases beyond the capacity of the nurse, medical aid and advice of a superior kind is also provided for. Where the child suffers for want of sufficient food or unhealthy surroundings means are found to remedy both. A complete and full history of every child is thus preserved and he is followed wherever he goes and whatever he does till he becomes adult. Before he arrives at school going age he is thus looked after by vigilant eyes and every help is rendered to the parents in looking after his health and in bringing him up. Food, clothing, pure air, recreation, kindergarten lessons, health literature for the mother, medical aid are looked after and provided for. The State and the City recognise these efforts and wherever needed or required supplement them. As soon as the child reaches the school age the State assumes the responsibility for his education. He must attend a public school. The education given to him is free.

Some States and Cities find everything for him free of cost, books, paper, ink, slate, even food in case when he is insufficiently fed at home. During this time the State and the private agencies spare no effort to see that he receives proper education, is properly fed, clothed and housed, and that his physical and moral development is normal and sound. In case of abnormal children, called defectives, special arrangements are made both for their treatment and education. Special agencies have been provided by the State, co-operating with philanthrophic organisations to look after the moral welfare of school going children. There are Inspectors invested with legal powers to watch children in the streets, in smoking and drinking saloons and in similar resorts. When caught they are brought before juvenile courts and treated as parents would treat recalcitrant children. The object is not to punish but to reform. The State makes laws against the employment of children in certain trades and industries or beyond certain hours whenever such employment is considered to be dangerous or detrimental to his healthy (physical or moral) development. There are regularly organised Associations or Leagues whose constant and sole duty is to watch the child labour laws. They keep a vigilant watch over legislation affecting child labour, suggesting measures or amendments or modifications in the interests of the children. Similarly, a close watch is kept on child employment agencies including such needy parents as benefit from the labour of their children. Sometimes children have to be protected from their parents, if the latter would "sweat" them, or would maltreat them, as for example, by employing them in dangerous trades or in immoral vacations or for employing them for a longer number of hours than the law allows or when they neglect to feed or clothe them and so on.

As soon as the child completes his school education he is looked after by the agencies which help him in prosecuting his studies further, in fitting him for some industry or profession, in providing means for the continuance of his studies during leisure hours; in short in placing facilities or opportunities within his reach by which he may further his prospects, make the most and get the best out of himself. Schools and colleges follow their *alumni* in life and help them by advice and otherwise in their careers throughout life.

All this is done by the State or by the State aided Agencies or by Agencies which have the fullest sympathy of the State. The State and the Community recognise that the children of the nation are their best and most valuable asset and that in the wise handling of that asset lies their prosperity; that the State and the Community owe it to themselves that every child should have the best training for the battle of life; that he should have the best possible or the best available training to develop on healthy and sound lines physically, intellectually and morally; in short that he individually should be able to make the most of his life and the State and the Community should also get the best and the most out of him; and that this should be achieved independently of the means and resources of his parents or of himself. The State and the Community recognise that it is the birthright of every child born in the United States to receive all possible help from them towards that end ; that his obligations and duties as a citizen only begin after his birthright has been conceded to him. This leads us to Vocational education.

6. *Vocational Education :* The people in the United States are just now almost mad about vacational education. The idea is to fit every child for some *special* occupation or business in life. The whole superstructure of education is being more and more built up on that supposition. The property and the wealth of a Community depend on the producing power of its members. To provide for the development and increase of this producing power is then the business and duty of the State and the Community. This is done in two ways, i.e., by mechanical improvements and by the improvements of the brains of the nation and by training every child to do the best he or she can in producing wealth. The object is individual prosperity as well as national prosperity. Every one must specialise for some trade or vocation or business or profession. He must definitely know his place in the national machinery and he must fit himself to fill that place to the best advantage for himself and the nation. This is achieved in various ways. First, each child must receive kindergarten instruction. Kindergarten schools are provided for by the State and are free. Then each child is given a certain amount of manual training as a part of his general education. The legs

and hands must get as much training as his mind or memory. Drawing and modelling is a necessary part of each child's education. Then he must receive his elementary instruction in some trade. It may be carpentry, smithing, bookbinding shoe-making or something of that kind in the case of boys; sewing, cooking, domestic economy (including washing table plate, laundry, table laying, attending at table, decorating a house, keeping rooms neat and tidy) in the case of girls. Gardening is taught to both. Mathematics is a part of general education. After completing his eighth grade course every child has to decide or those looking after his education have to decide whether he will prosecute his general studies in the High School and then in the College, preparatory to his having special or technical instruction in the business of his life or whether he will go in at once for the latter. If he chooses the latter course, then he must choose his vocation and join an institution which gives instruction in that vocation. Here he receives both kinds of education, general and vocational, but with special emphasis on the latter. A child entering life after his elementary course, i.e., after only eight years of school life, must remain an unskilled laborer unless and until he learns a particular trade or a particular vocation. Formerly this was mostly done by apprenticeship in different trades. Now it is being done in schools and colleges. The best and the highest interests of the nation demand that the number of children who enter life immediately after finishing the elementary school education should be the lowest possible and that every child should be trained to be a skilled laborer, or an artisan or a handicraftsman. Between the Elementary School educated and unskilled laborer and the highly finished product of Technological Institutes or Universities, there is another class of educational institutions which give specialised instruction to the majority of the nation's boys and girls in different vocations. These are called Vocation, Trade, Business, Industrial, or Agricultural Schools. Every kind of conceivable industry or trade or business is taught in these schools. The Agencies engaged in this work are State, State-aided, and Private. The Federal Government and the different States are spending colossal sums of money in furthering the cause of vocational education. Everything possible is being done to fix it on the mind of the nation. In the Educational Exhibit placed by the Federal Department of Education in the Panama Pacific International Exposition at San Francisco, I found the following exhibited in big capital letters as indicating the mind of the United States Federal Government on the subject :

(1) "The State that fails to educate dooms its children to industrial subjugation to those States that do educate. More than once have nations lost their land for lack of education.

Shall we prepare our children to hold this land ?"

(2) "Shall we equip an Industrial Army ?

The School, the University, the Laboratory and the Workshop are the battlefields of this new warfare. The weapons which science places in the hands of those who engage in great rivalries of commerce *leave those who are without them, however brave, as badly off as were the Derweshes of Omdurman against the Maxims of Lord Kitchener. Shall our children be Industrial Durweshes ?"*

In order to emphasise the need of vocational and industrial education the Congress of the United States has sanctioned the following scale of grants for furthering the cause of vocational education in the country from the Federal Revenues.

(1) Towards the salaries of Teachers and Directors and Supervisors of Agricultural Education in 1916. $500,000

(2) Towards the training of teachers of Agriculture, Trade, Industrial and Home Economic Industries in 1916. $500,000

(3) Towards the salaries of Teachers of Trade and Industrial Schools in 1916. $500,000

In the case of (1) & (3) this grant is increased by $250,000 every year till it reaches the figure of 3 millions in 1924. That figure then becomes an annual recurring figure.

Similarly in the case of (2) the figure is raised to one million in three years and is then to be maintained as an annual figure.

This is in addition to or besides what the States and Cities are doing or are expected to do in the coming years.

Too much of a good thing: Some people are so alarmed at the growing popularity of the Vocational Education as to consider it necessary to sound a note of occasional warning lest too much of a good thing in that line undermines the spirit of democracy which underlies the educational system of the United States. Only the other day Dr. Wheeler, the President of the University of California, an eminent educationist and a man of very great influence and position in the American world made the following remarks in a speech he delivered at the Convention in San Francisco of the State Teachers' Association. He said :

"I am wondering too, whether this most recent zeal of 'vocational training' with all the possibilities of good, may not respond to the spirit of caste and minister to it. As such it surely bears within it the seeds of sin and destruction. Does it propose that the life occupation of a child shall be determined for it early in life? That means that children shall follow mainly the crafts of their parents. It is the old device of monarchial-aristrocratic Europe for committing the young to manual and industrial pursuits. It is the old derailing switch which can be relied upon to shunt the children of laboring classes out into the labor field at the age of 12 and shut them off from the open road to highest attainment, even though they have the talent and the will for it. That is not democracy. It is just the opposite. Democracy is the matter of free opportunity, a fair field and equal chance. The teaching of a vocation to young children, furthermore, does not provide them with an equipment which will be available in the handicraft and industries of real life. It is misleading in making them think it does. The instruction of later years is another thing."

"At the very heart of present day belief in education is our people's faith in the common schools. They have developed *pari passu* with our democracy. Our people are persuaded that the maintenance of our peculiar institutions of popular government is dependent upon their existence, and the full and successful working of these institutions upon their efficiency."

7. *Some special features of the American system*: There are some special features of the American system of education which require mention.

(1) In the United States there do not exist any special schemes for the sons of the wealthy people. In this country there is no aristrocracy of birth. I mean, no recognised aristocracy. The United States Government confers no titles. But it is not in the nature of things that there should be no grades among men. The United States have men, who are possessed of fabulous wealth. Its Rockefellers, Carnegies, and Morgans can purchase Empires. Yet their sons are educated in the same schools in which the sons of the ordinary day laborers learn their A B C. The expression "public school" carries a different meaning in this country from what it does in the United Kingdom. The English Public School is meant for the sons of the aristocracy—meaning thereby the aristocracy of birth and the aristocracy of wealth. Etons, Harrows, and Rugbys are the places reserved for the education of the sons of the aristrocrats. Their expensiveness alone excludes the possibility of a commoner's son receiving education therein. In the United States a public school means a school open to all classes of the public and maintained from public funds, where all grades of American society receive their instruction in the three Rs. The only special classes of schools, are the schools for the children of Negroes, for Indians, for Defectives and the religious schools maintained by sectarian organizations.

(2) Another special feature of the American

system is that a very large part of the school education is in the hands of women. Most of the grammar schools, i.e., the eighth grade Elementary Schools, are almost exclusively staffed by women. Even in the High Schools the women are on the whole in a majority. Out of a total of 564,460 teachers employed in schools 451,118, or over four-fifths are females. Some people object to this preponderance of females in the teaching profession. A German Professor at the University of Harvard thinks that this is likely to affect the manhood of the nation. He seems to think that large or almost exclusive contact with women in the most impressionable part of a boy's life is likely to make him softer than is desirable in the larger interests of the nation. So far there are no signs of any lack of sternness in the manhood of the nation ; on the other hand, signs of sternness and vigour are clearly visible in the womanhood of the country. There can be no manner of doubt that the women are the best teachers for young children. They know how to win their affection and esteem. They enforce obedience by love. The discipline maintained or enforced mainly by fear of the rod brutalises as well as degrades human nature. We find ample evidences of that in India.

(3) The American boys and girls study in the same schools and colleges from the kindergarten upwards. This is again a matter on which there is some difference of opinion among educational experts. The preponderance of opinion, however, is in its favor. At every University where I have

been, I have made that a special point of investigation. I have been assured everywhere that the mixing of girls and boys in the same classes tends to refine the manners of the boys and adds to the dignity of the girls ; that it inculcates habits of self-control in both ; and that it adds to the pleasure of studies. The United States perhaps stands alone in the great countries of the West in the extent and the manner of enforcing this practice and I do not think there is any ground for saying that sexual relations are more loose or undesirable in the United States than in Great Britain or Germany. The United States certainly turns out a larger number of lady University graduates than any other country in the West and the women of the country make a material contribution to the wealth, prosperity, and the culture of the country. In fact, so far as the last is concerned, one begins to feel that the woman is the greater contributor of the two. The social and philanthrophic activities are mostly guided and controlled by women. The head of the Government Bureau foı the Welfare of Children is a woman—a very able and very sweet woman. Similarly, religious and ethical activities are mostly in the hands of women. Men are generally busy in making dollars. The women also contribute their share in that business, but religions, ethics, charity, social science, and philanthropy are very largely dominated by women. The founder of the Christian Science Church is a woman and that church is very powerful and influential in this country. Most of the heads of the social settlements in New York, Chicago and other places are women. In the Theosophical and Vedanta movements also it is women who take great interest. Among the writers on the question of the day one finds a good number of women. In the libraries, in lectures, and other centres of culture one finds a preponderance of women. The prohibition movement owes a great deal to the influence of women and so does the movement for the segregation of prostitutes and the abolition of the "red light" districts. In short the women play a great and a noble part in the life of the country, and this in spite of the fact that a very large number lead a frivolous and a purely gay life. But in this respect men are no better than women. That is due to general social conditions.

(4) That the American educational institutions are centres of social life. School buildings are freely used for social functions and public recreations, and the various States and City Councils take special interest in developing such a use of school and college buildings. The school gymnasiums and play grounds are open to the public on certain terms and under certain conditions such as may not interfere with their use by the school children. The halls and other parts of the buildings are freely lent for lectures, recitations, concerts, dances and other similar functions. The provision for public recreations is considered to be an important duty of the Education Department and it is expected to report on the progress of the social movement from year to year. I intend to describe in detail what is being done in that respect in one city as an instance of the

interest that is being done in the matter by public bodies.

(5) The games which are most popular in American schools and colleges are even more risky and dangerous than those prevailing in England. Some of them resemble very much the games that were popular in rural Punjab in pre-British days. Inter-school and inter-collegiate games and competitions constitute a very important item of American life and attract hundreds of thousands of spectators, may be millions, at times.

(6) The American schools and colleges give every possible encouragement to self-supporting boys and girls. The authorities take interest in them and allow them to complete their education by instalments. For example, a student may work for six months to earn money in order to enable him to study the next six months and so on. Thus a very large number of students prosecute their studies, who, otherwise, would never have been educated. The students are given jobs in the schools and colleges to earn their board and tuition fees, where the latter is charged; they are paid for work done in workshops; they attend at table at dinner time; they sweep and clean rooms; they work on playgrounds and in the garden, etc. The best part of this is that such students are not looked down upon either by the staff or by their fellow students. The fact of their doing some menial jobs in order to earn their tuition fees, in no way interferes with their activities in the school, on the playground or in social functions. Their position among their fellow students depends solely on

their personal merits and not on the position of their parents.

(7) But the very best part of the American Educational System is the government of the students. All schools and colleges are little republics in which the internal affairs of the student community are governed and administered by officers selected by themselves. Every year the students of each Department elect their officers and also a council which regulates all matters relating to discipline. All complaints of misconduct or misbehaviour are reported to them and their decisions are reported to the head of the Department for necessary action. Theoretically, the Head of the Department may or may not act on the recommendation of the students' council but in practice he *must*. The President of a University or a College can interfere with a decision of the students' committee no more than the King of England can with the decision of the Cabinet. As I am writing, an instance of this kind has just happened in the University of California. The Students' Committee has convicted a student of an attempt to steal and has recommended his expulsion. The student has appealed to the President for a *re-hearing*. The President has told him to put in his appeal. Several Professors told me that the President can not set aside the decision of the Committee. He, however, in consultation with the faculty which consists of the whole body of Professors and Assistant Professors in the Department, may recommend a rehearing, if he thinks that the case deserves a reconsideration.

(8) Another special feature of American institutions consists in the personnel of the Controlling Agencies. Every University is controlled by a whole-time President, who is a paid officer and attends college just as other Professors do. The University is managed by him in consultation with the faculty but in most matters his decision is final. He in his turn is controlled by a Board of Council of Trustees in the case of private institutions and by a Board of Management in the case of the State institutions. The Presidents of the American Universities wield the greatest possible influence on the public life of the country. The present President of the United States is a late President of Princeton University. Under the University President are Deans of the different faculties and the Heads of Departments. Most of the Deans are whole-time officers who do no teaching ; the Heads of Departments, however, take classes. Each subject constitutes a separate department, for example, the Department of Political Science, the Department of Sociology, the Department of Chemistry, of Agriculture, of Mining and so on. The Heads of schools are called Principals. Very few Principals, if any at all, do teaching work. The whole of their time is devoted to personal relations with the teachers and the students, to co-operation with the parents in looking after and advancing the interests of the students both in and out of school, to seeing visitors, to creating interest in the school in the community and to general administration.

A typical Recreation Department: I propose to

close this chapter by an account of the activities of the Recreation Department of the City of Oakland, California. This will show what interest the State takes in the physical development of its citizens and its children.

Recreation Department, City of Oakland, California: Oakland is known as a city of homes, schools, churches, factories and commerce, but when the day's work is done her citizens may turn to abundant opportunities for pleasure and recreation.

The average adult has from six to eight hours per day of leisure time. That is, one-fourth to one-third of one's lifetime. A large part of this time is given over to amusement, recreation and play of various sorts. Children spend an even greater part of their time in this way.

Healthy and normal play and recreation make for better and more efficient citizenship. Play is the important and vital part of a child's development, and some form of recreation is also necessary to the adult if he is to achieve his maximum-power. Even the old horse when turned out to pasture, plays and frolics and returns to work with renewed ginger.

Oakland may well be called the City of Playgrounds. The Oakland Recreation Department maintains thirty-eight playgrounds and recreation centers the year round. Thirty of these are school yard playgrounds and eight are large park recreation centers. In addition to the playgrounds for children, many sports and pastimes are provided for the adults. The recreation grounds are becoming more popular every day. Tennis, baseball, football, volley ball and folk dancing are the favorite sports for grown-ups. Social center buildings are available for club meetings, lectures, entertainments and dancing. Each recreation center or playground is in charge of trained supervisors whose duties are to lead and protect the children in their play and to promote and organise games, sports and other activities for all patrons of the grounds.

All of these opportunities are under the management of the Board of Playground Directors and are free to the public. Good behaviour is the only password. The following are some of the principal activities to be found in the recreation grounds:

Athletics: Both informal and organized athletic games of all kinds are provided on the playgrounds. A number of baseball leagues are conducted and any boy who wishes to may engage in the national game. There are ten public courts in Oakland, which receive constant use during the leisure hours of the people. The courts are frequently used for exhibition and match games by expert players.

Several basketball courts are provided at each playground and leagues organized in which as many as five or six teams are entered from a single playground. Volleyball is a new game but during the past year has become very popular, During the fall season football is given much attention.

Field and track meets are frequently held during the spring season. Classifications, and events, are provided in the above sports so that any amateur may enter, regardless of age.

The following is the yearly athletic schedule of the

Oakland playgrounds. Participation in these events is open and free to all :

Section 1. The games, sports and athletic events on the playgrounds shall be classified as follows:

(a) Major Sports—Baseball, track and field meets, soccer football, swimming, tennis, volley ball, German bat ball, hand ball.

(b) Minor Sports—Basketball, rugby football.

Contestants in the minor sports shall be classified according to weight; while contestants in major sports shall be classified as follows:

Bantams:	12 years of age; 4 ft., 10 in. in height.
Midgets:	13 years of age; 5 ft., in height.
Intermediates:	15 years of age; 5 ft., 5 in. in height.
Juniors :	17 years of age; 5 ft., 10 in. in height.
Seniors :	Under 21 years and no height qualifications, or older by agreement.

Section 2. Playground games, sports and athletic events, in accordance with the seasons, shall be played as follows:

1. Spring sports shall start the 15th of March and end with the close of school, and shall include:

Baseball: To begin the first Saturday in April.

Individual athletic tests: to be conducted from March 15th until the holding of the track meet.

Track meet: to be held in the latter part of April.

2. Summer sports shall start with the beginning of the summer vacation and end with the opening of school.

Baseball.

Tennis tournament.

3. Fall sports shall start with the opening of

school and close with the beginning of the Christmas vacation.

Swimming meet—Last Saturday in August.

Handball tournament—September 1st.

Rugby football—September 1st.

Basketball—For the 80, 95, 110 and 120 pound classes to start October 15th.

4. Winter sports shall start with the Christmas vacation and end March 15th.

Soccer football.

Basketball for the 130, 145 and unlimited classes.

This schedule applies to the large formal leagues only. Literally hundreds of other varieties of games are played all the year round.

Gymnasium. Outdoor gymnasium apparatus is provided on nearly all the playgrounds. Here the supervisors instruct on the rings, bars and in tumbling, wrestling, etc.

Manual Training. On several of the recreation grounds opportunities for boys' and girls' occupation work are offered. Model building, clay modelling, basketry and raffia are the principal branches taught.

Small Children's Department. Supervisors are required to teach a great number of circle, singing and running games for the benefit of small children coming to the playgrounds. Story-telling hours are occasionally held when professional story-tellers from the Oakland Library Department come and entertain the children with tales of adventure, fairies, and folklore. The sand box is always in evidence and is well patronized by the little tots.

Folk Dancing. Folk dancing is an important

department for girls and small children. Almost every day on each playground classes are held and the children learn to dance the folk dances of the old and new world.

Clubs. A favorable method for handling groups on the recreation grounds is by organizing them into clubs for various purposes. There are outdoor women's clubs for the mothers, older sisters and friends of the children, groups of Campfire Girls for girls between twelve and eighteen years of age, Blue Bird groups for girls under twelve, boys' clubs formed for numerous purposes, and dramatic clubs.

The clubs are organized with a president, secretary and various committees and are responsible for their own activities with such assistance as may be given them by the supervisors.

Any person may join a club by vote of the members, or new club may be organized when a large enough group is formed.

Field Houses. The field houses on the various playgrounds are equipped with shower baths, dressing rooms, toilets, lavatories and lockers. Clean towels are supplied for the shower baths. There is also maintained on each playground a supply of athletic materials, such as baseballs, footballs, basketballs, bats and games. These supplies are issued to the patrons very much in the same manner as books are issued from the Public Library, except that all supplies must be used on the playground and must be returned before closing time each day. All these facilities are free to the public.

Recreation Center Buildings. Several recreation center buildings are maintained by the department and are equipped with halls, game rooms, committee meeting rooms and dressing rooms. These buildings are used for club meetings, dramatics, entertainments, games and social purposes. Free permits for the use of these buildings may be obtained by any responsible organization which will comply with the rules and regulations.

In the six months of the year 1915 this department maintained 38 grounds, and spent about one lakh and thirty thousand rupees in the maintenance of these grounds and about a lakh of rupees on their improvements. During these six months well nigh seven lakhs of persons attended these playgrounds. The City of Oakland is by no means one of the biggest cities of the United States. Its population is a little over 200,000.

The ideal aimed at can be gathered from the following standard laid down for each locality by the Federal Bureau of Child Welfare and exhibited at the Exposition.

Public play and recreation demand four centers.

(1) Play Retreats for each city block for mothers and children under 7.

(2) Play Centers around grade schools of boys and girls.

(3) Athletic and Game Centers under Public Recreation Department for older boys and girls.

(4) Social Recreation Centers for evening recreation of older people.

Every Government in Europe and America insists

on States and cities making ample provision for public playgrounds and recreation centers. The smallest school has a playground and a gymnasium. Public parks, public baths and public swimming tanks abound in every part of the most crowded cities like London, Berlin, Paris, New York, Chicago, etc. and the Cities and States have spent millions of pounds and dollars in making them and keeping them in good condition, but a Public Recreation Department is perhaps a special feature of American life.

A Warning.

The preceding account of education in the United States might lead my readers to suppose that America must be a paradise on earth, entirely free from sin, poverty, squalour, immorality and physical degeneration. By no means so. So far as sin and immorality are concerned, America has as much of it as any of the community on the face of the earth; poverty and squalour perhaps she has less; physical degeneration perhaps the least. The fact is that considering the elements which make up her population she might be very much worse but for the care she takes in looking after the education, and moral and physical welfare of her children. Her educational system is her saving and well might the other communities of the world take a leaf out of her book if they want to improve the intelligence, the morals and the physique of their people. The children of a nation are her capital and in the *proper* investment of that capital consists her prosperity and life.

There is at least one State in the United States where they have abolished examinations altogether. Students are promoted and transferred from grade to grade, from school to school and from school to University on the certificates of teachers. No examinations are held. Certificates of graduation are, however, issued. I have omitted from this article all mention of education among the Negroes, education among the Indians and education in dependencies. These I propose to deal with in separate chapters.

EDUCATION IN THE UNITED STATES: II

In the last Chapter, I have given some facts and figures for the whole country. In this I propose to supplement the information by a few additional facts and figures for the whole country and then give an account of the educational activities of the City of New York. What is being done for education in the City of New York is with some slight variations being done in all the principal cities of the United States. My object in giving this information is to provide data for the guidance of those engaged in furthering the cause of education in our big cities.

Some more general facts and figures :—

I have before me a publication containing the results of a comparative study of Public School systems in the 48 States of the Union up to 1910.

The first diagram shows the number of children of school age in public schools, in private schools, not in any school, in each State. School age in the United States, is the period between 5 and 18 years. The diagram shows that in some States over 90 per cent of the children of school age attend school. There is only one State in which the figures fall below 60, viz., 55. There are six States where the figure is less than 70.

The next diagram shows the school revenues of each State. The maximum figure is of over 16 crores of rupees raised and spent in the State of New York. There are only 5 States, mostly in the extreme South, where the revenues are less than 30 lakhs of rupees, though nowhere is it less than 17 lakhs of rupees. That was in 1910. Since then much progress has been made in the Southern States as well.

The compiler of the report remarks : "Our expenditures for public education have more than doubled in the past ten years, no other investment produces so large a return. More money means better schools. Better schools mean more efficient citizens. More efficient citizens produce more money." Again he adds : "A free common school education is the common birth right of every American child and this is provided for by the taxation of property without reference to whether the owner has children to be educated or not. American experience shows that school tax legislation should provide

(a) Sufficient local taxation to encourage local pride and initiative,

(b) Sufficient State taxation (provincial revenue) to equalise educational advantages by aiding poorer communities,

(c) A distribution of school funds based both on the number of teachers employed and the aggregate days of attendance of the school children,

(b) The stimulation of progress through additional grants to communities providing such advantages as continuation schools, evening schools, playgrounds, medical inspection.

The third diagram shows the comparative investment made by each State in school plant. This varies from 345 Rs. per child in Massachusets to Rs. 12 per child in Mississippi. The Southern states containing the bulk of the Negroes again show a bad record. There are not more than 10 States altogether where the expenditure per child on school plant is less than 50 Rs. The figure is arrived at by taking the total value of the public schools of a State together with their sites and equipment and dividing that sum by the number of children of school age in that State. So the value of school plant shown in the diagram does not represent per child in school. That would necessarily be higher in States where the number of children of school age, not in school, is the largest.

Then comes the expenditure per child of school age. Again note, it is not the actual expenditure per child in school, that would be higher. At the head of the diagram is a State that spends 90 Rs. per child of school age within its borders. At the low end is one which spends 9 Rs. per child.

Then comes information about compulsory education legislation. At present 36 States of the Union have passed laws in favour of compulsory education. In six others education is compulsory only in parts. There are only six States which have made no laws at all.

There are some States which spend from ½ to ¾ per cent of their total wealth (estimated total value of all real personal property in the State) on education.

The average annual salary paid to public school

teachers in the United States as a whole is 485 dollars, i.e., about 1500 Rs. There are hardly any teachers that get much less than 450 Rs. a year, but as compared with the average wages of a skilled and unskilled labourer, these figures are very low.

In 1910 there were only 77 in a thousand illiterates in the United States among persons of 10 years of age or more. In some States the figure is as low as 1·7 or 2 or 3 in a hundred. Only in one State is it higher than 25, i.e. 29. Only in 4 is it higher than 20.

Free Text Books.

In 1910 there were 12 States that supplied free text books throughout their public elementary schools and in most cases in their high schools. In 15 States the laws provide for free books in all except certain districts of the State.

Medical inspection of school children in the United States was begun in Boston in 1894. So rapidly and convincingly did the movement establish itself that it was soon provided for by laws in the more progressive States. Seven States have passed mandatory laws, ten have passed permissive laws and in two States and in the District of Columbia Medical inspection is carried on under regulations having the force of laws.

The movement for the medical inspection of school children is a world-wide movement. Laws providing for medical inspection are needed because extended experience has demonstrated that efficient medical inspection betters health conditions among school children, safeguards them from disease and renders them healthier, happier and more vigorous.

Every such law makes provision for frequent inspection of children by duly qualified school physicians (*a*) to detect and exclude cases of contagious disease, (*b*) to detect any physical defects which may prevent the children from receiving the full benefit of their school work or which require that the work be modified to avoid injury to the child. It empowers school physicians to examine teachers and servants and inspect buildings, premises, and drinking water to insure their sanitary condition. In addition school nurses are provided, because they are the most valuable adjunct of medical inspection and the most efficient link between the schools and the homes.

The main ideas that underlie all this educational activity are thus briefly summarised :

(*a*) *People are more important than things.* The merchant, the artisan and the farmer are more important than the store, the tool, and the plough. So is education more important than any mere pecuniary interest or industry.

(*b*) In the school of the future, compulsory education will spell compulsory health.

(*c*) All children should be trained for, not away from, the economic age in which we live.

(*d*) The object of education is to develop physical health, enhance economic efficiency and increase intellectual vigour.

Education in the City of New York (1913).

(a)

In 1913 the city had a population of about 54 lakhs. It had a population of 13 lakhs between 5 and 18 years of age, 61.11 per cent of which was enrolled in the schools. To what extent the city is growing may be gathered from the fact that in one year its population increased by two lakhs. But while the increase in population was only 3·86 per cent, the increase in Public Schools was 14.97 per cent. The total enrolment in the year was 8 lakhs. Attendance on register for boys 89.77, for girls 89.13 per cent.

(b)

School attendance (not enrolment) according to grades.

Kindergartens	31,396
Elementary Schools	6,29,999
High Schools	45,059
Training Schools	1932
Vocational Schools	985

On the 30th June 1913 there were, besides the above, 81,495 pupils receiving part-time education.

Besides the whole-time and the part-time schools, there are 123 evening schools with an enrolment of 1½ lakhs of pupils and 1988 teachers. Then there are 3 summer evening schools for foreigners with 4703 pupils ; 33 vacation schools with average daily attendance of 26898. Besides these the department of public instruction has 217 vacation playgrounds and 56 Evening Recreation centres. The aggregate attendance at the former stood at 60½ lakhs with an average daily attendance of 133,035 pupils and 1853 teachers. At the latter, about 25 lakhs attended with an average daily attendance of 21,399 pupils and 265 teachers.

The Department organised 5398 lectures at 172 centers which were attended by about 11½ lakhs city of persons. The Elementary School Libraries in the of New York alone, have 5,13,300 volumes in Class Libraries and 148,219 in Reference Libraries, over and above 93,234 volumes in High School Libraries.

The superintending and the teaching staff is as below :—

	MEN.	WOMEN.	TOTAL.
Superintendents	33	2	35
Directors of Special Branches	5	4	9
Assistant Directors of Special Branches	3	6	9
Inspectors and Asstt. Inspectors	3	6	9
High School Principals	20	0	20
High School Teachers	869	921	1,790
Training School Principals,	2	1	3
Training School Teachers,	23	86	109
Vacation School Principals and Teachers	11	10	21
Elementary School Principals	217	196	413
Not engaged in teaching Asstt. Principals,	18	441	459
Elementary school teachers	1,133	14,151	15,284
Special teachers of special branches,	148	341	489
Kindergarten	0	848	848
Total	2,485	17,013	19,498

At the end of the year, 20,128 were engaged in the work of teaching in the City of New York.

Notes—Superintendents, Directors, Asstt. Directors, Principals and Asstt. Principals do no teaching work.

The State of New York alone, awards 750 scholarships for Collegiate studies, on the results of High School examinations which are tenable for four years.

Medical inspection of school children is at present conducted by the Health Department, but it is under consideration to establish a separate Department of School Hygiene with a full complement of physicians and nurses. In connection with evening schools special lunch rooms and kitchen facilities have been opened to provide cheap suppers for pupils who come to evening schools for their occupations without having time to go to their homes for an evening meal. Social and recreation centers are maintained in connection with evening schools.

Classes for Defectives.

Special classes are maintained for the training of children who are mentally or physically defective.

These include Mental defectives, Cripples, Blind, Deaf & Dumb, Anæmic and those suffering from Tuberculosis and infectious Eye Diseases. 140 such classes existed in the city of New York in the year 1912-13.

I have already said that school buildings and school gymnasiums are open to the use of the public through social centres, and recreation centres. The following facts and figures will show how and to what extent it is done in the city of New York.

Playgrounds are kept open during the summer months when the regular schools are closed.

In 1912-13, 111 schools allowed their indoor playgrounds to be used in the summer months. Over 37 lakhs of attendances were recorded. Seventy schools were used by mothers and babies. The aggregate attendances figured to over 11 lakhs. Sixteen schools had open-air playgrounds open to the public. Aggregate attendance came to over 3 lakhs. In six Kindergartens the aggregate attendance was 44513 and in 14 evening Roof playgrounds 834,801. In 56 evening recreation centres the aggregate attendance was about 25 lakhs.

What is a Social Centre.

The social centre is managed chiefly by committees of citizens who are not officially connected with the schools, while the recreation centre is exclusively under the jurisdiction of teachers. The recreation centre with its games, athletics, study rooms, gymnastics, folk dancing, etc., appeals chiefly to young people, while the social centre appeals to persons of all tastes and all ages.

Among the many activities of these social centers in 1912-13 were the organisation and training of orchestras, musical clubs, social dancing, *the holding of political meetings by all political parties*, the delivery of lectures to parents on social and economic subjects, the giving of popular concerts, amateur dramatics, the holding of exhibitions and the organisation of all sorts and conditions of clubs for social, intellectual and recreation purposes.

The State also maintains a nautical school for training in navigation. The School was established on board the *Saint Mary*, a ship owned by the "National Government." Several members of the staff of instructors were detached for the purpose by the Secretary for the Navy. Tuition was free, the only expenses to the students being for necessary clothing at the time of admission. The total number of students on roster in 1912 was 102.

Expenditure on Public Education in the City of New York in 1912-13.

The total amount spent was *12 crores* (in rupees). The average cost per capita from General and Special Funds (not including the Bond account) based on average daily attendance was 155 Rs., *i.e.*. about *13 Rs. per child per month.* The average cost in Elementary Schools was 115, in High Schools 315, in Training Schools 468 and in Vocational Schools 279 per pupil.

Note—The per capita cost of supplies alone		
in the High Schools was	Rs.	30
in Training Schools over	,,	36
The per capita cost of a pupil		
in vocational schools over	,,	260
Per capita cost in a Trade School		
for girls was	,,	336
,, in the nautical school was	,,	3000
,, in the evening schools		
Elementary	,,	36
High Schools	,,	90
Vacation Schools	,,	9
Vacation playgrounds	,,	3
Evening Roof ,,	,,	2½
Evening recreation centers	,,	13½
Truant Schools	,,	609

Conclusion.

The information given above relates only to Public Schools. Private denominational schools are not included in it, nor are the Colleges and Universities, of which there are a large number in the city both for boys and girls. It would be seen how vital a part of civic life the Public Schools of New York are and what huge amounts of money are spent on them. If one were to include all that is done for education by the State, the charitable endowments and private benefactions in the city of New York alone, the total cost of education in the city of New York might well nigh come up to very near 25 crores of rupees per year, if not more.

Colleges & Universities—General Statistics.

The total number of Universities, Colleges and Technological Schools in the United States in 1913 was 596.

The total number of Instructors and Professors engaged in them were, men 24,982, women 5,913.

The total number of Students in 1913—men 216,626, women 118593.

Total receipts for educational purposes exclusive of addition to Endowments	93,545,381 dollars or say about 38 crores in Rupees.
The Libraries in these institutions contained	17211649 bound volumes

The buildings were valued at 260,353,851 dollars i.e., over 78 crores in rupees.

Value of scientific apparatus and machinery was estimated at	64,204,619 dollars or say roughly about 20 crores in rupees.
Productive funds in endowments figured at	350,038,287 i.e., over 105 crores in rupees.

To this were added benefactions of 16045474 dollars, i.e., roughly speaking of the value of a little less than 55 crores of rupees in the year 1912.

Over seventy-five of these Universities or Colleges are State institutions on which the States spend millions of dollars every year. Some are maintained out of city funds; others are private or denominational institutions. The total income (from all sources) of the University of Columbia, which is a private institution, is a little over 67 lakhs of dollars (or over 2 crores of rupees), that of Harvard, another private University, is about 90 lakhs of rupees. The University of Wisconsin, a State University, has a similar income. The University of Chicago, another private University, has an income of over a crore a year, and the University, of Illinois, a State institution, above 85 lakhs. Both of these Universities are situated in the same State.

BOOKER T. WASHINGTON.

THE EDUCATION OF THE NEGRO

One of the things that prompted me to pay a second visit to the United States of America, was my desire to study the Negro problem on the spot and to acquaint myself with the methods that are being adopted for the education and uplift of the Negro population of these States.

The Negro is the PARIAH of America. There is some analogy between the Negro problem in the United States of America and the problem of the depressed classes in India. The two cases are not on all fours with each other, but there is a great deal common in both. The social problem in the United States is in some of its phases very similar to the social problem in India. Hence my desire to study it in all its bearings on the spot and to come into contact with the Negro leaders in these States, so as to know their point of view by first-hand knowledge.

In this chapter I do not propose to discuss all the phases of the social problem in the United States of America, nor even those relating to or affecting the Negro. For the present I intend to confine myself to the education of the Negro and to the efforts that are being put forth by Negroes as well as such among the white people as are favourably disposed towards the race. I propose to give a brief sketch of the history of education among the Negroes of the United States of America.

It should be remembered that the vast bulk of the Negroes that are to be found in the U. S. A., were brought here as slaves, or, to be more accurate, their ancestors, who originally came to this country, were slaves. It was after the civil war of 1860 that they were freed and slavery was abolished for good from all the States of the Union. During the period of slavery, literacy among the slaves was systematically discouraged; nay, in some cases it was positively prohibited. For example, in the state of Alabama, the law of 1832 provided that "any person or persons that shall attempt to teach any free person *of colour*, or slave, to spell, read, or write, shall upon conviction thereof by indictment be fined in a sum of not less than $250 (equivalent to 750 rupees) & not more than $500."

Similarly in 1833, "the mayor and aldermen of the city of Mobile were authorized by law to grant licence to such persons as they might deem suitable to instruct for limited periods *the free colored creole children* within the city, and in the counties of Mobile and Baldwin, who were the descendants of colored Creoles residing in said city and counties in April 1803, provided that such children first receive permission to be taught from the mayor and aldermen and have their names recorded in a book kept for the purpose." This signifies that other Negroes besides the Creoles mentioned above were not permitted to receive any sort of education. This exception was made in favor of the Creoles, as set forth in the preamble of the law, because there were many colored there, whose ancestors under the treaty between France and the United States in 1803, had the rights and privileges of the citizens of the United States secured to them.

In Georgia, the following law was enacted in 1829: "If any slave Negro, or free person of color, or any white person, shall teach any other slave Negro, or free person of color to read or write either written or printed characters, the said free person of color, or slave, shall be punished by fine and whipping, or fine or whipping, at the discretion of the court; and if a white person so offend, he, she, or they, shall be punished with a fine not exceeding $ 500 (1500 rupees) and imprisonment in the common jail, at the discretion of the court." In 1833, the city of Savannah adopted an ordinance "that if any person shall teach or cause to be taught any slave or free * person of color to read or write within the city, or shall keep a school for that purpose, he or she shall be fined in a sum not exceeding $100 (300 rupees) for each and every such offence, and if the offender be a slave or a free person of color, he or she may also be whipped *not exceeding thirty-nine lashes.*"

* Even before the emancipation that came about between 1860 and 1865 A. D., there were some Negroes that were free. At that time the colored population consisted of the following classes: (*a*) Negro slaves, (*b*) freed Negroes, (*c*) colored persons who were the offsprings of white people from Negro women, either freed or slaves; these were called Mulattoes (from mule) or colored persons.

In 1828, the State of Florida passed an act to provide for the establishment of common schools, but white children only of a specified age were entitled to school privileges.

In the State of Delaware a law was passed in 1863 against all assemblages for the instruction of *colored* people.

In Kentucky, the school system was established in 1830. In this provision the property of *colored* people was included in the basis of taxation, but they were excluded from school privileges.

By an act of January 1813, the legislature of Mississippi provided that the meeting of slaves and Mulattoes above the number of five at any place or public resort or meeting house in the night, or at any school house for teaching, reading, or writing in the day or night, was to be considered an unlawful assembly.

The legislature of Missouri in 1847 provided that no person should teach any schools for Negroes or Mulattoes.

In 1740 South Carolina enacted "that all and any person or persons whatsoever, who shall hereafter teach or cause any person of color, slave or slaves, to be taught, or shall use or employ any slaves as scribe in any manner of writing whatever, hereafter taught to write, every such person or persons shall for every such offence forfeit the sum of £100 (1500 rupees) current money." In 1800 free colored people were included in this provision. In 1836 it was provided that "if any person shall hereafter teach any slave to read or write, or cause or procure any slave to be taught to read or write, such person, if a free white person, upon conviction thereof shall, for each and every offence against this act, be fined not exceeding $100 and (suffer) imprisonment not exceeding six months; or if a free person of color, shall be whipped not exceeding 50 lashes."

Similar punishment was also provided for all free persons of *color* or slaves keeping schools or places of instruction for teaching any free person of *color* or slave to read or write.

Similarly the general assembly of Virginia, in 1831, declared that "all meetings of free Negroes or Mulattoes at any schoolhouse, church, meetinghouse, or other place for teaching them reading or writing either in the day or night, under whatsoever pretext, shall be deemed an unlawful assembly."

I have picked out a few of the typical Southern States, where slavery existed until the war of emancipation abolished it. In the Free States of the North, the Negro had a "more picturesque and exciting educational experience. The Northern States did not expressly forbid the education of colored persons, but the hostility to such movements is attested by many a local outbreak."

"It was amid such dangers and difficulties," continues Dean Kelly Miller of the Harvard University in his book of Race Adjustment, "that the Negro began his educational career. It must not be for a moment supposed, however, that the laws above referred to were rigidly enforced. It is known that the pious and generous slaveholders quite generally taught their favorite slaves to read, regardless of the inexorable provisions of law. Quite a goodly number also learned the art of letters somewhat after the furtive method of Frederick Douglass; in the cities, schools for Negroes were conducted in avoidance, connivance, or defiance of ordinances and enactments." The account of how Douglass learnt the art of letters is so interesting that I cannot resist the temptation of giving the following long quotation from his autobiography. He says:

"The most interesting feature of my stay here (in Baltimore) was my learning to read and write under somewhat marked disadvantage . . . My mistress, checked in her benevolent designs towards me, not only ceased instructing me herself, but set her face as a flint against my learning to read by any means.

"She would rush to me with the utmost fury and snatch the book or paper from my hand with something of the wrath and consternation which a traitor might be supposed to feel on being discovered in a plot by some dangerous spy. The conviction once thoroughly established in her mind, that education and slavery were incompatible with each other, I was most narrowly watched in my movements. If I remained in a separate room from the family for a considerable time, I was sure to be suspected of having a book and was at once called to give an account of myself. . .

"The plan which I mainly adopted . . . was that of using my white playmates, with whom I met in the streets, as my teachers. I used to carry almost constantly a copy of Webster's spelling book in my pocket and when sent on errands or when playtime was allowed me, I would step aside with my young friends and take a lesson in spelling."

The following will explain how he learnt to write:

"I was much in the shipyard, and observed that the carpenters after hewing and getting ready a piece of timber to use, wrote on it the initials of the name of that part of the ship for which it was intended. When for instance a piece of timber was ready for the starboard side, it was marked with a capital S ; a piece for larboard was marked L ; larboard aft was marked L.A ; starboard aft S.A ; starboard forward S.F. I soon learned these letters and for what they were placed on the timbers. My work now was to keep fire under the steambox and to watch the ship yard while the carpenters had gone to dinner. This interval gave me a fine opportunity to copy the letters named...With playmates for my teachers, fences and pavements for my copy-books and chalk for my pen and ink, I learned to write."

The reader will thus observe the educational difficulties and restrictions under which the Negro laboured before the Civil War. In the face of these difficulties it is very creditable to the race that in 1850, 32,627 of them were attending schools in both free and slave States, and in 1865, when emancipation came, "there was to be found in every Southern community a goodly sprinkling of colored men and women who had previously learned how to read and write."

But in the language of Dean Miller, broadly speaking, it might be said that fifty years ago the systematic education of the Negro race in the United States began near the absolute zero point of ignorance. "The real intellectual awakening of the race," adds he, "began with the overthrow of slavery. When the smoke of war had blown away, when the cessation of strife proclaimed the end of the great American conflict...there emerged from the wreck and ruin of war 4,000,000 of human chattels, who were transformed, as if by magic in a moment, in the twinkling of an eye from slavery to freedom, from bondage to liberty, from death unto life. These people were absolutely ignorant and destitute. They had not tasted of the tree of knowledge... Ignorance, poverty and vice, the trinity of human wretchedness, brooded over this degraded mass and made it pregnant............ At that time not only the policy, but the possibility of educating the Negro was in the bonds of dialectic doubt and denial. It was the generally accepted dogma of that day that the Negro was not amenable to the intellectual and moral regime applicable to the white child. The institution of slavery made requisition upon the Negro's physical faculties alone, and therefore the higher susceptibilities of his nature were ingeniously denied and prudently suppressed. Ordained intellectual and moral inferiority is the only valid justification of political and social subordination. Hence, this became the ultimate dogma of the pro-slavery propaganda...... It was deemed dangerous to communicate to the despised Negro the mystic symbols of knowledge which reveal all the hidden secrets of civilization. This policy was based upon the well-founded fear of primitive jealousy "lest he should stretch forth his hand and partake of the tree of knowledge and become as one of us." All this was however doomed, when the law put the Negro on an equal footing with his hitherto master, the white man. The emancipation brought him equality and liberty and his desire for the acquisition of knowledge which was so long suppressed, found an outlet and opportunity in the schools and colleges established by the religious and benevolent associations of those who had won liberty for him, viz., the people of the Northern States. "The missionaries who first came down from the North," says Dean Miller, "were not generally educators according to the requirements of the modern education. They brought the technical terms of knowledge in their left hand. In their right hand they brought religion, culture, civilization."

Almost all the institutions for higher education, high schools and colleges, that exist in the South for the education of the Negro were founded by these religious and missionary organizations or by other benevolent associations of the North. According to Dean Miller, "if we should subtract from the development of Negro life the influence contributed and attributable to these much berated Negro colleges and universities, the remainder would be niggardly indeed."

The educational facilities open to the Negro at the present moment may be summarized as below:—

In the North, all the universities, high schools and common schools are open to the Negro and he has the same facilities for education as other children have.

In the South, the ordinary colleges and schools maintained by the State for the white children are not open to the Negro. White children are not allowed to mix with colored.

The colleges which impart university education

to the Negro on the Arts side are generally denominational institutions maintained and managed by denominational organizations. They are in some cases aided by the States, in others not. The Howard University at Washington is one of the state-aided universities, where about 1800 Negro students, male and female, receive high education.

Similarly the Atlanta University for colored people used to be a State-aided institution until the grant made to it by the State was stopped on the ground that it admitted white students also. The story may be briefly told as follows : Some years ago when the State committee came to inspect the university, they found that among the students were two or three white children. The committee called upon the principal to refuse admission to white children as they disliked white children being brought up along with the Negroes. The principal refused to agree to this proposition and the State Committee recommended a discontinuance of the State grant, which was accordingly done.

At Atlanta, there is another university for the higher education of Negroes called the Morehouse College, and presided over by a very able graduate of Harvard, himself a colored person. This is a purely unaided institution. Similar institutions founded and maintained principally by Northern philanthropy or denominational organizations are to be found in almost every important city in the South, but the States do little for the higher education of the Negroes as compared with the provision they make for the higher education of the white children.

This is due to the reaction that followed the boom of the emancipation days. For some years the Southern States have been actively engaged in disenfranchising the Negro and reducing his influence on the elections. In some States educational qualifications have been fixed so high as to exclude most educated Negroes from the register.

In 1911, the Atlanta University published a book containing the results of an investigation made by them into the educational position of the Negroes in the United States. On the strength of the evidence collected in this book, the following conclusions were then drawn and laid before a conference of Negro leaders, who passed resolutions recalling the attention of the authorities to the facts elicited by this investigation:

1. That the overwhelming majority of Negro children of school age are not in school.

2. That the chief reason for this is the lack of school facilities; and a further reason is the poverty and ignorance of parents.

3. That those Negro children who are in school are as a rule poorly taught by half-prepared and poorly paid teachers and through short terms of three to six months a year.

4. That the schoolhouses and equipment for Negro schools are for the most part wretched and inadequate.

5. That the Negro schools as a rule receive little or no helpful superintendence from the school authorities.

6. That the result and apparently one of the

objects of disfranchisement has been to cut down the Negro school fund, bar out competent teachers, lower the grade and efficiency of the course and study and employ as teachers in the Negro schools those willing tools who do not and will not protest or complain.

7. That in the attempt to introduce much needed and valuable manual and industrial training there has been introduced into the curriculum of the Negro common school a mass of ill-considered, unrelated work which has over-burdened the teacher and pushed into the background the vital studies of reading, writing and arithmetic. In a large measure this has been done with the avowed object of training Negroes as menials and laborers and of cutting them off from the higher avenues of life.

8. That the forward movement in education in the South during the last ten years has been openly confined almost entirely to white people. The movement for local school taxes, better high schools, consolidation of schools and transportation of children has with small exception been encouraged and made possible among the whites and not among the Negroes. In many cases the Negroes have been taxed for the improvement of white school facilities, while their own schools have not been allowed to share in these improvements.

9. That along with this curtailment of elementary public education for Negroes has gone a tendency to decry the work of those schools which are devoted to the higher training of the Negro youth, to lower their curricula, to cut off northern benevolence and to

MAJOR J. B. RAMSEY

Commandant, Tuskegee Institute, Alabama.

decrease the supply of intellectual leaders for the Negro race.

Yet in spite of these complaints I am of opinion that, generally speaking, the Negro has better and larger facilities for education than the Indians have in their own country. Dean Miller, so often quoted in this paper, has thus summarized the results of the last fifty years of Negro education:

(1)—"In the first place," he says, "it has settled for all times the Negro's capacity to comprehend the rudiments, as well as the higher reaches, of knowledge and apply them to the tasks of life.

(2)—"In the second place, the colleges and universities have furnished the teachers, doctors, lawyers, editors, and general leaders, who are now directing the activities of the Negro people and stimulating them to higher and nobler modes of life."

(3)—"In the third place, the illiteracy of the race has been cut down to 45 per cent., which marks the most marvellous advance in the technical elements of knowledge in the annals of human progress."

There is another feature of the education of the Negro which puts an Indian to indescribable shame, viz., the education of the Negro women. The facilities which exist in this country for the higher education of Negro women, are decidedly larger, better, and more liberal than those that exist in India for the education of Indian women. Firstly, most of the Negro colleges and high schools are open to the girls. In some, the girls are actually in the majority. Secondly, there are special schools for girls which are even better equipped than similar schools for boys. I saw one such school at Atlanta, called the Spellman School. This school covers an area of twenty acres of land with a number of magnificent buildings for teaching and residential purposes. Ten brick buildings provide ample room for the boarding department, the literary and the industrial work. Reynolds Cottage is the residence of the president of the institution. In Rockefeller Hall are the office, the high school department, and a chapel with a seating capacity of a thousand. Mac Vicar Hospital is modern and completely equipped, with a fine operating room, a ward each for surgical and medical patients, and a lecture room for nurses in training. The Nurses Home contains eleven bedrooms and a reception hall. Giles Hall was planned especially with reference to normal work. It contains two spacious assembly rooms, with twenty recitation rooms for the practice school, besides study and class rooms for student teachers, and a gymnasium. Four other halls, viz., Morgan, Packard, Morehouse and Rockefeller, furnish accommodation for three hundred boarders. A large library and reading room containing about four thousand volumes, and a hundred current periodicals, occupies the lower floor of one wing of Packard Hall. In its basement are commodious rooms for classes in domestic science and dressmaking. A building in the rear contains the printing office and music rooms. In the laundry are eighty-five porcelain tubs, each with hot and cold water attachment. There are also drying and ironing rooms. A steam and electric plant furnishes heat and light for the whole establishment. In 1913 the school had 703 students on its rolls with 13 in the college department, 205 in the high school, 25 in the teacher's professional department, and 379 in the normal practice school.

In the Atlanta University in the same city, more than one half of the students are girls. There are two other high schools in the same city where girls read along with the boys and form the bulk of the school population. Similarly in the Howard University at Washington, with a population of about 1500 students, about half are girl students. What has been said of Atlanta and Washington, is true of every important city having a decent population of Negroes.

But what is of still more significance, is the provision made by States and private beneficence for the industrial education of Negro boys and girls, throughout the country. The question of industrial education has been receiving considerable attention in the U.S.A., more than twenty years, and the cry for "vocational" education is every day increasing both in volume and intensity. In the case of the Negroes, however, this cry has a special significance. The enemies of the Negro race have from the first deprecated the idea of educating the Negro. The Southern white hates the philanthropy of the North, which started educating the Negro and placed facilities for high education within his reach. He characterises this philanthropy as mischievous, misplaced, and calculated to embitter the racial feeling even to a greater extent than it was before the Negro was educated. The Negro owes not only his emancipation, but also his education to the North, and is naturally grateful to the same for all it has done for his welfare. The South has always resented this "meddlesome interference of the North in their affairs." The South considers the Negro question a local issue, and "has stubbornly and sullenly insisted that it alone possessed the requisite knowledge and experience" to deal with the problem. "The fact that the colored race has followed the guidance of the white man of the North has given rise to deep and bitter complaint. Ever since the Negro has begun to animadvert upon his own condition, the North and South have seemed to him to be as wide apart as the poles on questions touching his welfare. In the momentous conflict of thought and conscience which preceded the arbitration of arms, the North stood for liberty, the South for slavery. At countless cost of blood and treasure, the North broke his chains against the equally strenuous endeavour of the South to rivet them more tightly....... Northern statesmanship placed legislation upon the statute books recognising the equality of all men before the law, every line of which met with strenuous opposition and obstruction on the part of the South. Northern philanthropists have given their substance and their service for the intellectual and moral betterment of the black man, while the South has for the most part looked on with icy indifference and often with ill-concealed disapproval. The South knew the Negro as docile, obedient, submissive, unprotesting, and contented with whatever was given to him by way of food and clothes. He never could think of a time when the Negro would be otherwise and claim equality with him. This has however happened, mostly as the result of the meddlesome interference of the North and the education which the Negro has received principally through the instrumentality of the North. The South, therefore, and very naturally, lays all his racial troubles at the door of the North and the education which the Negro has received. He maintains that it was a mistake to educate the Negro ; but to give him higher education was even a greater mistake. He complains that after 25 years of higher education "the race problem has become rather intensified than abated in acuteness" ; and that the unpractical literary education imparted to the Negro has only produced so many swelled heads, with impossible aspirations and unreasonable demands of absolute equality. This attitude of the Southern white towards the higher education of the Negro has received a certain amount of support from that class of educational philosophers who decry high education and extoll "vocational education," as they call it. These philosophers have no use for the "mere theorists" produced by high liberal education unrelated to the needs of life. They want only such education as would raise the efficiency of the nation's workers as producers and distributors of wealth, and as pursuers of vocations which add to the material prosperity and material comforts of the nation. They estimate education by the amount of dollars it brings to the educated and the contribution which it makes to the wealth of the nation, and its efficiency as a wealth-producing community.

This change in educational values has affected the question of Negro education also, and just now that party seems to be in ascendancy, which champions the cause of industrial education among the Negroes as against high liberal education. Dean Miller complains that "our whole educational activities are under the thrall of this retrograde spirit. We are marking time rather than moving forward," and that "whenever the higher education of the Negro is broached, industrial training is always suggested as a counter-irritant." The Negroes as well as their well-wishers are thus divided into two camps, one who stands for the industrial training of the Negro, and the other who stands for his higher education. The advocates of higher education insinuate that those who champion the industrial training of the Negro at the cost of facilities for higher liberal education, do so with the motive of keeping him down. Their ideal of an educated Negro is an efficient servant, an industrious and intelligent mechanic, or carpenter, or mason. They do not want Negro thinkers, or writers, or publicists; nor do they want the Negro in the higher professions, which produce politicians and leaders. They are prepared to educate him according to his present position in life, to improve his earning capacity up to a certain limit; to increase his efficiency and value as an economic factor of the lower order; to enable him to live a clean, contented life on the lower rungs of the ladder. They do not want him to be so highly educated as to claim perfect equality with the white in all the departments of life, political, intellectual, religious, moral, and economic. Intellectual equipment of a high order leads to aspirations which are inconvenient to the ruling class and they, therefore, are anxious to dry up the very fountains from which these aspirations spring. The Negro leader complains that this interested view of Negro education has reduced the facilities for higher education which were heretofore open to the Negro youth. Northern philanthropists are changing the direction of their philanthropy not only by directing it, in the future, to the industrial training of the Negro, but even by withdrawing their aid from the colleges and institutions that have so far provided intellectual fare of a higher order for the Negro boy and girl.

This has frightened the Negro leaders, and they are protesting as well as making appeals for the continuance and multiplication of facilities for imparting high education to the Negro. Dean Miller has expressed these fears and sentiments of the Negro leaders in two articles, one called "Education for Manhood," and the other "A Brief for Higher Education." I propose to make rather lengthy quotations from these two articles in order to give my readers a clear idea of what the Negro leaders in the United States think of the conflicting claims of higher liberal education and industrial education.

"Education," says Dean Miller, "has two clearly

differentiable functions, (1) to develop and perfect the human qualities of the individual, as a personality, and (2) to render him a willing and competent participant, as an instrumentality, in the federation of the world's work. The one interferes in the nature of man and is conditioned only by the innate economy of human nature; the other is responsive to contemporary social demands. The one is independent of time, place and circumstances; the other is adjustable to these various elements. The one represents a pedagogical constant; the other presents the widest margin of variation. The one is generic in its embracement of all mankind; the other is specific in its application to the peculiar needs and requirements of each individual." "Education," he adds, "is not an end in itself, but is conditioned upon the nature of man and upon his place in the social scheme; it is not an independent and self-sustained entity, but is conducive to the fulfilment of ulterior aims."

After comparing the old idea of education, according to the old conceptions of human personality, with the modern ideas of education based upon the Darwinian theory of the survival of the fittest, and the modern requirements, Dean Miller remarks:

"There is a constant duel between the process of machinery and the spirit of democracy—the one tending to subordinate the human element to the mechanical process; the other insisting upon the higher rights and powers of man. Democracy banishes distinction between classes, and gives all men the same right to develop and exploit the higher powers and susceptibilities with which they may be endowed. Our educational system to-day is between the upper and nether stress of these conflicting influences. . . . The essential immediate aim of industrial education is to develop man as an instrumentality. The chief end of the so-called liberal education is to develop man as a personality. . . . . The advocates of industrial training would claim that their ultimate aim is the development of man as a personality through instrumentality. The higher education persumes instrumentality as a corollary of personality. . . . . . Under any present dispensation most men must devote the larger part of their powers to processes of producing and distributing wealth, while a smaller number, either through natural or artificial selection are set apart to the higher intellectual, moral, and spiritual tasks ; but however exacting the present necessities may be, it is incumbent upon each individual to have in view his best development as a personality. *

"The highest decree of the Godhead was—'Let us make man.' The true end of education is to develop man, the average man, as a self-conscious personality. This can be done not by imparting information to the mind or facility to the fingers, but felicity to the feelings and inspiration to the soul. Develop the man ; the rest will follow. The final, expression of education is not in terms of discipline, culture, efficiency, service, or special virtues, but in terms of MANHOOD which is the substance and summation of all. . . . . . When the manhood has been quickened, it may express itself in terms of character, efficiency, initiative, service, or enjoyment that occasion may require. None of these things represent final values in themselves, but are incidental manifestations of manhood from which they are derived and to which they conduce."

After laying down these general propositions and explaining them at some length, Dean Miller

* In my opinion this was true in all times. It was this idea which formed the basis of the original Hindu idea of the castes.

applies them to the Negro race in the U. S. A. and observes :

"The traditional relation of the American Negro to the society of which he forms a part is too well known to need extensive treatment in this connection. The African slave was introduced into this country as a pure animal instrumentality to perform the rougher work under dominion of his white lord and master. There was not the remotest thought of his human personality. No more account was taken of his higher qualities than of the higher susceptibilities of lower animals. His mission was considered to be as purely mechanical as that of the ox which pulls the plough. Indeed his human capabilities were emphatically denied. It was stoutly contended that he did not possess a soul to be saved. . . . Nor a mind to be enlightened. . . Under the dominion of this dogma education was absolutely forbidden him. It became a crime to educate this *tertium quid*."

"Then came the anti-slavery campaign which was based on the idea that the Negro was a human being endowed with heart and mind and conscience like other human beings. The anti-slavery philanthropists believed in the essential manhood of the Negro. Upon this foundation they not only broke the Negro's chains, but clothed him with political and civic prerogative as an American citizen. They established schools and colleges and universities for him because they believed in his higher susceptibilities. . . . They projected a scheme of education comparable with the standards set up for the choicest European youth for a race which had hitherto been submerged below the zero point of intelligence. These schools and colleges, founded and fostered on this basis, were the beginning of the best that there is in the race, and the highest which it can hope to be. But alas, the passion engendered by the war grew weaker and weaker, the corresponding belief in the Negro has also declined and the old dogma concerning his mission as a human tool has begun to reassert itself. . . . . Few indeed are left who have the intensity of belief and the intrepidity of spirit to defend the higher pretensions of the Negro without apology or equivocation. The old form of appeal has become insipid and uninspiring. . . . . Where now is heard the tocsin call whose keynote a generation ago resounded from the highlands of Kentucky and Tennesee to the plains of Carolina, calling the black youth, whose hopes ran high within their bosoms, to rise and make for higher things? This clarion note, though still for the nonce, shall not become a lost chord. Its inspiring tones must again appeal to the youth to rise to their higher assertion and exertion. If you wish to reach and inspire the life of the people, the approach must be made not to the intellect, nor yet to the feelings as the final basis of appeal, but to the manhood that lies at the back of these. That education of the youth, especially of the suppressed class, that does not make insistent and incessant appeals to the smothered manhood (I had almost said Godhood) within, will prove to be but vanity and vexation of spirit. What boots a few chapters in chemistry, or pages in history, or paragraphs in philosophy, unless they result in an enlarged appreciation of one's own manhood? Those who are to stand in the high places of intellectual, spiritual, and moral leadership of such a people in such a time must be made to feel deep down in their own souls their own essential manhood. They must believe that they are created in the image of God and that nothing clothed in human guise is a more faithful likeness of that original. This must be the dominant note in the education of the Negro. . . . The Negro must learn in school what the white boy learns from association and environment. The American white man in his ordinary state is supremely conscious of his manhood prerogative. He may be ignorant or poor or vicious, yet he never forgets that he is a man. But every feature of our civilization is calculated to impress upon the Negro a sense of his inferiority and to make him feel and believe that he is good for nothing but to be cast out and trodden under foot of other men. A race, like an individual, that compromises its own self-respect, paralizes and enfeebles its own energies... The old theologians used to insist upon the freedom of the will, but the demand of the Negro to-day is freedom and independence of his own spirit. Destroy this and all is lost; preserve it and though political rights, civic privileges, industrial opportunities be taken away for the time, they will all be regained... ....The Negro must develop courage and self-confidence.........The educated Negro must learn to state his own case before the bar of public opinion... ......The educated Negro to-day represents the first generation grown to the fulness of the stature of manhood under the influence and power of education ....The hope of the race is focused in them. They are the headlight to direct the pathway through the dangers and vicissitudes of the wilderness. For want of vision people perish. For want of wise direction, they stumble and fall."

The following incidental reference to India would, I am sure, be read with even greater interest there :

"The highest call of the civilization of the world to-day is to the educated young men of the belated races. The educated young manhood of Japan, China, India, Egypt, Turkey, must lift their own people up to the level of their own high conception."

The article is wound up with the following appeal:

"The white race is fast loosing faith in the Negro as an efficient and suitable factor in the equation of our civilization. Curtailment of political, civil and religious privileges and opportunities is but the outward expression of this apostacy. As the white man's faith decreases, our faith in ourselves must increase. Every Negro in America should utter his prayer with his face turned towards the light, 'Lord, I believe in my own inherent manhood; help Thou my unbelief.' The educated Negro must express his manhood in terms of courage, in the active as well as the passive voice; courage to do as well as to endure; courage to contend for the right while suffering wrong; the courage of self-belief that is always commensurate with the imposed task. The world believes in a race that believes in itself, but justly despises the self-bemeaned."

It is thus that the Negro leader protests against the growing opportunism of the friends of his race in their tendency to foster the industrial training of the Negro at the cost of higher liberal education among them. I have thought it best to let him speak for himself as there is always a danger in one's reproducing other people's thoughts in language other than their own. I need not say that, although I may not agree with everything said by Dean Miller, I am in full accord with most of the principles enunciated by him, and I wish my countrymen to know his view of them. I could not put them in better, more forcible, and more spirited language than he has done and that alone should be sufficient to justify the labours of those who have educated the Negro. There are hundreds of educated Negroes in the U. S. A., who can think and write as lucidly and vigorously as Dean Miller. Some of them perhaps do better, but in any case Dean Miller represents a fairly high water-mark of Negro ability and intelligence in this country, and he is perhaps one of those who have the least white blood in their veins, if any at all. In his other article, called "A Brief for the Higher Education of the Negro," Dean Miller examines the matter from a different point of view and says:

"Indeed, one of the strongest claims for the

higher education of the Negro is that it will stimulate the dormant industrial activities of the race. The surest way to incite a people to meet the material demands of life is to teach them that life is more than meat. The unimaginative laborer pursues the routine rounds of his task, spurred on only by the immediate necessities of life and the task-master's stern command. To him it is only time and the hour that run through the whole day. The Negro lacks enlightened imagination. He needs prospects and vista . . . . . . If you would perpetuate the industrial incapacity of the Negro, then confine him to the low grounds of drudgery and toil and prevent him from casting his eyes into the hills whence come inspiration and promise. The man with the hoe is of all men the most miserable, unless, forsooth, he has a hope. But if imbued with hope and sustained by an ideal, he can consecrate the hoe as well as any other instrument of service, as a means of fulfilling the promise within him....... The most effective prayer that can be uttered for the Negro is 'Lord, open Thou his eyes.' He cannot see beyond the momentary gratification of appetite and passion. He does not look before and after. Such stimulating influence can be brought to bear upon the race only through the inspiration of the higher culture. It requires men of sound knowledge to conceive and execute plans for the industrial education of the masses. The great apostles of industrial education for the Negro have been men of academic training or of its cultural equivalent. The work of Hampton and Tuskegee is carried on by men and women of a high degree of mental cultivation. Dr. Booker T. Washington (note the title) is the most influential Negro that the race under freedom has produced. He is the great apostle of industrial training. His great success is but the legitimate outcome of his earnestness and enthusiasm. And yet there is no more striking illustration of the necessity of wise, judicious, and cultivated leadership as a means of stimulating the dormant activity of the masses, than he who hails from Tuskegee....... Mr. Washington possesses an enlightened mind to discern the masses, executive tact to put his plans in effective operation, and persuasive ability to convince others as to the expediency of his policies. He possesses no trade or handicraft . . . Tuskegee has been built on intellect and oratory."

About the need of special colleges for the Negro, Dean Miller says :

"The white college does not contemplate the special needs of the Negro race. American ideals could not be fostered in the white youth of our land by sending them to Oxford or Berlin for tuition. No more can the Negro gain racial inspiration from Harvard and Yale. And yet they need the benefit of contact and comparison and the zeal for knowledge and truth which these great institutions impart. The Negro college and the Northern institutions will serve to preserve a balance between undue elation for want of sober comparison, and barren culture for lack of inspirational contact with the masses."

To the charge that higher education lifts the Negro above the needs of his race or, in other words, denationalizes him, Dean Miller replies :

"The thousands of graduates of Negro schools and colleges all over the land are a living refutation of this charge. After the mind has been stored with knowledge, it is transmitted to the place where the need is greatest and the call is loudest and transmitted into whatever mode of energy may be necessary to accomplish the imposed task. . . . . No one can be too learned or too profound in whose hands are entrusted the temporal and eternal destiny of a human soul. Even if the educated Negro desired to flee from his race, he soon learns by bitter experience that he will be thrown back upon himself by the expulsive power of prejudice. He soon learns that the Newtonian formula has a social application. 'The force of attraction varies directly as the mass.'"

I have given these long quotations for another reason besides the one stated above. Our own educational problem in India is so difficult and complex, so full of anomalies and inconsistencies, that I would like my people to know the views of people engaged in the solution of similar problems in a different part of the world. Our problem differs from the problems of the Negro in the U. S. in important points. The Negro is not indigenous to the soil; he has no past, nor a language of his own, other than the language given to him by his erstwhile masters; he has no country to look to, other than the United States; and last but not least, he fears no competition except that of his own countrymen. Yet he belongs to a submerged race; whom enlightened, advanced, well-educated and well-supported neighbours threaten to elbow out of existence if he would not look up and fit himself and his people with the knowledge necessary to compete with them in the struggle for life and progress both individual and social. The objections advanced against the higher education of the Negro are very similar to those raised in our country by the Imperialist Jingo, with whom fall in, sometimes, well-meaning friends and short-sighted Indians, against the higher education of the Indians. Yet we cannot fail to notice that the absence of sufficient facilities for the industrial and commercial training of the Indians has been and is more harmful to India, than similar neglect in the case of the Negro would be to America. The industrial competition in the U.S.A. is more inter-racial than international, at least so far as the question affects the Negro, but in

PROFESSOR G. N. CARVER.

Head of Department of Research, Experiment Station, and Consulting Chemist, Tuskegee Institute, Alabama.

India it is different. In both cases it is as necessary as higher education in letters, but perhaps it is even more necessary in India from an economic point of view. The economic pressure from the outside has ruined the industrial population of India and driven them to unskilled labour either in fields or in factories, detrimentally affecting both their physique and their morals. On the other hand it has narrowed the spheres of educated people's economic activity.

The Negro was on the lowest rungs of industrial labour when his education began. His education has raised him immensely, opening out better and nobler careers for him. He is now to be found in every walk of life, though in the higher callings and in the professions signifying higher mental calibre he is not in sufficient numbers in proportion to the numerical strength of his race. No one can maintain that the Negro has overcrowded these professions. His strength in these callings is not sufficient even for the requirements of his own race. The objection against his higher education is not that there are too many of them in the higher walks of life but that they ought not to be there at all. The white man does not want his competition in these higher callings. He wants to keep for himself even the Negro clientele. He objects to the Negro's claim for equal treatment; he objects to his political aspirations; he denounces his cultural pretensions; and he wants to shut the doors of knowledge against him; but he does not object to take his money. In fact he wants as much of it as he can get, by hook or by crook. He wants his labour, his service, and his industry, but he does not want his leadership; nor does he want him to lead his own people, because that necessarily deprives him of the opportunities of exploitation which he otherwise has.

On the other hand there are well-meaning friends of the Negro, both white and of his own class, who think that the Negro cannot maintain his own in the racial struggle and economic competition unless he is industrially fit to occupy the higher rungs of the industrial ladder. It will not do for him to remain contented with unskilled labour and the pittance which he gets thereby. They say that his progress must proceed from below. He must be fitted to take the next step in the industrial and economic march. I am not prepared to say that they are wholly wrong; nor can I say either that the champions of the higher liberal education of the Negro are wrong. I feel, however, that this stimulus to industrial uplift might not have come, or might not have come so soon, without the higher education which produced thinkers and leaders, who have brought it into existence and are pushing it on with such remarkable success. I am confident that the ideas of the Negro leaders on education and their application of them in solving the difficulties which face them in their racial struggle, would be of more than academic interest to Indian patriots and nationalists. That is my excuse for giving them at some length and in their own language.

It is my duty now to present to my readers the case of the advocates of industrial training among the Negroes, and this, I think, I cannot do better than by giving extracts from the publications that were very kindly given to me by Dr. Booker T. Washington of Tuskegee. I do not propose to say here much about Dr. Washington and his ideas. These I reserve for another occasion. But the extracts I propose to give below fairly represent his views about the mission of the institute at Tuskegee, of which he is the founder and leader at the same time.

THE NORMAL AND INDUSTRIAL INSTITUTE AT TUSKEGEE.

This institution owes its origin to the initiative of the Federal Government, but its phenomenal success is entirely due to the energy, enthusiasm, spirit, and tact of Dr. Washington. Mr. Arthur M. Evans, an American journalist, is of opinion that Dr. Washington and this institute are doing for the Negro people what the University of Wisconsin is doing for its state. Public service is the fundamental ideal of both.

"Both are striving to get into close touch with the people and to exert an influence on the affairs of every day life; to teach the farmer how to raise larger crops and better herds; to instruct the housewife in domestic arts; to improve the home; to raise the standard of living; to develop raw labour into skilled labour; in short—to improve conditions of society in the mass."

"Tuskegee is not a school, in the ordinary sense of the word. It's a city in itself, a community that dominates a whole county. It's a great industrial plant with forty trades and industries, that consumes all its own products, that erects its own buildings (first making its own bricks), that grows its own food, makes its own clothes, writes and prints its own text-books, all by way of education."

It is a mammoth laboratory in which a race

problem is being worked out. The object of Tuskegee is to train its students to serve society by doing some useful thing with skill, to give them a three-phased education of "the head, the heart, the hand," to use the alliterative phrase of the Tuskegee teachers, and then to send them out to teach others what they have learnt—education by the endless chain system. Intelligent thrift, training in the activities open to the masses of the Negro race in the South, industry, self-reliance, self-respect, cleanliness, system, courtesy, these are the things Tuskegee is teaching. Its principles are epitomized by Emmet J. Scott, executive secretary of the Institute in "Tuskegee and its People." "There can be no liberty without intelligence ; no independence without industry, and no power for man and no charm for woman, without character."

The institution was established by the legislature of 1880 appropriating two thousand dollars to be used to pay the salaries of the teachers. The school was opened for its first session, July 4, 1881, in a rented shanty church, with thirty pupils and but one teacher. No provision was made by the legislature for a building. In 1884 the appropriation was increased to three thousand dollars, and in 1893 the institution was incorporated under the name of the Tuskegee Normal and Industrial Institute. During the first session, the present location, consisting at that time of one hundred acres, with three small buildings thereon, was purchased by Northern friends.

At the close of the school term, May 28, 1814, it

had registered a total enrollment of 1,527—896 men and 631 women—who came from 32 States and territories and 17 foreign countries, or colonies of foreign countries. In addition to the attendance in the Institute proper, the average attendance at the Children's House, the Training School, was 201; the average attendance during the Agricultural Short Course was 275, and the average attendance during the Summer School last year was 412. There are about 200 teachers, male and female, resident in the Institute, some with their wives living in separate houses built by them at their own cost on plots of land sold to them by the Institute; others living and messing with the students. In 1912, the educational plant consisted of 2345 acres of land; 107 buildings, large and small, used for dwellings, dormitories, class rooms, shops and barns, which together with the equipment, stock-in-trade, live stock and personal property, is valued at $ 1,295,213. This did not include 19,910 acres of public land remaining unsold from 25,500 acres granted by act of Congress, and valued at $ 250,000,00 nor the Endowment fund. In his report for the year ending in May 1914, the Principal made the following observation about improvements and extensions:

"The most important permanent improvements that the school has ever undertaken are now under construction. These improvements when completed will cover the following: Power distribution and fire protection system, including wiring of buildings and grounds; buildings for new power plant; boilers, chimney, engines, generators, electric wiring, transformers, etc.; power piping and steam conduits ; sewerage system and disposal plant ; ice plant ; cold storage plant ; railroad extension. The water supply and fire prevention system has been completed, but must soon be enlarged. Work is now going forward on the remaining portions of the general plan, but at least two years will probably be required to complete the whole."

FINANCIAL : The year's budget provided $ 250,957, i.e., over 7½ lakhs of rupees, for current needs and about $ 20,000, i.e. 60,000 rupees, for improvements and equipment. The total receipts for the year amounted to $473,766, i.e., about 14 lakhs of rupees. In May 1914, the permanent endowment fund stood at $ 1,962,112, i.e., in rough figures about 60 lakhs of rupees. The bulk of this amount has been contributed by wealthy white Americans to whom the ideals and the methods of the Institute have appealed and who appreciate Dr. Washington's spirit. The educational work of the school may be gathered from the following extracts from another article of Mr. Evans.

"All the students are required to take academic studies, and the effort is made to correlate all the studies with the industrial training. In English, for example, the boys and girls write essays on their work in the shops. At commencement time, instead of delivering orations on "Over the Alps" or "Standing on the Threshold of Life," the graduating class shows how a meal should be served or how a horse should be shod. It is a practical demonstration of what has been learned, a clinic on industrial education."

The students in the academic department are divided into day and night classes, about one-third of the students being in the night school, which is designed for those who are unable to pay the small charges made by the day school. When a poor student arrives he works during the day and studies at night, and whatever he earns in excess of his board is placed to his credit in the bank. As soon as he has saved enough, he enters the day school. The pupils in the day school attend class room exercises three days a week, and the other three days they spend in the shops. The expenses of day students above the cost of clothing and what can be earned is about $ 45 or $ 50 for the nine months' term. Many of the pupils earn all their expenses. The teaching in the academic department, which is about as advanced in work as the second year of a Northern high school minus the languages, is done by a faculty of fifty college graduates, many of them from leading universities of the country. The male pupils form two battalions, one of four companies of ninety men each containing the night students, the other of five companies of ninety men each made up from the day students. Drills and inspections take place every day in the week, the day students being divided into two squads, which drill on alternate days. An officers' court passes judgment upon all breaches of discipline not serious enough to be referred to the principal.

The industries are grouped into three departments, the school of agriculture, the industries for girls and the department of mechanical industries. The courses in agriculture are given in Milbank Hall, a modern building erected in 1909 at a cost of $ 26,000. Farming was the first industry started at the Institute, and the school farm in thirty years has grown until it embraces 2,300 acres. Of this, eighty acres form a truck garden on which is raised produce for the school, eighty acres constitute an orchard, 840 acres form the tract for general farming, while 1,300 acres comprise an area given over to pastures and woodland.

The dairy herd contains 227 head of cattle, breeders, yearlings and calves, with 105 milk cows "at the pail." The farm also has 562 hogs, and 145 horses, mules and colts, while the poultry yard contains 3,000 fowls. The farm work is carried on by 288 students, forty hired men and eighteen instructors.

Last year 632 tons of ensilage, 12,000 bushels of sweet potatoes, 3,500 bushels of corn and 3,650 bushels of oats were grown on the general farm, while the truck garden yielded 115,453 pounds of greens, 1,116 dozen bunches of lettuce, 465 bushels of onions, 3576 water-melons, 358 bushels of beans, fifty-three bushels of beets, 783 bushels of tomatoes, 321 bushels of rutabagas, 3150 dozen ears of green corn, 2,064 melons and cantaloupes, fifty-seven bushels of white potatoes, and 258 bushels of peas— this enumeration being given as an indication of the variety of the table at Tuskegee and the manner in which the pupils are being saturated in one of the many ideas of Tuskegee that one indication of civilization is variety of food production.

'One of God's objects in surrounding us with vegetables, with grain, berries and flowers,' says Booker Washington, 'is to help us to make our bodies better fitted for the uses of life, to make our bodies stronger, to make them more healthful. When I go to church and hear people preach for hours on all kinds of subjects, especially in country districts, where the soil is fitted for growing all kinds of vegetables, all kinds of fowl, how much I wish the minister would take a few hours and teach the people how to fill their bodies with some of the beautiful things with which nature has surrounded them.' "

Discipline: Industry is the spirit of Tuskegee and military discipline is its system of government. From the moment the rising whistle blows at 5 o'clock until the "lights out" bell sounds at night, every moment of the time is occupied; work is in the atmosphere; industry is made a habit—the great aim of the school. At Tuskegee refractory students are punished, not by setting them at extra tasks but by giving them no work to do. The great idea of the Institute is to drill into the students the principle that labor is a privilege, hence work is never prescribed as a punishment, for that would be an inconsistency. Enforced idleness proves penalty enough, and after less than a day of lounging, a misfit in a busy community, a drone among the workers, the disobedient student generally goes to the Commandant and begs to be put to work.

The discipline is admirable. Ever since the opening of the school the students have been on a military system of some sort. The first day the student body assembled thirty years ago it marched to chapel, and it has been doing so ever since, drilling in the morning, marching to dinner after a review at noon, marching to chapel at night, marching back to the dormitories after a review procession before the faculty on the platform, assembling on dress parade every Sunday morning and on alternate mornings during the week, marching and drilling and becoming impregnated with the idea of order, system, obedience, and discipline. It is a sight never to be forgotten to see 1700 students march into the great dining hall at noon said to be the largest dining room in the country, and stand at attention until grace is sung. Then the silence is broken, chairs are pulled out and conversation starts up with such a roar that the band is kept playing in the balcony to drown the noise. There is nothing boisterous, but 1700 voices engaged in simultaneous talk make rather a cataract of sound.

Visitors rarely fail to comment upon the table manners of the students. At Tuskegee table manners are as much a part of the curriculum as is work in the shops or recitation in the class rooms. The man at the head of the table does the serving, assisted by a student on each side. There is none of the grabbing, none of the meat spearing and the bread harpooning that is far from the unusual feature of the life in the boarding clubs of many a Northern college. The students are served and the rule of the school is that each shall eat every thing that is placed upon his plate without passing remarks upon the cooking, if indeed, such adverse remarks could be made. The food comes fresh from the institute farm raised by the students, cooked by the students, and eaten by the students, and the variety of edibles placed on the table serves as another object lesson of the benefits derived from skilful labor on the soil."

Dr. Washington's principles, on which the education of the boys and girls in this Institute is based, may be gathered from the following report of a sermon he gave one night to the students assembled in the chapel:

"One of the best lessons in civilization you can teach anybody, is to be uneasy and unhappy when a door-knob is even loose. In spite of all its antiquated and, in some cases, almost heathenish methods, it is hard to free ourselves from the slavery of the old-time book education. Every good citizen, whether he be teacher or is engaged in any other occupation, has something, should have something, to do with the education that is going on in his community. Whether you get an opportunity to exert the slightest influence, see to it that the house in which the teachers and children are assembled is made clean inside, clean outside; floors well swept, everything thoroughly dusted. See to it that every piece of furniture is put in the very best repair; see to it that, wherever it can be done, the paintbrush or whitewash brush is used on the inside.

"A great many people are content to put up a house and let it stand without paint, its weather-boards cracking and warping, a symbol of slovenliness. The whitewash brush and the paintpot are indexes of civilization. When you leave here, see to it that your homes and your farm buildings and your schools are fit to live in. If you can't afford paint, use whitewash. When you go into a school as a teacher, take a week's time to clean up. See to it that the yard is cleaned up, every piece of paper picked up, every paling put where it should be on the fence; that the gate hinges are all right, and all the broken window glasses are put in. Then begin using the whitewash brush or the paintbrush around the schoolhouse on the building, on the fence, on the gate, everywhere, to make the schoolroom an inviting, beautiful place, one that is fit for human beings to live and work in. Teach your pupils to be unhappy when one window pane gets a little cracked, and if a window pane is out, dismiss the school if necessary until that window pane is put in its place.

"After you go away from here I want to see you keep up this same thought, this same idea of activity and of keeping all your surroundings at all times and under all circumstances in good repair. See to it that you are not farmers unless the house in which you live is whitewashed or painted. See to it that when it begins to get a little out of repair, when the whitewash or the paint begins to get off, a little dull, see to it that a new whitewash, a new paint takes its place. See to it that everything you touch, every point in life that you touch, you keep in good repair, beginning with your own bodies, with your own dress, then with your surroundings in school and out of school. Be sure that you try to keep in good repair, in good shape, and then you will feel vigorous, you will feel that you can overcome difficulties.

"I don't believe it is possible for a person to be a good Christian with one suspender off, going around the country trying to wear one suspender. It lops him all over. He is one-sided from the time he gets up in the morning until he goes to bed at night. There is something wrong. He cannot act straight, he cannot think straight. There is something out of order all the time. A person does not indicate that he has the highest training, the highest civilization, who is satisfied to let a single button be off his clothes.

"Keep the grease spots off your clothes. I remember I had occasion some time ago to call a doctor in—and it was not a doctor here, I am glad to say, or anywhere near here—but I noticed he had a button off and he had two or three grease spots on his clothes. I do not know how much medicine he knew, but that button oft and those grease spots perfectly disgusted me in reference to that man. Keep the grease spots off your clothes, keep the buttons on, because no person who has the highest idea of civilization can go through life without being in proper repair in these respects.

"Make a study of the preparation of food. See to it that a certain ceremony, a certain importance, be attached to the partaking of the food, a certain time when each meal is to be served; then see to it that the food is not only prepared in the most tempting way, but that it is served in the most attractive and beautiful way. In most cases, as you know, the place where the food is taken is the most dismal, the most gloomy place in the whole house and people want to get out of it just as soon as possible. See to it that when you build your own home that the dining-room is the most beautiful, the most convenient, the most tempting room in the whole house."

Net result: In the thirty years of its existence the Institute has given two years of training to approximately 9,000 persons. The average earnings of persons trained at Tuskegee is $ 700 a year. Before attending Tuskegee they earned on an average about $ 100 a year. Thus the Institute has increased by about 600 % the earnings of all who have taken its courses. The earnings of the average Negro is placed at about $ 300 a year.

The economic value of the Institute to the entire South has been estimated. The average length of time the 9,000 students have been out of school is fourteen years, during which time their earnings have been $ 88,200,000, it is estimated. Without the industrial training the 9,000 would have earned in the fourteen years only $ 12,6000,000. So that the South, where most of the 9,000 are located, has had the advantage of an increase of $ 75,600,000 in the economic value of the 9,000 alone, to say nothing of what Tuskegee has done in improving the condition of the Negro outside the school walls by teaching the dignity of labour and by influencing the colored people of the South to sobriety, discipline, order, a better family life, a higher standard of living in general,—all items of economic value.

Practical Work at Tuskeegee.

Tuskegee, Alabama, April 25.—Macon County affords a tangible illustration of the way Tuskegee is constantly expanding its zone of influence. For years the work of the Institute has reached far beyond the schoolgrounds, each year bringing new ramifications, until to-day Tuskegee is conducting an extension work of twenty-six varieties that has two general aims—to change public opinion and direct attention to lines of industry that offer most opportunities for the colored people of the South and to educate the people in better methods of farming and so induce the children of Negro farmers to remain on the soil.

An idea of the scope of this work may best be given by a list of the extension activities, with the dates of establishment :

1884—Teachers' Institute.

1891—Annual Tuskegee Negro Conference.

1892—The Hospital, Greenwood Village.

1893—The Ministers' Night School.

1894—Tuskegee Town Mothers' Meeting.

1895—Building and Loan Association.

1896—The Town Night School.

1897—The Town Library and Reading room; Town Cooking Class; Russel Plantation Work; Farmers' Institute; Mothers' Clubs.

1891—The County Fair; The Town Y.M.C.A.; The Town Sunday School.

1900—The National Negro Business League.

1901—New Hospital Building—treatment of outside patients becomes a regular feature at Tuskegee.

1902—Village Improvement Association.

1904—The Jail work; the Farmers' Short Course; Rural School Improvement.

1905—The Weekly Farm Paper; The Ministers' Institute; The Circulating Library.

1906—The Jesup Agricultural Wagon—an agricultural school on wheels.

1907—Farmers' Co-operative Demonstration Work.

Macon County, in which Tuskegee is located, is one of the most prosperous and law-abiding in the South. It contains about 600 square miles and has a population of about 26,000, of which about 24,000 are Negroes. It is constantly growing, owing to the attractions afforded by its schools and by the assistance in farming methods given by Tuskegee Institute. The influence of the school is seen everywhere, particularly in the well-to-do condition of the Negro farmers. Macon county is said to have a larger area of land held by Negroes than any other county in the South. In 1910 Negroes owned 61,689 acres in Macon County. In Liberty County, Georgia, the next largest in Negro land holdings, the area was 55,048, while in Louisa County, Virginia, the third county in this respect, the colored population owned about 53,268 acres.

In Macon County there is no race problem—the Negro population, through the industrial education of Tuskegee, has become self-reliant. The county has fifty-seven colored public schools, of which forty-seven have been built through the aid and assistance of Tuskegee Institute, and the Negro patrons have paid for building, and taken advantage of this fact by influencing nearly every church community in Macon County to become a modern school community.

In various ways the school is teaching the farmers to increase the productivity of their lands, the principle underlying the system identical with the one that is the basis of the Tuskegee's labor—learning and teaching by doing and seeing. The Annual Negro Conference was started eighteen years ago, when Dr. Washington sent out invitations to seventy-five representative Negroes in Macon County; farmers, mechanics, school teachers and ministers. Instead of about seventy-five, above 400, most of them farmers, responded to the invitation, and the conference met with such success that it was made an annual feature. Negro farmers from all parts of the South attending. The school employs a conference agent, who organizes local conference in all parts of the state. The growth of this work is seen in the fact that 105 of these branch organizations have been established. Eight years

SOME TUSKEGEE STUDENTS.

ago a short course in agriculture was started with a view of giving farmers in the neighboring territory the advantage of two weeks' study of the work at the school farm. The first year there were eleven students, most of them older men; in 1911 there were 1,900, about 1,000 of them being young men and women.

A year after the short course had been established, the school launched a movement to take agricultural training to the farmers by means of a school on wheels, the Jesup agricultural wagon. The practical demonstrations given right on the farms by the men in charge of the wagons has been of great value in raising the standard of farming in Macon County. In 1907 the demonstration farming experiment, a work carried on by the Department of Agriculture at Washington, was started. Under this plan a number of farmers in a county, farm a small portion of their land under the direction of the department, using seed furnished by the department. Of the six Negro demonstration agents in Alabama, four were trained at Tuskegee, as was also the district agent who has charge of the work among the Negroes in Alabama, Mississippi, Oklahoma and Louisiana.

An idea of what the demonstration agents have done for the Negro farmer may be seen from the fact that in 1909 the average yield of corn per acre for the Negro farmers was less than eight bushels. Last year Negro demonstration farmers in Macon County grew an average of fifty-four bushels to the acre. In 1911 the average yield of cotton in

Alabama was about 600 pounds per acre. The highest average yield made on farms managed under a Negro demonstration agent was in Lee County, where an average of 1,867 pounds of cotton to the acre was raised. This was more than 1200 pounds per acre in excess of what was grown on the average farm of the State.

The last census figures gave an indication of how the influence of Tuskegee ramifies beyond the school gates. The census showed that while the counties in the black belt were losing in population, Macon county had made an increase of more than 10 per cent. New Negro families are continually coming into Macon—in five years fifty families bought $ 49,000 worth of land, in 1910 Negro farmers in the county bought 1,450 acres at a cost of $ 21,335, an indication of the prosperity. Macon County to-day is not only prosperous but it has so little crime that the sheriff complains of enforced idleness; it has no mob violence, no race problem; the white population co-operates with Tuskegee and with the Negro farmers in the development of agricultural methods, and the county is regarded as a model. The movement of the Southern Negro to the soil is evidenced in the fact that in the last ten years the colored people bought 4,000 additional farms in Virginia, 4,000 in Tennesee, 16,000 in Arkansas, 16,000 in Alabama, 35,000 in Mississippi, and 45,000 in Georgia.

No account of Tuskegee would be complete that did not mention the music at the school, the wonderful singing in the chapel, in which the student body is led by a choir of 150 voices, pipe organ, a piano and an orchestra of twenty-five pieces. Special effort is made to preserve the old Negro hymns and plantation melodies, orchestration for which have been made with great skill by the bandmaster, Captain N. C. Smith, who for nearly twenty years was leader of the Eighth Regiment Band in Chicago. Forty-seven students are in the band, which furnishes music for all occasions, and the surprising phase of the playing is the manner in which the students render classic music from the great operas. The leader drills the players in the story of the opera, telling them what every musical phrase means, before rehearsals are started, and with this as an inspiration the Tuskegee band plays almost as if it were composed of virtuosi.

Ambitions of the Principal: In his last report Dr. Washington remarks that "in the form of a temporary or permanent endowment we ought to add at least 3 million dollars, *i.e.*, 90 lakhs of rupees, to our present endowment," and he details only some of the present and most urgent needs of the institution as below:

1.—$ 50 a year for annual scholarships for tuition for one student, the student himself providing for his own board and other personal expenses in labor and cash.

2.—$ 12,000 for permanent scholarships.

3.—Money for operating expenses in any amounts, however small.

4.—$ 15,000 each for teachers' cottages.

5.—$ 40,000 for a building for religious purposes.

6.—$ 16,000 to complete the Boys' Trades Building.

7.—$ 50,000 for a Boys' Dormitory.

8.—$ 50,000 for a Girls' Dormitory.

9.—An addition to our Endowment Fund of at least $ 3,000,000.

Such, in brief outline, is the famous Institute of Tuskegee, started by the Federal State with an appropriation of $ 2000 a year towards the salaries of the teachers in 1881, worked and organized and brought to its present state by the genius and devotion of Booker T. Washington, with the sinews of war supplied in response to his appeal by generous-minded, wealthy Americans. The head that has planned and the hand that has reared up this magnificent structure are those of the Negro leader, while the food that has made it what it is, has been supplied by the white philanthropists of the country. It is no wonder then that out of the nineteen Trustees, sixteen are white people and only three Negroes or colored people. The staff, however, is almost exclusively colored.

I have seen the institution in working order; the academic teaching, the industrial training, the military drill, the midday parade, the work on the farms, in stables, in creamery, in shops. I have dined in company with the staff in the dining hall below and I have seen the student body taking their meals in the hall above and can say that the account given above gives a fair and accurate idea of the actual working of the Institute. The features that struck me most were the following:

EMMETT J. SCOTT,

Secretary, Tuskegee Institute, Alabama.

(1) The general neatness of the girls as well as of the boys;

(2) Their demeanor and bearing, which was at once respectful and dignified;

(3) The general air of cheerfulness that pervaded the institution throughout in all its departments;

(4) The earnestness that characterized the workers in shops, factories, and farms;

(5) The morning drill;

(6) The midday parade;

(7) The physique of the inmates. I hardly came across any boy or girl who looked pale or sickly. Most of them were in robust health, and all appeared to be in normal health.

To me it seemed that Tuskegee was a beehive where there were no drones and all were queens.

The Principal lives on the campus in a spacious house specially built for him, and lives on the income of a fund of six hundred thousand dollars specially gifted for the purpose by Mr. Carnegie. Two of his sons help him in his work; one as a teacher in the institute and the other as the travelling secretary of his father. His wife superintends the women's department and has a noble personality. Dr. Washington keeps a private poultry farm which he looks after personally, feeding his birds and pigs, and gathering the eggs himself. On the whole, I enjoyed my visit considerably and learned a good many practical lessons therefrom, but what the visit principally did for me was to raise the D. A. V.

College of Lahore and its first Principal, and the Gurukula of Kangri and its first Governor, at least 100 times more in my estimation than before. In endowments, in actual expenditure, in buildings, in grounds, in the extensiveness of its operations, the vastness of its industrial and educational activities, the Normal and Industrial Institute at the Tuskegee is far, far ahead of and very much larger than either of the Arya Samajic institutions in the Punjab. In fact, in these respects, there is no comparison between it and them. But in the solitary fact that the two institutions of the Aryas have been conceived, built, reared, provided for, by Hindus exclusively and that in so far they have been managed and staffed by them only, they stand on a higher level than the Negro Institute at Tuskegee. I say this in no spirit of carping criticism, nor do I mean it as a disparagement of Booker T. Washington's work. In the circumstances in which Dr. Washington's community is placed in these States, his work and success are grand, inspiring and unique. His community could not supply him the necessary sinews of war simply because they had them not. Yet the fact that he managed to get them from the white community which hates the Negro, stands to his everlasting credit. The glory of the D. A. V. College and the Gurukula, however, rests on a different footing. They represent the spiritual loftiness and grandeur of the ancient Aryas. They are the living testimony of that spirit. Though smouldering, it is still there and with one touch of a mighty soul like that of Dayanand, can be made to burst into a blaze. It is something, nay, it is a mighty good thing to be proud of, to have a Hansraj living all his life with a family of wife and children, on 50 Rupees a month, and a Munshi Ram, giving all his substance to the Gurukula, himself living on bread and milk.

THE NEGRO IN AMERICAN POLITICS

Slavery and bondage are unnatural as well as inhuman. They degrade and debase both the master and the slave. The former they turn into a brute, a bully, and a monster of greed and lust; the latter into a parasite, a hypocrite, and a mere animal. The institution of slavery saps the manhood of both. It kills the germs of humanity, generosity, and fellow-feeling in one, amd those of self-respect, confidence, frankness, and manliness in the other. Slavery is of several grades and kinds. The worst form is that where a man owns a man, body and soul; where he is sold and bought like a chattel, a block of wood, or a vegetable; where he has no choice of life, of profession, of work; where he subordinates for life his will to the will of another and where his body, his brain, and his soul, all, are at the bidding of another. In this state, even a conception of individuality ceases and the slave becomes a mere machine, worked, maintained, and exploited by another. Then there is political bondage, where one nation rules over another, holds it under complete sway, exploits and uses it as it suits her. The world has agreed to condemn the former, but not the latter. Civilization not only does not condemn, but in a way admires and glorifies the latter. It is an object which excites jealousy and rivalry among the "best" and the "most civilized" of the race.

Human foresight cannot see any time when the struggle between might and right, between force and fairness, between the strong and the weak, the oppressor and the oppressed, the mighty and the mightless, shall cease. Two-thirds of human history is made up of these struggles. That is what interests mankind the most, and a nation that ignores it is condemned by civilization as lacking in historical sense—a verdict which is often passed against the Aryans of India, the ancestors of the present-day Hindus.

Considering that these struggles are a permanent feature of human life and human activity, they are of permanent and absorbing interest to humanity at large and must forever continue to interest mankind. Indeed, from that standpoint, the history of the emancipation of the American Negro is of abiding interest to my countrymen, and I sketch it below as briefly as is possible in conformity with the scope of this book. Negro slavery in America is as old as America itself—not the land which we call America but the America conquered and owned by the white people. The first batch of twenty African slaves landed in America in what is now the State of Virginia in the year 1619, but there were Nego slaves in the country even before that. When the Spanish explorers and adventureres came to America, they brought with them many Spanish Negroes as servants and as slaves. It is probable that a few Negroes were sent out to the West Indies as early as 1501 A.D. At the beginning of the 19th century

England held in all her colonies in the New World 800,000 slaves, France 250,000, Denmark 26,000, Spain and Portugal 600,000, Holland 50,000, Sweden 600. There were about 900,000 slaves in the United States and about 2,000,000 in Brazil. Mr. Booker T. Washington thinks that "from the time America was discovered down to 1860 A.D. the number of white people that" had "immigrated from Europe to North and South America was less than the number of black people, who were brought over in slave ships during the same period."* In passing, it would be interesting to observe that in the early days of American settlement, slavery was not confined to the American Indian and the Negro. There were other human beings besides them, that were "bought and sold" and "in other respects treated as property" in America.† The historian Bancroft says that "conditional servitude under indentures or covenants had from the first existed in Virginia" and that "white servants" were "an article of regular traffic. They were sold in England to be transported and in Virginia were sold to the highest bidder ; like Negroes, they were to be purchased on shipboard as men buy horses at a fair." "It was surprising to me to learn," says Mr. Washington, "that a little more than 200 years ago Englishmen

* "The Story of the Negro" by Booker T. Washington, volume I, page 106.

† Diving into the remote past, we learn that centuries ago there had been white slaves in England and that "Pope Gregory, seeing some beautiful English slaves exposed for sale in the Forum at Rome, was so impressed by their sad conditon that he determined to undertake the conversion of Britain."

sold the prisoners taken in their civil wars in much the same way that the African people captured and sold people of their own race." At first the condition of the Negro slave was not in most respects unlike that of the white servants, but gradually the sentiment that "blood is thicker than water" asserted itself. "The condition of the white servants was continually improved, but that of the black slave grew steadily worse" until it became unbearable and resulted in occasional revolts. Very stringent laws were made to keep the Negro down, to prevent his escape, to secure his recapture after escapes, to assure the master a complete dominion over him. In 1829, when a master was indicted for beating a slave, the Supreme Court of North Carolina acquitted the former and "affirmed the master's right to inflict any kind of punishment upon his slave short of death." It was a mistake, the decision continued to say, that the relations of the master and slave were like that of parent and child. The object of the parent in training his son was to render him fit to live the life of a free man and as a means to that end, he gave him moral and intellectual instruction. With the case of a slave it was different. Chief Justice Ruffin summed up his opinion upon this point in these words:

"The end is the profit of the master, his security, and the public safety; the subject one doomed in his own person and his posterity to live without knowledge and without capacity to make anything his own and to toil that another may reap the fruits...... Such service can only be expected from one who has no will of his own, who surrenders his will in implicit obedience to that of another. Such obedience is the consequence only of uncontrolled authority over the body......The power of the master must be absolute to render the submission of the slave perfect."

The treatment which the Negro received at the hands of his master under the above conditions of law may better be imagined than described. It would be small wonder then that even before the great American Revolution that took place in 1776, something like 25 insurrections of the slaves should have taken place in the United States. These did not include the outbreaks that occurred in Louisiana (as it was not a part of the United States at the time of the Revolution) and in the other Spanish, French, and English colonies in the West Indies. But it would be quite wrong to conclude that these insurrections and revolts were due to the ill-treatment of those that revolted. The history of these outbreak leaves no doubt in the mind of the reader that they were in the main inspired by the human love of liberty and by the love which individuals cherish for their race and their community. We will narrate a few select events :

In 1800 two Negroes were the leaders of an attempted revolt in Virginia. The plot was discovered before the attempt could be made, and the leaders were caught and executed.

Twenty-two years later, an extensive conspiracy was organized by a free Negro, Denmak Vesey. Vesey's plot failed. He was caught, tried, and with thirty-four others put to death.

In 1831 came the outbreak under Nat Turner, a very remarkable Negro who believed that he had a mission to free the Negroes.

"He grew up to be a silent, dreamy kind of man, going, whenever he could, to the caves of the mountains, to brood over the condition of slaves. . . . . On August 31, 1831, with the belief that he was executing the will of God, Nat Turner started forth with six companions who were soon joined by others, making a force of 60 men."

Eventually the troops were called out and after more than 100 of the insurgents were killed, the uprising was crushed. Nat Turner was convicted and hanged.

John Brown was a white man who championed the cause of the Negro and organized a revolt in 1859. He had a number of colored men in his hand.

A great Negro leader, Frederick Douglass, says in his narrative published in 1845 that when he was a slave in Maryland on the shores of Chesapeake Bay, he often watched the ships as they sailed by and as they passed, he addressed them in this way:

"You are loosed from your moorings, and are free. I am fast in my chains and am a slave! You move merrily before the gentle gale, and I sadly before the bloody whip! You are freedom's swift-winged angels that fly around the world, I am confined in bonds of iron. O that I were free! O that I were one of your gallant decks and under your protecting wing!"

II.

The final abolition of slavery and the emancipation of the slaves did not come until 1865, as a result of the Civil War between the North and the

South. But before that there was a fairly large number of free Negroes in the United States. The emancipation of the Negro had practically begun with the Declaration of Independence in 1776. The Colony of Vermont adopted a constitution in 1777 abolishing slavery, Massachusetts in 1780, New Hampshire in 1783; Pennsylvania, Rhode Island, and Connecticut passed gradual abolition laws in 1799 and 1800. The South, however, was always opposed to the relaxation of property rights in slaves and passed law after law checking and limiting their emancipation. Yet the number of free Negroes continued to increase in the Southern States as well as the Northern in spite of these laws. Some persons during their lifetime voluntarily granted freedom to their slaves; others liberated their slaves by will. In other cases freedom was purchased by the slave first for himself and then for his family, by paying a price to the slaveholder. In addition to this, a large number ran away from their masters and settled in free colonies and countries. "In this and other ways," says Booker T. Washington, "there were at this time something like 30,000 fugitives in Canada, the number of free Negroes in the United States increased from 59466 in 1790 to 434,495 in 1860." It appears that for some time the free Negroes exercised about the same rights under the law that other free persons had, but gradually when their number began to increase, State after State began to impose restrictions and make discriminations.

Between 1792 and 1834, the four bordering States

Delaware, Maryland, Virginia, and Kentucky denied suffrage to the Negro. In 1835 North Carolina excluded them from the suffrage. New Jersey took away the suffrage of the Negro in 1807, Connecticut in 1814, and Pennsylvania in 1838. "These changes," says Booker T. Washington, "were all evidences of the steady growth in the United States both North and South, of a caste system which excluded the Negro from the ordinary privileges of citizenship exclusively upon the ground of his color. In 1802 Ohio demanded a bond of $500 for Negroes who came into the State. A Negro, even though a free man, could not at that time testify in a case in which a white man was a party, and Negroes were not admitted to the public schools." Similar provisions were made in other States. In 1833 it was judicially decided that a free Negro was a person and not a citizen.

"In some States they were forbidden to sell drugs, in others they might not sell wheat and tobacco, and in still others, to peddle market produce or own a boat was against the law. In several States it was against the law for a free Negro to cross the State line; in others a slave who was emancipated was compelled to immediately leave the State."

One good came out of all these restrictions and limitations and that consisted in the Negro coming to realize the value of co-operation and organization for common purposes. A remarkable instance of such organization was the "Underground Railroad", an account of the origin of which we take from a work called "The Negro in American History" compiled by a Negro professor of the Atlanta University. In Appendix E* of his work he says:

"The abolition of slavery in Massachusetts, Pennsylvania, New York and other States in the North was followed by unceasing attempts of the slave in the South to escape from bondage. He could not always use the well-established routes of travel, the public stage, the steamboat or, later, the railroad, for this would have invited attention and facilitated detection and apprehension to be followed by a return to more oppressive forms of bondage."

In the first administration of President Washington, in 1793, a Fugitive Slave Law was passed which "empowered the owner, his agent or attorney, to seize the fugitive and take him before a United States Circuit or District Judge within the county in which the seizure occurs."

But this law was ineffectual, for slaves in increasing number continued to escape to the North and to Canada. The time of their departure, and the route were not only not within the public eye, but beyond detection. The route was as much a secret as though underground, hence the term "Underground Railroad" was understood to include all the agencies and instrumentalities by which the slave received the direction and aid that enabled him to obtain his freedom.

The number aided and escaping by means of the Underground Railroad has been placed as high as fifty thousand by Rev. W. M. Mitchell, one who was an active agent in this work, author of "The Under-

* John W. Cromwell, "The Negro in American History," Appendix E, pages 246-247.

ground Railroad"; and J. H. F. Claiborne, biographer of John A. Quitman, placed the number as high as one hundred thousand.

A full and comprehensive history of this movement has now been published and reads like a romance. It narrates in the words of the fugitives themselves the difficulties, sufferings, fears of runaway slaves, and of the various devices which they used to escape from bondage to freedom. The man who preserved this record speaks of his own motives for keeping this record in the following words:

"Thousands of escapes, harrowing separations, dreadful longings, dark gropings after lost parents, brothers, sisters, and identities, seemed ever to be pressing on my mind. While I knew the danger of keeping strict records, and while I did not then dream that in my day slavery would be blotted out, or that the time would come when I could publish these records, it used to afford me great satisfaction to take them down, fresh from the lips of fugitives on the way to freedom, and to preserve them as they had given them." *

We give the following lengthy quotation from Booker T. Washington's book called the "The Story of the Negro," to illustrate the methods adopted by "The Underground Railroad" in helping fugitive Negroes:

"Sometimes these fugitives reached free soil packed in boxes, shipped as merchandise by rail or by steamship, from some of the nearby Southern ports. This was the case of Henry Box Brown, who was shipped from Richmond, Va., by James A. Smith, a shoe dealer, to William H. Johnson, Arch Street, Phila-

* B. T. Washington, "The Story of the Negro," Vol. I, pages 216—217.

delphia. Though the box was marked "This side up," in the course of his journey, Mr. Brown was compelled to ride many miles standing on his head. When the box arrived at the anti-slavery office, there was the greatest apprehension lest, in the course of the journey, the fugitive had perished and the society would find itself with a corpse upon its hands. Mr. Still described, in the following words, the scene when this box was opened in the presence of a number of prominent members of the Anti-slavery Society:

"All was quiet. The door had been safely locked. The proceedings commenced. Mr. J. Miller McKim, Secretary of the Pennsylvania Anti-slavery Society, rapped quietly on the lid of the box and called out, 'All right.' Instantly came the answer from within, 'All right, sir.'

"The witnesses will never forget that moment. Saw and hatchet quickly had the five hickory hoops cut and the lid off, and the marvellous resurrection of Brown ensued. Rising up in his box, he reached out his hand, saying, "How do you do, gentlemen?" The little assemblage hardly knew what to think or do at the moment. He was about as wet as if he had come up out of the Delaware. Very soon he remarked that, before leaving Richmond, he had selected for his arrival-hymn (if he lived) the psalm beginning with these words: 'I waited patiently for the Lord, and He heard my prayer.' And most touchingly did he sing the psalm, much to his own relief, as well as to the delight of his small audience. He was then christened Henry Box Brown, and soon afterwards was sent to the hospitable residence of James Mott and E. M. Davis, on Ninth Street, where, it is needless to say, he met a cordial reception from Mrs. Lucretia Mott and her household.

"Other attempts were made after that time to ship fugitive slaves out of the South as express packages. In 1857, a young woman was shipped from Baltimore to Philadelphia in a box of freight. After reaching Philadelphia, this box with its living freight, after having been turned upside down several times, was left standing nearly all of one night at the freight shed, and it was not secured by the persons to whom it was consigned until ten o'clock the next day. When the box was opened the young woman inside was unconscious and could not speak for some time. She recovered, however, and eventually escaped to Canada. Samuel A. Smith, who shipped Henry Box Brown from Richmond to Philadelphia, attempted, shortly after this successful venture to send two other slaves by express to the anti-slavery office. The deceit, however, was discovered and Smith was arrested, convicted, and sentenced to eight years in prison, and served out his time in the penitentiary.

"Frequently fugitives were secreted upon steamships and sailing vessels. There was usually a colored steward on these vessels who was willing to run the risk of assisting a fugitive to escape. Men dressed themselves as women, and women dressed themselves as men in order to escape from slavery. Sometimes fugitives travelled hundreds of miles in skiffs in order to reach free soil." *

III.

The final emancipation of the Negro, however, was due to the exertion of the Northern States. Principle, philanthrophy, the Christian teaching of the brotherhood of man, combined with expediency to pave the way for the reform. "The overthrow of slavery," says Dean Kelly Miller, "was due to economic as well as to moral and philanthropic causes." The free labour of the North was the first to awake to consciousness of the fact that he was made the competitor of slave labor, a

* B. T. Washington, Vol. I, pages 217 to 219.

condition which he resented and resisted to the bitter end. It is impossible to relegate the Negro to any status without at the same time affecting a sufficient number of white men to make up the full quota of that status. Any degradation placed upon the Negro laborer must react upon the white workman of the same grade.

The presidential election of 1860 was fought on this issue and resulted in the victory of the North. Then came the civil war. The white laborer had virtually been reduced to the position of the Negro, and his emancipation was as much an issue in the war as that of the Negro. On April 16, 1862, slavery was abolished in the district of Columbia by the payment of about a million dollars to the slave owners. On January first, 1863, President Lincoln issued the Emancipation Proclamation, declaring all slaves in the United States "henceforth and forever free." "Slavery," said Lincoln, "must be always and everywhere hostile to the principles of republican government. Justice and the national safety demand ter and complete extirpation from the soil of the Republic."

"The assassination of President Lincoln, April 15, 1865, following so closely upon the Fall of Richmond and the Surrender of Lee at Appomattox, precipitated a long and bitter conflict between Congress and Andrew Johnson, Lincoln's successor in office. April 9, 1866, a Civil Rights Law was enacted, conferring certain fundamental rights upon the emancipated race—the right to sue and be sued, to hold property, and to testify in the courts. The States lately in rebellion passed vagrant acts which virtually re-enacted many of the objectionable features of the Slave Code, and Congress decided to protect by legislation and constitutional enactments those freed by the sword. The Thirteenth Amendment, constitutionally legalizing emancipation, became a part of the Constitution, December 18, 1865; the Fourteenth Amendment, defining citizenship and declaring all Negroes to be citizens of the United States and of the States in which they reside, became incorporated in the Constitution, July 18, 1868. The right of franchise was given the Negro, first in the States that were engaged in rebellion by the Reconstruction Act organizing the seceded States, which passed March 2, 1867 and through the Fifteenth Amendment, preventing any denial of the right of suffrage on account of race, color or previous condition of servitude. This amendment was ratified March 30, 1870, and applied to the entire country. With its embodiment in the fundamental law and the restoration of all the States lately in rebellion to their constitutional rights and representation within the Union, the work of reconstruction was supposed to be complete."*

IV.

Then came the aftermath. The Negro was emancipated. Slavery was gone; but the free Negro was an even greater problem than the slave Negro. The emancipation of the Negro had been obtained at the point of the bayonet. The South had never agreed to it and had resisted it to the bitter end. The Republican North had attempted it by force. The questions that confronted the party in power were twofold : (1) what to do with the freed Negro: how to float him in the world. He was penniless and houseless, with nothing to eat, nothing to clothe himself with, no shelter from rain and sun, and no

* Cromwell: "The Negro in American History," page 23—24.

work to earn his livelihood by, even if he would. The white Southerner was sour and dour; the war had ruined him politically as well as economically. (2) The reconstruction and reorganisation of the South on the principles which had won the war.

The war had resulted in an extreme exhaustion of the South. It had impoverished the Southerner, dethroned the planter, enfranchised the poor white, emancipated the Negro, and had thus altered the whole basis of government and society in the south. The logic of facts made co-operation between the North and the South in the work of reconstruction extremely difficult, if not impossible. The Northerners believed they had been right. Did not their victory show that? The South had seceded and had by her rebellion and contumacy brought on the war. "Should she not be punished for it or at least forced to acknowledge that she had been wrong and compelled to take step that would prevent the recurrence of that wrong ?" Then the assassination of Lincoln intensified this feeling a hundredfold and the North began to insist upon "punishment" and revenge.

The Southerner on the other hand saw that "his estates were ruined, his fortune gone ; he saw Northern soldiers quartered on the poverty-stricken and exhausted country and knew that, whatever legal excuse was offered, they were "conquerors" and held him and his in subjection. Then the Negro and the poor white whom he had despised and ruled, were also thorns at his side. The war had raised the Negro to the level of both. He resented the interference of the North in his affairs and was not willing to co-operate in the work of reconstruction except on his own terms. The moment he got that chance, he showed his terms by actual conduct and by a policy of resentment and reaction. "The resentment and reaction of the South," says Mr. Usher in his book called "The Rise of the American People", "caused the insertion of clauses in the New Constitution denying with vehemence the equality of the white and the black races and affirming that Negroes could not be citizens of the United States. To coerce the Negroes into working "vagrancy", Acts were passed in several States in the fall of 1865 which declared it an offence for Negroes over 18 years old to be without "lawful employment or business" or to be found "unlawfully assembling themselves together either in the day or night time." Negroes under 18 years of age, "orphans or the children of parents who could not or would not support them" were to be apprenticed until 21 years old by the clerk of the Probate Court at his discretion, preferably to the former owner. Mississippi made a similar provision for Negroes who did not pay their taxes, and then levied a poll tax of one dollar a head on all Negroes "for the support of the poor." The criminal statutes provided fines and compulsory work to be done by the criminal for the man who would pay in return for the shortest period of service in such elastic offences as "malicious mischief," "insulting gestures," "seditious speeches," "or any other misdemeanor." These acts created an impression in the North that the Southerners intended to restore actual slavery under the guise of apprenticeship or as a punishment for debt or crime and, to hasten and facilitate the completion of the process, had put Acts on the statute book defining proverty and crime in broad and inclusive terms which ipso facto made every Negro guilty. They had provided compulsory work for Negroes in debt and had then passed laws which instantly put every Negro in debt. The South, besides, very naturally proceeded to elect those very men as senators and representatives of the United States Congress who had been prominent in the administrative and military service of the Confederacy and organized a State militia in whose ranks were naturally to be found a large proportion of confederate veterans who had fought in the war on their side. All this raised the suspicion of the North. They thought that everything gained by the war was likely to be lost if they were not vigilant; the South was still in rebellion and would do everything possible to reduce the Negro to the old conditions of slavery. 'There commenced the tug of war between the Republican Congress and the South which was to humiliate the South and place the power in the hands of those who accepted in full the principles of the North.

The Negro had in the meantime been put under the protection of an official bureau called the Freedmen's Bureau, whose duty it was "to care for the blacks and their interests, to shield them from the speculation and sharpers, white and black, already imposing on their inexperience and to allot to them the abandoned plantations and furnish enough tools and seeds to start them on the new life." To facilitate the work, jurisdiction was given the bureau over all controversies to which a Negro was a party, including family relations and marriage. In particular, the bureau was to take cognizance of all the means and methods by which the whites sought to secure the labour of the freedmen and was to guarantee them against contracts which should be the equivalent of slavery for life. . . . To the Southerner, the Bureau was a diabolical device to perpetuate the military conquest of the South and humiliate the whites before the Negro, a method of compelling by force recognition of the social equality with the blacks which the whites were determined not to concede." When the tug of war recommenced between the Congress and the South over the reactionary measures enacted by the latter, the first measures were intended to increase the power of the Freedmen's Bureau. The first step was to ensure the continuance of the republican parties' regime that had won the war, for sufficient time to enable them to crush the South and enforce their measures. These measures were calculated "to secure to the Negro full equality in civic rights and before the courts; to define the term 'Citizen of the U. S.' and include the Negro . . . to repudiate forever all claims to indemnification for loss by reason of the emancipation of the slaves; and to disqualify all confederates (those who had taken part in the war on the side of the South) for election to Federal office. Above all it was intended to prevent Southern States, when re-organized, from taking advantage of the increase in representation" to which they were entitled under the amended constitution, "without enfranchising the Negro. . . . ." In the States where the Negroes equalled or outnumbered the whites, the effect of the amendment was materially to decrease the old representation of the State in the House of Representatives and thus to ensure the control of that body by the Republicans, for any increase could be obtained only by the enfranchisement of the Negroes who could be depended upon to vote for the Republicans.

Thus the white Republicans of the North sided with the white Republicans of the South and the Negroes to frustrate the designs of the Southern slave-holders against the party in power. The result was what are called "Negro Governments" in the South. In South Carolina the majority of the legislature and of the most important officers were Negroes and the rest were, in the words of Usher, "rascally whites from the Northern or even more unsavory characters from the South." The tables were thus turned on the whites.

By 1871, the valuation of property held by the whites had decreased 40 %, the taxes had risen 500% and the state debt increased 400%. The taxes were often levied by the Negroes, of whom scarcely 20 % had any property at all and of whom 80 % were illiterate, and were paid by the whites, the vast majority of whom were disfranchised for participation in the war. To protect themselves against the alleged excesses of the Negroes, elated by this sudden accession of power, the whites set up secret organizations which meted out summary punishment to the offending Negroes. This tug of war continued until, in 1870, the Freedmen's Bureau was abolished, the corps of the army were soon after withdrawn, and the artificial support of the Negroes disappeared. Gradually, too, the whites who had been disqualified for participation in the war, were qualifying as voters, and, as the Negroes were in the numerical majority in only three States, it was clear that the whites would control the other States as soon as they could be re-instated. How the Negro majorities were reduced in these three States has been described by Usher.

The methods resorted to for reducing the Negro majorities have since been persistently followed to practically disfranchise the Negro population altogether. To-day the Negro is politically as much a zero in the South as he was before the emancipation. The present political position of the Negro in the United States may be stated in the words of another American writer, Mr. Paul Leland Haworth:

"The provisions of the fifteenth amendment prohibiting the denial to citizens of the right to vote 'on account of race, color, or previous condition of servitude" would seemingly stand in the way of any legal discrimination against the Negro's political rights; but, as everybody knows, ways have been found for evading the constitutional prohibition. Following the downfall of the Re-construction governments the Negroes in the Southern States were virtually disfranchised by force or fraud, but in 1890 Mississippi evolved a plan whereby the end sought could be attained in a quasi-legal manner. To-day every one of the former Confederate States, except Florida, Arkansas,

Tennessee and Texas, have suffrage requirements which practically eliminate the Negro from politics, while even in the four States named as exceptions he is not much of a factor. By educational or property tests the mass of ignorant and poor Negro voters are excluded, while loopholes are provided for ignorant and poor whites in the shape of "Grandfather clauses," or "Understanding clauses," which last white registration officers can apply rigidly to Negroes and leniently to whites. The avowed purpose of these "suffrage amendments" was to eliminate the Negro from politics and, in spirit, they certainly violate the fifteenth amendment and also lay the States which have adopted them liable to that section of the fourteenth amendment which provides for a reduction in representation in proportion to the number of citizens excluded from the suffrage ; but the Supreme Court has always carefully evaded the constitutional issue, while Congress has not seen fit to reduce the representation of any State. In view of the existing political situation it is improbable that anything will be done to nullify the suffrage requirements."

But that is not all. In addition to disfranchising the Negro and eliminating him from politics "by force or fraud," the Southern legislatures have passed numerous discriminating laws against him. In 1910, 26 States (out of 52) either by statute or constitution forbade the inter-marriage of Negroes with whites. Such mixed alliances are declared void, while the contracting parties are held guilty of a "misdemeanor" in some States, of "felony" in others, and of "infamous crime" in yet others. The punishment varies from imprisonment for ten years at one extreme in certain Southern States to a minimum fine of $ 50 in one and to no penalty on the Negro participant in another.

"A few States impose heavier penalties for illicit relations between whites and blacks than for such offences between persons of the same color. In Alabama, for example, a Negro and a Caucasian convicted of living together for one day with intent to continue the relation are liable to the same penalty as for intermarriage, namely, imprisonment in the penitentiary for not less than two nor more than seven years. In Florida and Nevada the penalties may be no heavier than a simple fine, but Louisiana has a more drastic statute, passed in 1908, which provides that concubinage between a Negro and a white person is a felony, punishable with imprisonment of from one month to one year." *

Besides these, "Jim Crow laws" are in force in all the former slave States providing for separate accommodation for the races on railways and (in some States) on steam boats and street cars. Separation in waiting rooms and railroad dining rooms is also the general rule. Separate cars are usually provided, but on street cars the white passengers are usually assigned to the front seats and colored passengers to the rear seats. It is usually impossible for a Negro passenger, however rich, to obtain a sleeping berth on railroads, and in case such a passenger, in Illinois for example, crosses the Ohio river into Kentucky, he must give up his berth and retire to the colored coach. Too often also, the railway companies provide better accommodation for white passengers than for their colored ones, even though they both pay the same fare.

No Southern State permits colored and white children to attend the same public schools and some

* Haworth, "America in Ferment," page 131-132.

States extend the provision to private schools also. One State only recently enacted a law forbidding white persons to teach in colored schools or vice versa.

Legal distinctions and discriminations are mostly confined to the South, but race prejudice is to be found practically throughout the United States. Negroes are excluded from hotels, Young Women's Christian Associations, Young Men's Christian Associations, theaters, saloons, and are even refused interment in white cemeteries—in some cases in direct violation of local laws. In the absence of legal regulations, public sentiment results in the Negro attending separate churches and registering at separate hotels, confines him to special seats in the theaters, segregates him in cities and even in country places and tends to keep him apart from white people in all relations of life. The Negro is the pariah of the United States.

Race prejudice frequently prevents colored men from obtaining justice and causes white men to wink at and condone flagrant impositions on him. The practice of peonage was broken up by federal courts but in more than one Southern State the laws regarding contracts and leases are so drawn up that the Negro is virtually at the mercy of unscrupulous white men.

The worst form taken by this race prejudiee is the "lynching" of Negroes accused or suspected of crimes against white people, before they have been tried and adjudged guilty by any court of justice. The extent to which it has been indulged in and the alleged causes which furnished occasion for it will appear from the following figures reproduced from a tract on the subject issued by the National Association for the Advancement of Colored People :

NOTES ON LYNCHING :

1. Statistics.

COLOURED MEN LYNCHED WITHOUT TRIAL.

1885	......	78	1901	......	107
1886	......	71	1902	......	86
1887	......	80	1903	......	86
1888	......	95	1904	......	83
1889	......	95	1905	......	61
1890	......	90	1906	......	64
1891	......	121	1907	......	60
1892	......	155	1908	......	93
1893	......	154	1909	......	73
1894	......	134	1910	......	65
1895	......	112	1911	......	63
1896	......	80	1912	......	63
1897	......	122	1913	......	79
1898	......	102	1914	......	69
1899	......	84			
1900	......	107			
		Total		......	2,732

Number of Crimes.

The alleged causes for 1914 were :

			p. c.
Murder	......	30	44
By rioters and nightriders	......	13	19
Personal assaults	......	10	14
Rape, attempts to rape, and presence in women's rooms	......	8	11½
Robbery and theft	......	5	11½
Arson	......	2	
Resistance to search	......	1	

We give the figures above from the Chicago *Tribune*.

"The Crisis" (the organ of the National Association for the Advancement of Colored People) believes that at least 100 colored people were lynched during the year 1911, and that the number given by the *Tribune* is estimated too low.

2. ILLUSTRATIVE MATTER, 1911.

THE CRIME OF BEING A NEGRO

ACCUSED OF KNOCKING A WHITE MAN DOWN

October 20, Manchester, Ga.—Because he was accused of knocking down a white man last night, Jerry Lovelace, a Negro, was taken from jail at 2 o'clock this morning and lynched. There were about thirty men in the mob.

WOMAN AND CHILD HANGED.

May 26, Okemah, Oklahama.—A colored woman accused of having shot a sheriff was taken by a mob and, together with her fourteen-year-old son, was hanged from a bridge. The woman was raped before she was hanged.

A NEGRO A DAY KILLED.

November 2, Birmingham, Alabama.—Four miles north of Birmingham a reign of terror exists. Six white men and eleven Negroes have been assassinated within the past eighteen months. Six of the Negroes have been killed within the past six days, an average of one a day since last Saturday.

FIVE INNOCENT MEN LYNCHED.

May 20, Lake City, Fla.—Six men were taken from jail and lynched "for complicity in the murder of a prominent citizen." The lynchers came in automobiles and showed the sheriff's young son, who had been left in charge of the jail, a forged telegram purporting to come from the governor and ordering that the prisoners be given up. On investigation it was found that only one of the six men murdered was even accused of a crime. A quarrel between a white man and a colored man had been brought up before a local court and the colored man had been exonerated. Immediately afterward the white man went into the colored man's yard with a gun. Shots were exchanged and the white man was killed. The colored man gave himself up at once and the five men with him were being held merely as witnesses.

WOUNDED NEGRO BURNED TO DEATH.

August 13, Coatesville, Pa.—There is no need to repeat the story of the Coatesville horror. You all remember the man who was taken from a bed in the hospital and burned alive for having shot a watchman when drunk. His writhing body was poked back into the flames as he tried to drag himself away. His teeth and charred bones were kept for souvenirs. All arrested for this frolic have been ACQUITTED.

WHAT A JUDGE SAID.

July, Lawrenceville, Ga.—Judge Charles H. Brand of Lawrenceville, Ga., refused to call for troops to protect two Negroes who came before him for trial, one on a charge of an alleged attack on a white woman; the other for "loitering in a suspicious manner."

They were lynched, one was taken from a train where he was in charge of two officers (the train stopping while the passengers saw the lynching); the other was dragged out of jail by a mob several hundred strong.

Judge Brand defended his failure to secure a safeguard for the prisoners, saying:

"I don't propose to be the engine of sacrificing any white man's life for all such Negro criminals in the country. . . . I am in perfect accord with my conscience and my God. I would not imperil the life of one white man to save the lives of a hundred such Negroes."

WHAT GOVERNOR BLEASE SAYS.

November 11, Honeapath, S.C.—Governor Blease of South Carolina says, in regard to a recent lynching in his State, that rather than use the power of his office in deterring white men from "punishing that Nigger brute," he "would have resigned his office and come to Honeapath and led the mob."

The above facts have, I presume, given the reader some idea of the magnitude of the problem of the Negro in the United States of America. Both the parties to the question, the whites as well as the blacks, are conscious of the gravity of the situation. There is a great deal of conflict of the rights and wrongs of the actual state of things and about the future. The whites themselves are divided into three classes: first, those who have nothing but condemnation for the prejudice; second, those who condemn the prejudice, but palliate it on the ground that there is such a distance between the white man and the Negro that it is impossible for the former to treat the latter as an equal. These people would discriminate in favour of the better class of Negroes, the educated and the cultured among them; last, but not least, is the class which condemns the Negroes on racial grounds and would under no circumstances have any sort of social relations with them. This class believes that "no amount of education of any kind, industrial, classical, or religious, can make out of a Negro a white man or bridge the chasm which separates him from the white man in the evolution of human history."

Among the Negroes themselves there is unanimity only up to a certain point. The prevalence of crime, ignorance, superstition, laziness, thriftlessness, are all ascribed to environments and circumstances. "The Negroes were brought to America as dejected and expatriated individuals. The imported slaves represented the conquered and subdued, the despised and outcast of their own country and race." In America, during the period of slavery, they were denied freedom of education, freedom of motion, means of intercommunication and the privilege of unrestrained assemblage. Generally speaking, everything which tends to civilize a man was denied to him. The master was bound by no law or morality in his treatment of the slave, man or woman, and to-day a large number of colored men in America are the standing proof of the immoral lawlessness of their former white masters. Under the institution of slavery the Negro was suppressed below the level of self-respect. The black woman often felt her superior importance by becoming the mother of a tawny child. The white master or overseer felt no legal, social, or conscientious constraint in victimizing the female chattel. "The Negro in this country," says Dean Miller, "is the sacrificial race. He is the burden bearer of the white race. He constitutes the meek sill of society and suffers the ills of that lowly place. He performs the rough work of society. He suffers the affliction and even commits the crimes which always fall to the lot of his status."

In another place the same writer says:

"The Negro woman has been made to bear the brunt of the evil passions of all the races of men living or sojourning in this country. Within the veins of the so-called Negro race there course traces of the blood of every known variety or sub-variety of the human family. Not only within the limits of the race itself, but even within the veins of the same individuals, the strains of blood are mingled and blended in inextricable confusion."

Under the circumstances, Dean Miller claims that the advancement of the race during the past fifty years since the emancipation, has been marvellous. Fifty years is entirely too short a time to measure the potency and promise of the race. "In the economy of racial life a half century is scarcely more than a single year in the experience of an individual." Yet the following facts show that the progress made by the Negro in America within the last fifty years is a marvel.

Judged by the standard of physical persistence, the 4½ million slaves of 1860 have doubled their number under the strain and stress of conditions that would have caused any of the weaker breeds of men to pine away and die.

Coming to the test of literacy and education, in a period of 50 years a considerable majority of its members have learned the use of letters.

"The accumulation of houses and lands and material goods on the part of the Negro has been commendable and encouraging. If his landed possessions could be formed into one continuous area, it would make a territory larger than many a far famed principality in ancient and modern annals.

"In industry he has pushed his way into every line of listed occupation and contributes his full share to the nation's industrial equation.

"He has developed a professional class who sprang into existence suddenly like Melchisedeck of old, without antecedent or beginning of days. This professional class must stand in the high places of leadership and guidance of the masses and direct them aright amid the stress and strain of a strenuous civilization. It is easy to predict the speedy undoing of a race that fails to produce its own competent leaders, but a people that can produce safe and sagacious leadership can never be undone.

"In religion, the race has developed a priesthood whose increasing power and piety will enable them to hold this vast Christian constituency in definite organic relation to the great religious movements of the age.

"In morals, manners, social customs and habits he conforms to the prevailing standards, with no greater variation than grows out of his status in the general scheme. The Negro shows his near kinship to the great body of white Americans by speaking the same language, worshipping the same God, striving after the same ideals, longing for the same destiny. None but the most confirmed pessimist can say that that past half century has not given a satisfactory indication that he will be able to meet every exaction that the coming years may impose upon him."*

Nor is the record of the Negro from the point of view of eminent Negroes, in any way such as to prove the inherent intellectual inferiority of the race. Several lists of distinguished Negroes have been prepared and are in existence and a race which can produce a Booker T. Washington and a Du Bois need not be ashamed of its intellectual capacity.

So far, all parties among the Negroes are agreed, and so are they on the question of race prejudice. When it, however, comes to a question of remedies, they differ.

"Mr. Washington represents in Negro thought the old attitude of adjustment and submission ; but

* Kelly Miller : "Out of the House of Bondage," pp. 37-38.

adjustment at such a peculiar time as to make his programme unique. This is an age of unusual economic development, and Mr. Washington's programme naturally takes an economic cast, becoming a gospel of Work and Money to such an extent as apparently almost completely to overshadow the higher aims of life. Moreover, this is an age when the more advanced races are coming into closer contact with the less developed races, and the race-feeling is, therefore, intensified ; and Mr. Washington's programme practically accepts the alleged inferiority of the Negro races. Again, in our own land, the reaction from the sentiment of war time has given impetus to race-prejudice against Negroes, and Mr. Washington withdraws many of the high demands of Negroes as men and American citizens. In other periods of intensified prejudice all the Negro's tendency to self-assertion has been called forth ; at this period a policy of submission is advocated. In the history of nearly all other races and peoples the doctrine preached at such crises has been that manly self-respect is worth more than lands and houses, and that a people who voluntarily surrender such respect or cease striving for it, are not worth civilizing.

"In answer to this, it has been claimed that the Negro can survive only through submission. Mr. Washington distinctly asks that black people give up, at least for the present, three things,—

"First, political power,

"Second, insistence on civic rights,

"Third, higher education of Negro youth,—

and concentrate all their energies on industrial education, the accumulation of wealth, and the conciliation of the South. This policy has been courageously and insistently advocated for over fifteen years, and has been triumphant for perhaps ten years. As a result of this tender of the palm branch, what has been the return ? In these years there have occurred :

1. The disfranchisement of the Negro.

2. The legal creation of a distinct status of civil inferiority for the Negro.

3. The steady withdrawal of aid from institutions for the higher training of the Negro.

"These movements are not, to be sure, direct results of Mr. Washington's teachings ; but his propaganda has, without a shadow of doubt, helped their speedier accomplishment. The question then comes: Is it possible, and probable, that nine millions of men can make effective progress in economic lines if they are deprived of political rights, made a servile caste, and allowed only the most meagre chance for developing their exceptional men ? If history and reason give any distinct answer to these questions, it is an emphatic NO. And Mr. Washington thus faces the triple paradox of his career:

1. He is striving nobly to make Negro artisans, business men, and property owners; but it is utterly impossible, under modern competitive methods, for workingmen and property-owners to defend their rights and exist without the right of suffrage.

2. He insists on thrift and self-respect, but at the same time counsels a silent submission to civic inferiority such as is bound to sap the manhood of any race in the long run.

3. He advocates common-school and industrial training; but neither the Negro common-schools nor Tuskegee itself, could remain open a day were it not for teachers trained in Negro colleges, or trained by their graduates.

"This triple paradox in Mr. Washington's position is the object of criticism by two classes of colored Americans. One class is spiritually descended from Toussaint the Savior, through Gabriel, Vesey, and Turner, and they represent the attitude of revolt and revenge; they hate the white South blindly and distrust the white race generally, and so far as they agree on definite action, think that the Negro's only hope lies in emigration beyond the borders of the

United States. And yet, by the irony of fate, nothing has more effectually made this programme seem hopeless than the recent course of the United States towards weaker and darker people in the West Indies, Hawaii, and the Philippines,—for where in the world may we go and be safe from lying and brute force?

"The other class of Negroes who cannot agree with Mr. Washington has hitherto said little aloud. They deprecate the sight of scattered counsels, of internal disagreement and especially they dislike making their just criticism of a useful and earnest man an excuse for a general discharge of venom from small-minded opponents. Nevertheless, the questions involved are so fundamental and serious that it is difficult to see how men like the Grimkes, Kelly Miller, J. W. E. Bowen, and other representatives of this group, can much longer be silent. Such men feel in conscience bound to ask of this nation three things:

1. The right to vote.
2. Civic equality.
3. The education of youth according to ability.

"They acknowledge Mr. Washington's invaluable service in counselling patience and courtesy in such demands; they do not ask that ignorant black men vote when ignorant whites are debarred, or that any reasonable restrictions in the suffrage should not be applied; they know that the low social level of the race is responsible for much discrimination against it, but they also know, and the nation knows, that relentless color-prejudice is more often a cause than a result of the Negro's degradation; they seek the abatement of this relic of barbarism, and not its systematic encouragement and pampering by all agencies of social power from the Associated Press to the Church of Christ. They advocate, with Mr. Washington, a broad system of Negro common schools supplemented by a thorough industrial training; but they are surprised that a man of Mr. Washington's insight cannot see that no such educational system ever has rested or can rest on any other basis than that of the well-equipped college or university, and they insist that there is a demand for a few such institutions throughout the South to train the best of the Negro youth as teachers, professional men, and leaders.

"This group of men honor Mr. Washington for his attitude of conciliation toward the white South; they accept the 'Atlanta Compromise' in its broadest interpretation; they recognize, with him, many signs of promise, many men of high purpose and fair judgment, in this section; they know that no easy task has been laid upon a region already tottering under heavy burdens. But, nevertheless, they insist that the way to truth and right lies in a straightforward honesty, not in indiscriminate flattery; in praising those of the South who do well and criticising uncompromisingly those who do ill; in taking advantage of the opportunities at hand and urging their fellows to do the same, but at the same time in remembering that only a firm adherence to their higher ideals and aspirations will ever keep those ideals within the realm of possibility. They do not expect that the free right to vote, to enjoy civic rights, and to be educated, will come in a moment; they do not expect to see the bias and prejudices of years disappear at the blast of a trumpet; but they are absolutely certain that the way for a people to gain their reasonable rights is not by voluntarily throwing them away and insisting that they do not want them; that the way for a people to gain respect is not by continually belittling and ridiculing themselves; that, on the contrary, Negroes must insist continually, in season and out of season, that voting is necessary to modern manhood, that color discrimination is barbarism, and that black boys need education as well as white boys." *

* W. E. B. Du Bois: "The Souls of Black Folk," pp. 50-55.

NEGRO ORGANIZATION.

To-day, throughout the length and breadth of the country, there is a vast network of organizations for the protection of the interests of the Negroes. One of the principal organizations of that kind is the National Association for the Advancement of Colored People. A copy of its treasurer's report for the year 1914 will give an idea of its resources. The Association has an organ of its own, called "The Crisis," which had a circulation of over 30,000 copies in December, 1914.

REPORT OF THE TREASURER.

N. A. A. C. P. Revenue and Expense Account, 1914.

EXPENSES.

Salaries	...	$	7,395·34
General expenses	...	,,	2,606·15
Printing	...	,,	1,613·53
Travelling expense	...	,,	879·51
Postage	...	,,	868·88
Depreciation on furniture	...	,,	96·80
		$	13,460·16
Net gain			570·54
		$	14,030·70

REVENUE

Membership	...	$	5,661·19
Donations	...	,,	8,334·81
Literature sold	...	,,	18·70
Profit on pins sold	...	,,	16·00
		$	14,030·70

BALANCE SHEET, DECEMBER 31, 1914.

ASSETS

Cash in banks	... $	1,374·04
Petty cash fund	... ,,	25·00
Due from "Crisis"	... ,,	9·30
Pins on hand	... ,,	130·92
Furniture and fixtures	... ,,	876·65
	$	2,415·91

LIABILITIES

Special funds reserved :		
Maclean Memorial	... $	302·90
Fed. Aid Educational	... ,,	195·63
	$	498·53
Net worth		1,917·38
	$	2,415·91

It is gratifying to note that the Association can report itself out of debt with a substantial balance in bank. Its net gain for the year is almost $600 and its net worth over $1,900,

An analysis of the membership list shows that eighty per cent. are colored and twenty per cent. white.

The preceeding financial report by a certified public accountant shows expense and revenue only. It is interesting to note in this connection that since the Association's books were opened in May, 1911, its income has been as follows, that for 1914 being within about $ 300 of that of the previous year despite the financial depression :

1912	... $	11,815·15
1913	... ,,	15,526·85
1914	... ,,	15,237·98

A fair idea as to the scope of the work done by the association can be obtained from the following extracts from the report of the secretary as to the activities of some of the various branches of the association during the year 1914.

The Boston branch persuaded the Boston School Committee to withdraw from the schools a book entitled "Forty Best Songs" which contained words objectionable to colored people.

The Northern California branch was successful in having discriminating signs removed from cheap restaurants.

The Cleveland branch took the initiative in getting two colored people on the General Welfare Council of the city.

The Detroit branch smothered an anti-intermarriage bill in the Michigan Legislature in February, and secured the appointment of two colored detectives to the police force.

The District of Columbia branch work resulted in: The reinstatement of a colored government employee who had been dismissed; successful agitation to compel the commencement of work on the new colored high school; the checking of discrimination in the restaurant of one of the large department stores; securing assurances from the Board of Education that moving pictures on educational topics for the public schools should be enjoyed by colored pupils.

The Harrisburg branch won an encouraging victory over a local moving picture theatre. According to witnesses, the proprietor of this theater had the following notice posted at the ticket office:

"The balcony of this theatre is provided for our colored patrons. If you do not wish to sit in the balcony, do not purchase tickets, as they will not be honored in any other section of the theatre."

In giving his decision in the case, the judge ruled that to reserve a certain section of a public amusement house for the special accommodation of the white race and to deprive colored patrons of the right to occupy that particular section, is a discrimination against the colored race and a violation of the criminal statute and punishable by a fine. This decision is the first of its kind rendered in Dauphin County.

The Howard branch was the first college chapter chartered. As a student organization, it has devoted itself especially to the study of the race question and to spreading the propaganda of the N. A. A. C. P. by sending speakers to other colleges, by correspondence, and by distributing literature broadcast. The dispatch with which briefs protesting against the Afro-Exclusion amendment to the Immigration Bill were distributed to members of Congress was largely due to the energy of the students of the Howard Chapter.

Kansas City branch was successful in its agitation against segregation and Jim Crow street cars and successfully contested state bills against intermarriage.

The Providence, R. I. branch made a successful protest against color discrimination in the Y. M. C. A.

The St. Paul, Minn., checked discrimination in a private circulating library and in a school of shorthand and also prevented the introduction of an anti-intermarriage bill into the legislature.

The chairman, Board of Directors of the Association, closes his report for 1914, as follows :

"The record of the American people on the race question now stands as follows. During the year just passed some seventy colored men and women were lynched without trial and in many cases with barbaric torture. Segregation ordinances restricting the property rights of colored people have passed or are pending in some of our largest cities, including Baltimore, Richmond, Louisville, and St. Louis. Legislation opposed to the interests of colored people has been introduced into the legislature of nearly every state in the Union during the last few years. Farm segregation is being agitated in the South. It is not unfair to say that at this very moment an orgy of Negro baiting is going on in Congress. Out of eleven million people, including 1,600,000 men of voting age who can read and write, only 550,000 were permitted to vote at the last Presidential election. The Supreme Court of the United States has virtually declared that the colored man has no civic rights, and has refused redress on one ground or another in every case that has come before it. All this does not take account of the daily humiliations, persecutions, and wrongs to which the American Negro is subjected, or the political, economic and social opportunities which are withheld from him. . . . Our task like that of the old Abolitionists is to 'alter public opinion.' . . . We fight side by side with men whom we know to be 'essentially like ourselves.' Our weapon is 'not only the old idealism but the new science. We know . . . . that race is but historical opportunity, and nationality but funded ideals."

Besides the above-mentioned activities of the M.A.A.C.P., the Negroes hold many periodical conventions where they discuss their affairs and decide the line of action to be followed by the community as a whole. They have their own philanthropic, industrial and financial organizations, such as banks, insurance companies, stores, real estate companies, Brotherhoods, Friendly Societies, etc. There are 30,000 Negro religious organizations reporting over 3,600,000 communicants. The value of property involved amounts to 56,000,000 dollars. In the larger cities there are splendid church buildings ranging from 50,000 to 100,000 dollars in value, with an annual fiscal budget of from 5000 to 20,000 dollars.

"The last word in caste."

The situation as it stands today has been stated by Dr. Du Bois in his essay, bearing the above title, and in his "Immediate Program of the American Negro." Concerning economic discrimination against the Negro, he states:

"So far as work is concerned we again find the barriers up and not tending to fall. The attempt to establish a strict caste of occupations in the South has not been successful, but it has been possible to keep the majority of Negroes in the most disagreeable and poorest-paid occupations, and in the lowest positions of most occupations."

"Just as soon as the Negro city labourer, working on a wage scale lower than that of any other single group of people, saved out of his meagre earnings enough to move out of the alleys and slums to the front streets, there immediately arose the question as to who should bear the economic cost of race prejudice."

The whites insisted that "it is largely a social matter," and "let the Negroes develop their own settlements," and out of this attitude developed the city segregation movement. A further argument was brought forward:

"Let the Negro stop crowding into the cities. Here they have in the country and in the South a wonderful chance for development. They can get hold of land; they know how to raise a great staple crop and many auxiliary crops. Here is an open economic field; let them take advantage of it."

Tuskegee's insistence on industrial training of the Negro and the movement fathered by the late Morris K. Jessup, along with other causes, strongly enforced these arguments. Consequently the movement toward farm life among Negroes in the last decade has been phenomenal. While farms conducted by white farmers have increased 9½ per cent. between 1900 and 1910, farms conducted by colored farmers have increased nearly 20 per cent. There were 7½ per cent. more white farmers conducting their farms in 1910 than in 1900, but there were 17 per cent. more colored owners conducting their farms. The land in Negro farms increased from 42,000,000 to 47,000,000 acres in that time, and the land in the hands of Negro farm owners from 16,000,000 to 19,000,000 acres. To-day 29 per cent. of the farms in the South are conducted by colored men, not counting the vast number of farms conducted by white men with colored labor. The value of the farm property owned by Negroes between 1900 and 1910 increased from $108,000,000 to $410,000,000, or 145 per cent. Negro land ownership has increased from about 3,000,000 acres in 1875 to 6,000,000 acres in 1880, to 8,000,000 acres in 1890, to 15,000,000 in 1900, and nearly 20,000,000 in 1910.

"We find on the part of the dominant South not only absence of all enthusiasm for this increase of Negro agricultural well being, but a distinct air of disappointment and something worse. Indeed, this air of disappointment is so widespread that one can not help wondering if the Negro has not been urged to take advantage of Southern agriculture just because some Southerners were convinced that he could not take such advantage, and that in the country districts of the South he could be held in his place politically, socially, and economically."

The Negro was asked to give up his political rights for the sake of economic advance.

"He finds that with the giving up of his political rights his educational rights are curtailed, the right to work is increased but inadequately, his right to hold property in cities is being questioned, and now finally, there is a movement in the South to curtail his right to own agricultural land."

The cry "The South for the White Race!" is rising and gaining in volume. Various means are sought to accomplish this end: (1) It is suggested that 'Jim Crow' laws be put into effect in the rural districts, and that Negroes buy land adjoining and settle in communities to themselves; (2) that laws be enacted prohibiting future sale of land to them in white communities. "Atlanta has just passed a law saying that a majority of property owners in a city block can say that in future no land shall be sold to a person of a different race from them, why not pass laws giving similar privilege to country people?" writes Mr. Clarence Poe, editor of the *Progressive*

Farmer, as quoted by Du Bois. Mr. Poe goes on to say:

"We report that if our people make up their minds that segregation is a good and necessary thing, they will find a way to put it into effect just as they did in the case of Negro disfranchisement despite an iron-bound amendment specifically designed to prevent it."

Mr. Dubois concludes his article on "The Last Word in Caste" as follows:

"The South says here: We despise the Negro because he is down and yet we connot allow him to rise; we cannot educate him lest he grow intelligent, we cannot allow him in industry lest he compete with us and save money; we cannot allow him to buy property because he will be independent and live beside us; we cannot let him live by himself because we want his labor, and because we dare not give him political power enough to establish and protect his own segregated communities.

"The South is not wholly to blame for this logic. The North shares the blame. The high and only tenable ground of the past was: Educate the Negro, give him work and wages, give him civic rights, give him a vote and let him make his own way as a free man.

"This ground the North has joined the South in undermining; they have half ruined his schools, they have curtailed his work and lowered his wages, they have made him a legal pariah and social outcast, and now they are cooly proposing to steal the bits of property which by the sweat of his face he has saved.

"For stealing it is. Everybody knows that segregation is confiscation. Have we not the shameful treatment of the Indian (American) to prove this?

"How fine a program of solving the race problem this is which, after twenty-five years of trumpeting and advertising, lands us right in the same black slough of despond out of which we are just starting to raise the robbed and raped Indian. Fine statesmanship for the twentieth century—fine cowardice for the land of the free."

In his article on "The Immediate Program of the American Negro," Du Bois names three "shackles" of which the Negro must rid himself: (1) He must be free from the political tyranny of white folk, and must have the right to vote; (2) he must have a voice in the new industrial democracy; (3) he must have the right to social intercourse with his fellows.

"What now are the practical steps which must be taken to accomplish these ends?"

"First, we must fight obstructions; . . . we must . . make American courts either build up a body of decisions which will protect the plain legal rights of American citizens or else make them tear down the civil and political rights of all citizens in order to oppress a few."

"We must secondly seek in legislature and Congress remedial legislation."

"Third, the human contact of human beings must be increased . . . . . closer contact and mutual knowledge" of "the white and black people of this land."

"Fourth," the "publication of the truth repeatedly and incisively and uncompromisingly" to "secure that change in public opinion which will correct these awful lies."

"Such is the program of work against obstructions. Let us now turn to constructive effort. This may be summed up under (1) economic co-operation (2) a revival of art and literature (3) political action (4) education and (5) organization."

"Under economic co-operation . . . we must seek not simply home ownership, small land-holding and saving accounts, but also all forms of co-operation, both in production and distribution, profit sharing, building and loan associations, systematic charity for definite, practical ends, systematic migration from mob rule and robbery to freedom and enfranchisement, the emancipation of women and the abolition of child labor."

"In art and literature we should try to loose the tremenduous emotional wealth of the Negro and the dramatic strength of his problem through writing, the stage, pageantry and other forms of art. We should resurrect forgotten ancient Negro art and history, and we should set the black man before the world as both a creative artist and a strong subject for artistic treatment."

"In education we must seek to give colored children free public school training. We must watch with grave suspicion the attempt of those who, under the guise of vocational training, would fasten ignorance and menial service on the Negro for another generation."

"For the accomplishment of all these ends we must organize. Organization among us has already gone far but it must go much further and higher. Organization is sacrifice. It is sacrifice of opinions, of time, of work, and of money, but it is, after all, the cheapest way of buying the most priceless of gifts—freedom and efficiency. I thank God that most of the money that supports the National Association for the Advancement of Colored People comes from black hands; a still larger proportion must so come, and we must not only support but control this and similar organizations and hold them unwaveringly to our objects, our aims and our ideals."

RELIGION IN THE UNITED STATES.

If one were to judge of the religious life of the Americans by the number of churches, chapels, religious societies and organizations and the amount of money spent on home and foreign missions, one would think that America is intensely religious. On the other hand, if one were to judge of Americans by the number of saloons and cabarets that exist in American cities, by the commercial spirit that dominates all American activities, by the materialization of American life and the utter lack of spirituality in the vision of the average American, one would pronounce America to be thoroughly irreligious. Yet neither is the whole truth.

If religion means devotion to a principle, material or spiritual, America has plenty of it. There is enough of single-mindedness in American life. The average American is devoted to the acquisition of wealth, the Dollar is his God, because the Dollar brings him power and pleasure, the two things for which he cares and lives. He will devote a whole life to the discovery of a new mechanical contrivance or a scientific truth which, when put in the market, will bring him enough money to live well and wield that power over men and the State which money secures in this conntry or, for the matter of that, in all the countries of the West. The average man seems to have no time for any other idea. He will occasionally take a holiday to recruit his health. He lives to have a good time after a hard day's work; he cares for all sorts of pleasures and enjoys a good drink, a hearty laugh, an exciting show, and a jolly company; but the ruling idea of his life is to be rich. He puts forth the best of his mind and brain in that pursuit. He is affected by a sort of money mania. Thanks to his education, he has aesthetic tastes, as well as a liking for manly games, but his mission in life is to make money, become a millionaire and then have pleasure and wield power.

This trait of American character is so predominant that a foreigner takes no time to find it out. Even the best and the most lofty side of American life is more or less affected by this dominating note. Yet it will be unjust and unfair to conclude that there is nothing beyond it. It is true that the commercially minded American—a mixture of a Jew, a German and a Saxon—is perhaps devoid of God-consciousness, still more of Christ-consciousness; that he has no use for ethics or morality that does not help in, or that stands in the way of, acquiring wealth; or that he thinks he can make his peace with God, or purchase immunity for his sins of omission and commission by lavish gifts of money to churches and charities after he has become rich. It is equally true that the American generally leaves religion or the cultivation of higher or spiritual life to his women-folk pending his accumulation of the good things of the world; he considers it to be a fair division of labor that he should create wealth and that his wife should look after their souls.

Sometimes one is inclined to think that the American's faith in profitable investment leads him to believe that he can well provide for his soul by giving large sums of money for the conversion of the heathen and by making it possible for a number of men and women missionaries to devote their lives to ministering to the religious wants of other people. He thinks that is his spiritual investment. His religious advisors (professionals) have evidently led him to think that wise. It is a significant feature of American life that while a horde of missionaries (men and women, some of them high class persons of lofty motives and high-minded) are sent abroad and millions (or perhaps billions) of dollars are spent every year in the maintenance and endowment of foreign missions, Christianity and church-going is on a steady decline in the States or for the matter of that in all Christian countries. "The Alarming Leakage in the Churches" was the subject of a series of lectures by Reverend George Duncan, D. D., pastor of Zion Church, London, not long ago. "It is an alarming sign of the times," the leakage of the churches, says he, and "a sad reflection" on them which may indicate something wrong in their doctrines or spirit or form or methods of life. He states his position in a series of obvious and simple propositions which we give below :

I. That there is a wide-spread defection from all our Christian Organizations.

That is the stern and even appalling fact which confronts us. There is no exception in any church, for if there be no actual report of decrease in numbers, the numbers in no case are proportionate to the increase in the population and are very far from being what the efforts put forth give us a reasonable right to expect. The facts are patent to all who care to look at them. . , . . Churches seem to be waning powers in the land, and that fact in every way is a most deplorable one.

II. That this wide-spread defection is on the increase.

It is no temporary lull in the tide of prosperity, no mere local defection while generally the work goes forward. No, each year has a more dark state to record and deplore. This has continued now for some years and all the signs of the times indicate that no change for the better need be expected. The power of Christian organizations has waned much and is waning still more.

III. That this wide-spread defection seems to be irrevocable.

The various churches have braced themselves for the occasions. They have had on the subject—

Committee meetings.

Conference.

Books, pamphlets, sermons.

Missions, door to door appeals, but all of little avail.

The church either does not know her duty in the matter, or else she cannot or will not do it, and so she is face to face with the fact that in an avowedly Christian land she finds those outside her organizations and who resolutely mean to remain there vastly more numerous than those within her borders. Not one-third of the people identify themselves with Christian organizations though they know that those very organizations exist for the sole purpose of doing good to every one who will accept good at their hands. That is a marvellous moral problem which surely demands an earnest and effective solution.

IV. That this widespread defection is based on various manifest grounds.

The obvious reasons are,—

Spiritual indifference,
Thorough worldliness,
Slavery to vice,
Evil companions,
A hateful environment,
Doubt, infidelity,
Discontent with Christian teaching,
Contempt for the average character of Christians.

The reverend father thinks further,—

"V. That infidelity has but little attraction for those who have forsaken the Christian Church.

VI. That this wide defection is often a departure not from Christ himself, but from the churches only.

VII. That one cause of this wide defection is accounted for by the fact that an enormous number of men can no longer believe some of the dogmas which we preach, and

VIII. That surely we can do something more and something better for those that have deserted us on doctrinal grounds, than we have thus far done."

At this stage we are not concerned with the remedies suggested by him. We may consider them later on. For the present we intend to cite some more testimonies on the subject of the decline in the influence of the churches in Christian countries.

Dr. Newman Smythe, another great divine, says:—

"For a hundred years we have been breaking up creeds rather than making them ... The Protestant faith is losing mastery over the controlling forces of modern life ... It has lost the old authority of the church. It has lost it in its own families ... It has lost it in the state ... I am not speaking of the causes for this ; I am facing the facts. What do they mean?

What is the significance of the failure of the Protestant ages but this—the new age is coming? 'I see', said the last Bampton lecturer in the pulpit of St. Mary's, at Oxford,—'I see the signs of a new religious order, the greatest that the world has ever known, drawn from all the nations and all classes and, what seems stranger yet, from all the churches.' (Dr. Newman Smythe in a Christmas sermon.)

A writer (Julian K. Smythe by name) in the *New Church Review* of October, 1914, remarks :—

"A crisis in the Christian world has certainly come. There is hardly a minister but feels it. The layman feels it just as truly......The complaint goes up from nearly every quarter that the churches have lost their power. The masses, it is said, are not reached. They have lost faith in the church. The Christian pulpit, it is said over and over again, has lost its prestige. It no longer speaks with the power of a great conviction. 'The trite criticism,' exclaims an earnest man, 'that while Peter converted three thousand men with one sermon, it now takes, according to the painful figures of the denominational year books, almost three thousand sermons to convert one man, is hurled at preachers who are already humiliated by their apparent lack of effectiveness.' The churches in self-defence sometimes declare that the blame is to be laid to 'the hard and uncircumcised heart' of our twentieth century civilization; that the age is material in its aims; that it lacks high aspirations, and is ungodly in the extreme; that it is 'full of pleasure-seekers and social agitators who, in their different ways, have done much to draw away the attention of thousands of people from the Christian Church.'

"The more thoughtful recognize that the churches in Protestantism have lost their teaching power. They stand before the world today without any generally accepted theology. Where some declare that men are tired of theology and wish for none of it, others see that the Church, as a teacher of spiritual truth, has no clearly defined doctrine to impart."

Another observer is quoted to have remarked that "its course reminds one of a mighty shell fired by an enormous charge. While it held together its momentum was terrific; but as it broke into fragments each fragment possessed less energy. When these in succession subdivided, their potential energy became still feebler. The explosive power which impelled it originally was the sense of individual liberty—liberty of conscience, liberty of thought, liberty of action." And yet liberty is a dangerous spirit to raise unless controlled by Truth. And here the various parts of protestantism hesitate and fumble. In the words of one of its leaders :

> "A century ago each had a confession, or a system of truth which satisfied it. It had a message, which, whether true or faulty, it could deliver when challenged. But now the very spirit of intellectual freedom which was invoked has examined these doctrinal structures, and in the name of truth has condemned them."

> "Even the Bible," continues Mr. Julian Smythe, "has lost its authority, and some of its fundamental teachings, such as the Divine incarnation of Jesus Christ and the unique character of His Divinity, are being not only challenged, but openly discarded. As a result, Protestantism today is uncertain and hesitating in its message ; its rivalries and consequent wastefulness tend to render it feeble ; 'it has lost the controlling position it once held in schools, colleges and universities ; the laboring classes have largely drifted beyond the sound of its voice ; the middle classes are less and less keeping holy its Sabbath day.'"

The following is from an address delivered by Professor Hamack to the Prussian clergy on the religious situation in Germany:

"Never before were so many men filled with such longings as today for firm and consistent convictions. Men are ready today to give anything for a conviction that is a real conviction—for a belief that really is believed in. The demand is for a faith in which there is a real faith; men require convictions as to the meaning of life."

The following is a passage of an English author who is widely read:

"Men long for a basis of life which shall be as credible to the intellect as it is inspiring to the soul. They want a religion into which their whole manhood can go. And this is what at present they have failed to find. The Church, they say, feeds the heart at the expense of the brain. . . The disaster that has happened to it is that people have come to repeat its creed in a quite different sense from that in which they repeat the creed of electricity or mechanics. This last is actual belief, a belief by which they run trains or build bridges. The other is, in part at least, make-believe. . . The Church offers peace at the expense of truth. And this at a time when the world, by its training in science, is beginning to appreciate truth as never before, as among the highest of all possible goods, as the first essential of the soul's prosperity." (Brierly, "Our City of God," pp. 106 et seq.)

Having given these quotations from church sources, the writer of the article in the *New Church Review* concludes by giving one from a financial journal. He says:

"These quotations are from church sources. Have we any right to suppose that the secular world cares anything about a lack of spiritual conviction? Does it ever enter the mind of the financial world, for instance, to question whether the decline of faith could have the slightest interest or significance to it? Let me quote these words from an editorial in a well-known New York financial journal. The writer is wise enough to see and to say that if there has been a decline in religious faith, especially Faith in the Future Life, that fact 'alters the basic conditions of civilization,' it 'changes the standards and affects the value of things,' it 'becomes a factor in the markets,' and concerns the immediate interests of those who never had such a faith almost as much as it does the lives of those who have had the faith and lost it."

And then it speaks out as follows:

"The question, therefore, of immediate, practical, and tremendous importance to Wall Street quite as much as to any other part of the world, is, has there been a decline in the faith, in a future life, and if so, to what extent is this responsible for the special phenomena of our time—the eager pursuit of sudden wealth, . . . the growth of greed, . . . the social unrests, the spread of demagogy, the appeal to bitter class hatred."

The conclusion is thus given:

"The supreme need of the hour is not elastic currency or sounder banking or better protection against panics, or bigger navies or more equitable tariffs, but a revival of faith, a return to a morality which recognizes a basis in religion and the establishment of a workable and working theory of life that views man as something more than a mere lump of matter." (*Wall Street Journal*, quoted in *Literary Digest*, Feb. 2, 1907).

These quotations give the reader some idea of the unrest and disquietude that prevails in the religious circles of Christian lands. The war has accentuated the feeling even more intensely. The cry has risen almost from all quarters and all classes of thoughtful persons, that Christianity has failed and that the church has collapsed. In the first months of the war, a hot controversy raged in the press, (secular as well as religious) as to the proper attitude of tolerant Christians toward war; and as to the effect of war on Christianity. The religious leaders of each country decided that it was a part of their religion to fight for their respective countries and that their respective countries were right in fighting what each believed to be a righteous war. Some of them joined the fighting ranks and exchanged the pulpit for the trenches. The British schools of theology and the bishops have since refused to ordain candidates of military age. The pulpit and the religious platform have been freely used to encourage enlistment and to exhort Christians to go and fight for their respective countries. In sermons and in articles it has been freely remarked that the Christian religion does not prohibit war and that Christianity demands war in a righteous cause. Did not the Lord say, it is argued, that he had come with a sword in his hand? Some contended that the war had established the greater need of Christianity and the churches and religion. Others said that the war was not due to a failure of Christianity, but to the material spirit of the modern civilization, though this is a practical confession that materialization has triumphed over Christianity and the latter has failed.

The Christian theologian is not prepared to admit as much because that deprives him of an argument which he has often very effectively used in his efforts to convert the heathen. He has so often pointed to the glories of the modern civilization as a proof of the excellence and superiority of Christianity as against and over the other religions. All this, however, is hardly convincing, and thoughtful people in all countries are agreed that the present war, its dimensions, its cruelties, and its incidental happenings, are proof positive that there is something wrong with the churches. A Christian writer, a follower of Swedenborg, has explained the war in a rather ingenious way. Starting with the remark that the war has caused great disappointment in the Hague conferences and that "Christianity itself has been put on trial as a failure and asked to show how it can account for such a condition of Christian nations who profess to be disciples of the Prince of Peace," he explains how rulers and nations were hurried on into bloody battles by "Great and Hidden Spiritual Forces, without any personal guilt, when the time was ripe for the great spiritual battles of religion of the Christian church, to be ultimated by correspondence—to burst forth in the wars of nations." In his opinion it was "necessary for the salvation of humanity that a great crisis of judgment should take place in the spiritual world and the power of ultimates could be operated only by means of this great war in the natural world." It had to be, continues he, in order that the lesson of hell in the spiritual world might be so powerfully set forth on earth that a new impetus of religion should be given, a mighty reaction of good against evil which should bring new victories of the former over the latter, overturn all institutions of the past, the fruits of form of the Christian religion which had become perverted and is now brought to judgment. . . .

But one of the best (and at the same time quite moderate in its views and tone) articles I have read on the subject was the one that appeared in the *Century Magazine* for February 1, 1915, under the heading "Has The Church Collapsed?" To the article is prefixed a note from the editor to the effect that "while the *Century* is not in accord with many of the ideas presented in this article, it has, with thinking people in general, a very keen realization of the fact that all is not well with the Christian church." The article begins with the significance of the grounds on which the bombardment of the Rheims Cathedral by the Germans was denounced by the world. The cry that went up from the enlightened lands was that "a work of art had been destroyed," and not that "a house of God" had suffered disaster. The beauty of the nave, he says, has outlasted the religion of the altar.

"Apollo has triumphed over Christ. All this has come about as naturally as ripe fruit falls from a bough. For no one imagines that it is the sudden shock, the excitement of war, that has diverted attention from the church. That which we have witnessed is simply a unique registering of an ancient fact. For, as we all know, it was during years of peace that the spirit of the church was bombarded."

A little later he adds:—

"While never before, probably, was such a tribute paid to art in its general character, it is the profound change which this indicates in the Christian world which surprises us most, not because we were not aware that a profound change had taken place, but because now for the first time we are face to face with the thing that registers infallibly the full ebb of the tide. And very clearly it is not an ebb from one shore, with a corresponding flow upon another, as it invariably is with the movements of the ocean, but an ebb complete and world-wide."

Then he traces the different stages through which the Christian church has passed in its development and points out how in each development the creed or the outward manifestation of it, in philosophy or art, usurped the place of religion, how "wine or bread or cups or altars or buildings" were confounded with the real teachings of Christ, and finally concludes as below :

"Is it any wonder that the tide has gone out and left the church utterly powerless; that the whole vesture of Caesarism with which she once overawed the millions has been stripped off piece by piece; that art has become art, still capable of arousing men to its defence; that philosophy has become philosophy, honorably installed in our educational system; that organization is still active in politics and industry; and that the church is nothing? Is it not a comment upon the hollowness of her pretensions that as civilization has advanced the church has receded and that annually her remaining millions ooze away and are lost in secular affairs?

"All this would be of little moment and would merit the unconcern with which it is popularly regarded were there not a tremendously serious side to the matter. For nineteen centuries society has left in the hands of the church the direction of the moral forces of the world. And now, after all these centuries, we find ourselves falling into the same moral vacuum into which the Roman Empire fell. After eighteen hundred years it is as easy for men to thrust bayonets into one another as it was in the heathen world. Is it not apparent that the church has collapsed?"

We have selected these expressions of opinions from within the church itself avoiding the stern judgment of the rationalists, naturalists, and free thinkers. Yet, as I said in the opening, the religious activities of the United States both at home and abroad are on a collossal scale.

According to the returns of 1906, the population of the United States was about 92 millions. The last enumeration of religious bodies relating to the year 1906 showed a total of nearly 33 million communicants or members, of whom 20 millions were Protestants and 12 millions Roman Catholics. In the "World Almanac" for 1915, the number of communicants or members is given as 38 millions, of churches 223,735 and of ministers 176,624. It will be thus seen that the American people maintain an army of over one hundred thousands and three quarters of ministers (full time, regularly paid) for the salvation of their souls. The total number given in the Almanac, i.e., 176,624, included some non-Christian ministers also, but if you put the figure of Christian ministers at 175,000, you will not be erring on the side of overestimation. If you add an equal figure for those who are not ordained ministers, but connected with religious organizations and regularly paid for work connected with the religious organizations, you will get some general idea of the enormous army of religious preachers and ministers that administer to the religious wants of the people of the United States.

and are regularly paid for by fixed salaries for the services rendered by them. Counting by main heads, the number of Christian denominations having churches and organizations stands very near half a hundred, but if you count the various subsections into which they are subdivided, it will come to very near 200, and if you count the still minor subdivisions, it will come to several hundreds.

Federal Council of the Churches of Christ in America.

The Federal Council of the Churches of Christ in America alone represents thirty Protestant denominations, with a membership of over 16 million communicants, 101,552 ministers and 138,155 churches.

According to the constitution of this council, it has no authority over the constituent bodies adhering to it, and its province is limited to the expression of its counsel and the recommendation of a course of action in matters of common interest to the churches, local councils and individual Christians. It has no authority to draw up a common creed or form of government or of worship, or in any way to limit the full autonomy of the Christian bodies adhering to it. The following details about the organization may not be without interest :

The Federal Council meets quadrennially and consists of about four hundred qualified delegates officially elected by the various denominational assemblies or other constituted authorities.

Its Executive Committee consists of about ninety of these delegates and acts for the Council during the Quadrennium between its sessions, holding regular meetings.

The Executive Committee has an Administrative Committee holding regular monthly meetings, which acts for the Executive Committee between its sessions.

The national office and its executives, under the Administrative Committee, carrry on the continuous work of the Council.

The united work undertaken by the Council is indicated by the titles of its Commissions.

These Commissions are as follows: State and Local Federations, Foreign Missions, Home Missions, Christian Education, Social Service, Evangelism, Family Life, Sunday observance, Temperance, and Peace and Arbitration, The Commission of the Church and Social Service.

The Commission of the Church and Social Service has been, up to this time, the most effectively organized, because its work seemed to offer the larger immediate field for common action. This Commission also has a Committee on the Church and Country Life. The Commission on Peace and Arbitration and Evangelism also have offices and executive secretaries.

Other special Commissions, such as the Joint Commission on Theological Seminaries, on Interdenominational Movements and on International Relations, are appointed from time to time to take up special activities calling for action upon the part of the churches.

The Council has a whole time secretary and more than one assistant secretary with a staff of clerks to carry on their work.

The budget figures for 1914 provided Rs. 75,000 for special commissions.

SOME OF THE MODERN SCHOOLS OF RELIGIOUS THOUGHT.

America is the land of fads. We in India have been accustomed to think that we had a monopoly of credulity and superstition. Travelling abroad, I have learnt that we are by no means the most credulous people on earth; that want of education and illiteracy is not the sole cause of credulousness. The number of teachers of religion in America is perhaps as large as in India. Anyone can set up a school of thought of his own. Any one may found a sect or a seminary or a college and may give lessons in anything. He is sure to find some followers and some admirers. He must know how to advertise and must invest some money in hand-bills and what are called "circulars" and "schedules" in this country.

Mysticism particularly appeals to the imagination of the occident most intensely. Anything mystic is bound to attract a following. Hence the great charm that oriental systems of thought have for the people of America. The oriental religious thought has deeply affected the thought of the West and many a modern religious sect could be traced to some idea borrowed from Buddhism or Vedanta. Even the new schools of Christianity bear the marks of contact with the East.

Bahaism is as much in vogue as Buddhism or Vedanta. Of this an Oriental may well be proud. But over and above this, many a fraud is being practised in the name of the Orient by unscrupulous persons. The parties most culpable among the latter are Americans themselves. Many an American uses oriental names, oriental signs and mystic symbols, as aids to advertising. Sometimes he gets hold of a needy Oriental, a Hindu, a Muslim, or a Chinaman, makes a tool of him, uses his name, keeps him in the background, credits him with occult powers, advertises his holiness and achievements and carries on a roaring trade. Sometimes books or treatises, written by Americans, are published over Oriental names and sold largely under false pretenses. "Professor" is a most misused term in this country and so is "doctor". Professors and doctors are as common as blackberries. It is a pity that it should be so, because a large number of professors in the universities and holders of the degree of doctor are learned men well deserving the title of a professor or a doctor. The title carries a social status with it which is being exploited by unscrupulous adventurers. A young Hindu told me how an American tried to use his name for his own purposes. He wanted to publish books in his name and to advertise him as a savant of high order and mystic powers. An American lady told me of a similar attempt having been made in relation to another Indian. That some of these attempts bring a certain amount of success both in disciples and in money is proof enough of a widespread desire to probe into the inner meaning of life and a hankering after things beyond the reach of the intellect, and of the failure of the prevailing forms of religion to satisfy this hankering. I am of opinion that this hankering is not altogether unintelligent, though to me it looks as if even the more serious developments of religious thought in America exact a great deal of ready faith, not necessarily based on reason, on the part of those who believe in these developments and adopt them for their guidance and enlightenment. In the following paragraphs I propose to notice a few of these developments briefly.

MORMONISM.

Mormonism, or The Church of Jesus Christ of Latter Day Saints, is an offshoot of Christianity. It was founded by one Joseph Smith on the 6th day of April, 1830, in the town of Fayette, Seneca County, State of New York. The founder claimed a special dispensation from God himself, beginning with "a vision and revelation, given in answer to his earnest prayer to know which of the religions was true and which of the contending sects was the acknowledged Church of Christ that he might know which to join." The answer of the Lord was :—"He must join none ; they were all wrong ; their creeds were an abomination in His sight ; the professors thereof were corrupt ; they drew near to their Lord with their lips, but their hearts were far from Him," and ending "with divine appointment and commission" "to organize the Church and teach the true Gospel of Jesus Christ to all the world." The principal doctrines of Mormonism may be given in their own language* :

* Mormonism, Its Origin and History, an authorized brochure issued by the Church, pp. 9 & 10.

"I. WE BELIEVE IN GOD, THE ETERNAL FATHER, AND IN HIS SON JESUS CHRIST, AND IN THE HOLY GHOST.

Of this it should be said that while the church preaches that these three divine persons constitute the God-head, the one creative and governing power in heaven and earth, she also teaches that each person of the God-head is distinct from the others. That is, each person is a distinct individual. She teaches that the Father and the Son are personages of tabernacle, personages of flesh and bone; and that their bodies are as tangible as man's; while the Holy Ghost is a personage of Spirit. In Mormon theology the "oneness" of the God-head consists not in the absolute identity of the substance of the three persons, but in the absolute agreement of mind and purpose and will subsisting among them; by which the mind of the one is also the mind of the others; they are also one in wisdom and holiness; and so in all qualities and attributes of mind; but are distinct persons or individuals.

God, the Father, then according to "Mormon" theology, is the Father of the spirits of all men; not in a mystical sense, but actually—the spirit of men is really the offspring of Deity. Hence God's interest in man is everywhere proclaimed in the appointments and economy of the earth. The church also teaches that from the Fatherhood of God, as pertaining to the spirits of men, arises the brotherhood of man—not a mere sentiment more or less pretty and conventional, but a reality, resting upon the actual fatherhood of God; *that the spirit of man had a pre-existent estate, that is that he existed, as a spiritual personage,** the offspring of God before he tabernacled in the flesh; that the earth was created, and a temporal existence provided for man wherein he would be allowed a probation in the midst of conditions which would give him an experience necessary to his eternal progress.

* The Italics are mine.

2. We believe that men will be punished for their own sins, and for Adam's transgression.

3. We believe that, through the atonement of Christ, all mankind may be saved, by obedience to the laws and ordinances of the gospel.

4. We believe that the first principles and ordinances of the gospel are: first, Faith in the Lord Jesus Christ; second, Repentance; third, Baptism by immersion for the remission of sins; fourth, Laying on of Hands for the Gift of the Holy Ghost.

5. We believe that a man must be called of God, by "prophecy" and by "the laying on of hands," by those who are in authority, to preach the gospel and to administer in the ordinances thereof.

6. We believe in the same organization that existed in the primitive church, namely, apostles, prophets, pastors, teachers, evangelists, etc.

7. We believe in the gift of tongues, prophecy, revelation, visions, healing, interpretation of tongues, etc.

This belief in the continuance of the spiritual gifts of the gospel is one of the chief characteristics of Mormonism, and one of the things which most clearly distinguish it from all the Christian sects. Mormonism holds that all the spiritual powers ever attendant upon true religion—the gospel of Jesus Christ—belong to it now; that whatever the gospel of Christ is, and in whatever age it is found, there also will be the power of God as well as the forms of godliness; that the spiritual gifts and graces of the gospel of Christ are as inseparable from it as warmth and brightness are inseparable from the sun; and it is a miserable blunder and the apology of apostate churches, or the excuse of false religions, to say that the powers of godliness as manifested in the spiritual gifts of the gospel enumerated in the scriptures are to be separated from the religion of Jesus Christ, as things transitory and to be done away.

8. We believe the Bible to be the word of God, as far as it is translated correctly; we also believe the Book of Mormon to be the word of God.

It has been alleged that Mormons do not believe in the Bible; that they discard it, and substitute for it the Book of Mormon, often spoken of as the "Mormon Bible." The Latterday Saints, however, believe the Bible, the Jewish scriptures—the Old and New Testaments, to be the word of God; to it they appeal in support of their doctrine; it is an authority with them in matters of faith and morals and church government; but they do not overlook the fact that there are errors and inaccuracies of translation in the English versions. Moreover they cannot help but know that there are omissions of whole books of scripture from the collection of books called the Bible; books written by prophets, seers and apostles. Direct reference is made to such books in some parts of the Bible. The inaccuracies growing out of errors of translation on the one hand, and the omission of whole books of scripture from the collection on the other, with here and there parts of the sacred text designedly mutilated for sectarian purposes, render it necessary to say, in expressing their belief in the Bible, that they accept it as the word of God as far as it is a collection of sacred books, its texts uncorrupted, and its translations accurate. In saying that "they also believe the Book of Mormon to be the word of God" the Saints, of course, mean that it is a volume of scripture of equal authority with the Bible. Modern Christendom would have the world believe that the Bible alone contains all the revelations of God. But it is evident that not only the Eastern hemisphere, but the western hemisphere also was peopled by the children of God, although the existence of the people of the western hemisphere was unknown to Europeans until a little over four hundred years ago.

9. We believe all that God has revealed, all that he does now reveal, and we believe that he

will yet reveal many great and important things pertaining to the kingdom of God.

10. We believe in the literal gathering of Israel, and in the Restoration of the Ten Tribes ; that Zion will be built upon this (the American) continent ; that Christ will reign personally upon the earth ; and that the earth will be renewed and receive its paradiseacal glory."

Besides these, there are some additional doctrines which form the distinguishing features of Mormonism. One of them is a provision for the salvation of the dead by "attending to outward ordinances—baptisms, confirmations, washings, anointings and sealings—all being appointed by revelation and direction of the Lord, and all sealed and ratified by the power of the priesthood of God which binds on earth and in heaven."

The other is their marriage system, which has drawn so much attention to them. They claim that their doctrine on marriage was revealed to their prophet, Joseph Smith, by which the Saints learned that—

"In celestial spheres the marriage relation exists eternally ; and that the pleasing joys of family ties and associations, coupled with the power of endless increase, contributes to the happiness, power and dominion of those who attain to the celestial glory. Instead of the God-given power of procreation being one of the things to pass away, it is one of the chief means of man's exaltation and glory in eternity. Through it men attain to the glory of an endless increase of eternal lives, and the right of presiding as priest and patriarch, king and lord, over his ever-increasing posterity. Instead of the commandment 'Multiply and replenish the earth' being an unrighteous law, to be regarded askance and as something evil, it is one by which the race of man is to be eternally perpetuated ; and it is as holy and pure as the commandment 'Repent and be baptized.' The new marriage system, then, or, rather, the old marriage system of the patriarchs restored to earth through this revelation, consists in the eternity of the marriage covenant ; that is, the marriage covenant between a man and his wife is made for time and all eternity, and being sealed by that power of the priest-hood 'which binds in earth and in heaven,' the covenant holds good in heaven as well as on earth ; in eternity as well as on earth ; in time ; after as well as before the resurrection from the dead ; and by reason of it men will have a claim upon their wives and wives upon their husbands throughout eternity."

"Celestial marriage also includes under certain conditions, restrictions and obligations, a plurality of wives. Such prominence indeed has been given to this feature of the marriage system of the Church that to a great extent it has obscured the grandeur and importance of the principle of the eternity of the marriage covenant. Plurality of wives, of course, was a great innovation in the marriage system of the world as marriage for eternity was. It comes in conflict, too, not only with the education and traditions of the modern world, but in conflict with the prejudices of the Saints themselves ; yet God had commanded its introduction into the world, and though the prejudices of the Saints revolted against it, the faithful to whom it was revealed resolved to obey it, and in the introduction of this principle of the marriage system of the Church, the prophet Joseph Smith himself led the way. * Its introduction into the Church originally was confined within a small circle of the faithful brethren and sisters ; and it was not until the Church had settled in the Rocky Mountain valleys of Utah, that it was publicly proclaimed as a doctrine of the Church unto the world. The practice of it was then

* He had a large number wives.

made public. The whole Church—and at that time (1852) the members of the Church comprised nearly the whole community of Utah—approving the principle, which was at once recognized as a proper religious institution."

"For ten years the practice in Utah of this system of marriage met with no opposition from the United States Government. But in 1862 a law was enacted by Congress to punish and prevent the practice of 'polygamy' in the territories of the United States. The penalties affixed were a fine, not to exceed five hundred dollars, and imprisonment not to exceed five years. For twenty years, however, this law remained practically a dead letter. . . . In 1882, however, the law enacted twenty years before was supplemented by what is known as the 'Edmunds Law.' In addition to defining the crime of 'polygamy'—for which it retained the same penalties as the law of 1862—the 'Edmunds Law' also made the cohabiting with more than one woman a crime, punishable by a fine not to exceed three hundred dollars, and by imprisonment not to exceed six months. This law also rendered persons who were living in 'polygamy', or who believed in its rightfulness, incompetent to act as grand or petit jurors: and also disqualified all polygamists for voting or holding office. This law of 1882 was again supplemented by the 'Edmunds-Tucker Law —enacted in 1887—which made the legal wife or husband, in cases of polygamy or unlawful cohabitation, a competent witness, provided the accused consented thereto; it also enlarged the powers of the United States commissioners and marshals, and required certificates of all marriages to be filed in the office of the probate court. The penalty for the violation of this last provision was a fine of one thousand dollars, and imprisonment for two years. The law disincorporated the Church, and ordered the supreme court to wind up its affairs, and take possession of the escheated property."

"The laws were rigorously enforced by the

United States officials, special appropriations being made by Congress to enable tbem to carry on a judicial crusade against the Saints. The prominent Church officials were driven into retirement; others into exile. Homes were disrupted; family ties were rent asunder. Upwards of a thousand men endured fines and imprisonment in the penitentiary rather than be untrue to their families. Every effort of the government to deprive the Saints of their religious liberty was stubbornly contested in the courts until the decision of the supreme court of the United States was obtained. While some of the proceedings of the courts in Utah in enforcing the anti-polygamy laws were condemned, the laws themselves were sustained as constitutional. The court also held that the first amendment to the Constitution, which provides that Congress shall not prohibit the free exercise of religion, cannot be invoked against legislation for the punishment of plural marriages. Meantime government was relentless, and still more stringent measures than those already enacted were threatened. In the midst of these afflictions and threatening portents, President Wilford Woodruff besought the Lord in prayer, and the Lord inspired him to issue the manifesto which discontinued the practice of plural marriage. And the semi-annual conference in October following, the action of President Woodruff was sustained by unanimous vote of the conference, and plural marriages were discontinued in the Church."

The following figures taken from one of the authorized publications of the Church give the present status of the Church:—

"The Church was organized on the 6th day of April, 1830, with six members; in six months it had increased its membership to about seventy; it now (1902) has a membership in the organized stakes of Zion of several hundred thousands, and more than fifty thousand in the various missions. In the stakes of Zion are eighty-five thousand children under eight years of age.

"The latest reports concerning the number of men holding the Priesthood in the Church show that there are three of the First Presidency; twelve Apostles; two hundred Patriarchs; 6,800 High Priests; 9,730 Seventies; 20,000 Elders, a total who bear the Melchisedek Priesthood of 36,745; while 25,700 bear the Lesser Priesthood, making a grand total of those who hold the Priesthood of 62,445.

"In the auxiliary organizations of the Church there are 30,150 members of the Relief Society; 10,000 officers and 115,000 members in the Sunday Schools; 28,000 members of the Young Men's Mutual Improvement Associations; 36,000 of the Young Ladies' Improvement Associations, with about 20,000 who belong to the Religion Classes; making a total of 264,150 belonging to these auxiliary organizations.

"As a people the Saints are thriving and prosperous, and are continually extending their settlements throughout the inter-mountain region from the Province of Alberta, Cananda, in the North, to the northern states of Old Mexico. They have 20,000 farms, 18,000 of which are free from mortgages and encumbrances; and ninety per cent of the whole Church membership own their own homes, while the average number of people who own their homes in the United States is something like five per cent."

In the census returns their numbers are given as below:—

Ministers 3560,

Churches 1520,

Members 356,000.

In its early history, the Church underwent a great deal of persecution at the hands of the orthodox Christians. Originally established in a town of the State of New York, they soon transferred themselves to Missouri State and formed a considerable settlement there. In November, 1833, they were practically turned out of that State. An organized mob assembled, burned their houses, "tarred, feathered, and whipped" many of their adherents and "finally drove them from their habitations." It is stated that this proceeding was winked at by the government and although they had warranted deeds for their lands, no redress was given. The next settlement was formed in Clay County, where they remained for three years, to be eventually turned out as before. They then settled in Caldwell and Daviess Counties. Here again in 1838 they were attacked by mobs, an exterminating order was issued by Governor Baggs, and under the sanction of law, an organized banditti ranged throughout the country, which robbed their followers of cattle, sheep, horses, hogs, etc. The authorized account adds:—

"Many of our people were murdered in cold blood, the chastity of our women was violated, and we were forced to sign away our property at the point of the sword and after enduring every indignity that could be heaped upon us............were driven from our firesides" and deprived of lands and houses.

The next settlement was formed in the State of Illinios where, in 1844, the prophet and his brother were arrested on a charge of treason. But before the trial could be held, they were 'ruthlessly murdered' by a mob on June 27, 1844. Within two years of this event the community was chased out of the boundaries of the United States and forced to migrate westwards. Crossing the Mississippi and the Rocky

Mountains, they settled in what is now known as the Utah State and founded a city called the "Salt Lake City" where now they have their principal temple and the headquarters of their Church. Utah now forms part of the United States and is a flourishing state of the Union. About one half of the population of Salt Lake City is Mormon and the Church and the community own considerable property in the city and the state. They have considerable influence in the civil life of the state and are generally prosperous and contented. The Christian world still looks on them with contempt and calls them 'infidels,' 'renegades,' or 'heretics.' Their temple is closed to the public ; nor do they admit strangers to their ceremonies. But their grounds and offices and halls are open to visitors and are shown by an official guide who answers all questions about the Church and its history and its organisation.

THE UNITARIAN CHURCH.

The Unitarian Church is perhaps one of the oldest of the reformed churches in the West. Its position in Christianity is very much like that of our own Brahmo Samaj in Hinduism. The Unitarians do not believe in the Divinity of Christ nor in the in-infallibility of the Bible. They believe in God and stand for the greatest possible freedom and tolerance in religious thought and practice. Their principal organization is located at 25 Beacon Street, Boston, Massachusetts, and is known as the American

Unitarian Association. The Association has a whole time paid staff of

1 President,
1 Secretary,
1 Treasurer,
1 Assistant Secretary,
4 Departmental Secretaries,
3 Field Secretaries, and so on.

Their activities may be judged from the following facts gleaned from their report for 1914:—

"The Publication Department printed and circulated during the year 1913-14

400,000 tracts,

Seventy new books, including the New Hymn and Service book and the new Ministers' Hand Book,

45,000 Word and Work,

52,000 copies of the "Calendar,"

360,000 copies of The Beacon, (a weekly organ), and 19,443 manuals, service books, etc., for Sunday Schools were sold.

Aid has been granted by the Directors to some ninety-six churches and missions in all parts of the United States and Canada.

Five new churches have been organized.

New churches, parish houses, and parsonages have been built, and considerable changes and improvements have been made in fifteen other churches.

The Association has purchased lots for new churches in four places.

Officers and representatives of the Association have personally visited practically all the aided churches and the new missions, and in their journeys have covered the whole country.

Work has been carried forward among the Icelanders in Manitoba, where seven Icelandic societies are organized in the Icelandic Unitarian Conference, among the Swedes and Norwegians in Minnesota, among the Finns in Minnesota and Montana, and a new work inaugurated among the Italians in New York and Philadelphia.

The Church of the Messiah, among the colored people in Greater Boston, has had a successful year. Free tracts are published in German, French, Swedish, Norwegian, Finnish, and Spanish.

The Association has carried forward the work in Japan under the direction of Mr. MacCauley and his fellow-workers.

Support has been given to the Unitarian work in Hungary, Denmark, Germany, and in Bulgaria.

The work of the Association of Free Believers in Italy has been developed and sustained.

A successful session of the International Congress was held in Paris last summer, and a missionary Conference was held in Boston in November.

Plans have been formulated for a series of conferences in India, China, Japan, to be held when possible. The arrangements for these meetings have been forwarded by the journey of Dr. Sunderland, as Billings Lecturer, around the world."

The report of the Treasurer of the Association for the year ending April 30, 1914, has in it many interesting figures. The table of Income and Expenditure for immediate use shows receipts and payments of about $ 200,000, i. e., 6 lakhs of rupees. The gifts and bequests added to permanent funds show receipts of $ 158,000, i. e., more than 4½ lakhs of rupees in the year.

The writer has been the recipient of kindness and hospitality from Unitarians all over the United States and has spoken at several of their meetings.

The American Bible Society.

As a sample of the huge scale on which work is done by some of the Christian agencies of America, we give below the figures relating to the work of the American Bible Society.

The total issues of the Bible during the year (1914) amounted to 5,251,176 volumes. The total issues of the Society in the 98 years of its existence amount to 103,519,891 volumes.

The trust funds of the Society amount to $ 2,461,652, i. e., close to about 75 lakhs of rupees. During the year the trust funds increased by over 2¼ lakhs of rupees.

The last receipts of the year 1914 are given below :

From individuals	28,409 dollars
,, churches	78,701 ,,
,, auxiliaries	22,695 ,,
,, Legacies	42,258 ,,
	161,923

The income from trust funds, etc., was $ 120,969, i. e., very nearly 6 lakhs of rupees, bringing the total income for current expenses up to $ 282,992.

The Bible Society makes it a point to introduce copies of the Bible to persons of all classes and conditions whom it can reach. As seen from the picture facing this page, it is even reaching immigrants in their own tongues soon after their arrival in the United States. It is a question if the Hindu laborers in the United States as represented in this picture make any use of the Bibles given to them.

THE NEW CHURCH OF JERUSALEM OR SWEDENBORGIANISM.

Before giving an account of its fundamental teachings, I would state in the words of the

HINDUS IN OREGON.

There Poor Laborers are given the Bible in their own tongue.

authorized publications of the church what it is not :—

"It is not one of the many sects of Christendom. Presbyterianism means the authority of the presbytery, the equality of the ministry, and the doctrine of the Divine decrees. Episcopalianism means a graded ministry, deriving its authority from the apostles. Catholicism means the authority of the Bishop of Rome. Methodism emphasises the Divine grace aud upholds human freedom in spiritual matters. The Baptists stand mainly for a certain form of baptism. The Second Adventists hold that Christ is yet to come into the world in person. But all these, and the many others which are based upon the Bible, rest upon the same general foundation, the same underlying scheme of essential doctrines, believed to be taught by the Bible, and revealed by Jesus Christ in His advent of 1800 years ago. No considerable sect believes that God has revealed Himself since the last book of the Bible was written, except to individual souls. All the Christian bodies are but different branches from the same stock, and are divided only on nonessential questions.

"Swedenborgianism, on the other hand, stands for a belief that the Lord Jesus has fulfilled his promise, made in the Bible, to come a second time. It is not a phase of the old Christianity, but a new Christianity, spoken of in our text, and predicted in the last two chapters of the Bible, where the city, New Jerusalem, is described, descending from heaven.

"Now, underlying doctrines of Swedenborgianism —the foundations, walls, and bulworks of its Holy City :

I. The first and most central truth of Swedenborgianism—that is to say, of the Lord's New Church—is that our Lord and Savior Jesus Christ, in His glorified nature, is the one and only God,—the object of our supreme love and worship. In its earliest days, Christianity seems to have believed this, or to have believed nothing contrary to it; but since then, Christ has become a subordinate and separate Person; and the purpose for which He came, which originally was understood to be to save men from their sins (Matthew i. 21), finally came to be understood to be to save men from the just wrath of a superior Divinity, through a vicarious atonement.

II. The next great and new truth of Swedenborgianism, or the Lord's New Church, is its doctrine of Sacred Scripture, or the Bible. The Bible is the Word of God, and, as the Word of God, must contain a Divine spirit and Divine and infinite meanings. 'The words that I speak unto you,' said Jesus, 'they are spirit, and they are life.' The New Church doctrines present to us the idea of the Bible as the 'language of God in the language of men.' From its infinite origin in the 'light inaccessible' of the Divine love and wisdom, it descends according to the law of creation, by being clothed upon in lower planes or atmospheres with forms of truth adapting it to the different planes of human life. It dwells in heaven among the angels. It comes down to men of different degrees of spiritual life, even to the lowest and most sensual; and on the surface it presents ideas suitable to those who are 'of the earth, earthy.'

III. The third great truth of Swedenborgianism is that respecting a good life. Religion is a life in accord with God's commandments. There is no instantaneous salvation, no sudden and miraculous transformation of human nature, although there may be a sudden revelation of the truth which awakens a desire for a higher life. There is no entrance into heaven through God's immediate mercy, although God's yearning love for man would save every man if man would consent to live in heaven and would be happy there. But unregenerate and wilful men would only be wretched if compelled to live among the unselfish in heaven. Religion is a life. Regeneration is a development of character along the line of Divine truths or laws revealed in the Word, and now unfolded rationally in the New Church doctrines. According to the quality of these truths is the quality of heavenly life or character. 'In the Father's house are many mansions,' according to the grade of Divine truths which have been followed as the highest laws of life during our abode in this world. And the new truths, revealed from out of the World to-day, must lead inevitably to a higher life than the truths which have been held hitherto, for they awaken new and higher motives or purposes, and these constitute character.

A man may keep God's commandments merely for the sake of a good reputation, or for fear of suffering the loss of some earthly good. There is no heaven in such a life.

IV. And the final great truth of Swedenborgianism of which I shall speak is that respecting our future life. This, like all the other fundamental teachings of the New Church, is new. It was a new thing for a human being to be openly admitted to the scenes of the other life, to converse with spirits and angels, to live in both worlds at the same time, to pass from the natural to the spiritual state at pleasure. It is a new thing to learn from a human eye-witness of what we shall be and what kind of a world we shall live in hereafter. It is a new thought that the spiritual world is a real, substantial world, filled with forms and things that are familiar, but capable of indefinite development. It is new that we shall be real men and women hereafter, preserving our identity, our individuality, our ruling desires and affections, which we have chosen here. It is new that our cast off material bodies are cast off forever, and will be needed by us no more, because we shall be raised up immediately after death in our spiritual bodies. It is a new thing that the judgment follows death, and consists in bringing to light our ruling love, our interior and hidden life, good or evil, which we have chosen during our earthly probation. It is a new idea that no one is cast into hell by the Lord, but that it is the freely chosen home of all who enter there."

This is Swedenborgianism,—"new truth revealed for new age; new truth revealed for a new church or dispensation now beginning; a new Christianity" revealed by Swedenborg.

THE THEOSOPHICAL SOCIETY.

Through the agency of Madame Blavatsky, a westernized form of eastern thought and belief has been introduced into America in 1875. Madame Blavatsky, born in Russia, had studied Buddhism in India. In New York she found a considerable number of adherents who formed the Theosophical Society. Soon afterward, a split divided this society into different sections. The most important one has since located at Point Loma, California, under the direction of a Mrs. Tingley. They have there estalished a very flourishing co-operative community and school on land owned by the society.

The members of the society gradate themselves into eso- and exoteric degrees. They accept the authority of their leader as absolute, considering such leader to be the direct agent through whom unseen masters guide their destiny. The leader receives instruction by means of supernatural revelation.

This movement, never very extensive, does not seem to be gaining greatly in adherence, for Americans, as a rule, do not like to place themselves under the sway of personality such as this form of religious organization permits of.

SPIRITUALISM.

Spiritualism, the belief in physically inexplicable phenomena and in communion with the spirits of deceased people, is quite prevalent in America. The movement started with two mediums, the Fox sisters, New York, who about the middle of the 19th century claimed the establishment of communion with lost relatives and eminent deceased men and women. It is claimed that such communication with the dead reveals matters of great spiritual significance, and therefore spiritualism has been elevated to the position of a religion by a great many of its adherents.

There is hardly a town in America which does not possess its "spirit-circles," which always attract old believers and newly curious inquirers. Many of these meetings have developed a definite form of worship, if so it may be called. They open with the singing of some hymn or song, a short lecture or reading. Then the lights are turned out and the members present sit in semi-circles with joined hands. Through the agency of a medium present, single members will then call for communication with certain relatives, ask them questions, and receive some answer through the lips of the medium. At other times spirits are supposed to materialize before the very eyes of the audience as luminous, veiled forms, ask for certain persons present and transmit to them their message. These messages are usually of the tritest kind and it is surprising to notice with what seriousness they are received.

The writer was present at one of these meetings

when a number of departed spirits "materialized." One of these called for the writer, wishing to transmit the message. Nothing remains to be said but that the handclasp of this particular spirit was most physical, and little calculated to transmit spiritual knowledge.

Christian Science or The Church of Christ, Scientist.

Thirty-six years ago, in Boston, Massachusetts, a woman, Mrs. Mary Baker Eddy, together with a group of her students, founded "The Church of Christ, Scientist." This church, formed in the spring of the year 1879, was reorganised in 1892, renamed "The First Church of Christ, Scientist," and Mrs. Eddy accepted the call to become pastor of the new church. Under her guidance and incessant efforts, this church soon gained numerous adherents not only in Massachusetts, but throughout the whole United States, spreading even to most foreign countries, and forming to-day one of the most influential religions of America. One tenet of its by-laws forbids absolutely the publishing of the membership of the Christian Science Church, but one may arrive at an estimate of its great strength by looking through the pages of its official organ, "The Christian Science Journal." The number for July 1915 lists about 1200 established branch churches and societies —an average of over thirty newly established churches per year. The service in these churches is conducted by "first and second readers" (ministers) and, judging from the number of churches, there are about 2500 "readers" conducting services to-day. About 6000 officially recognized "healers" and about 100 nurses are listed, besides fourteen societies at universities and colleges.

Mrs. Eddy writes :

"In the year 1866, I discovered the Christ Science or divine laws of Life, Truth, and Love, and named my discovery Christian Science. * * * The term Christian Science was introduced . . . to designate the scientific system of divine healing. The revelation consists of two parts :

"1. The discovery of this divine Science of Mind-healing, through a spiritual sense of the Scriptures and through the teachings of the Comforter, as promised by the Master.

"2. The proof, by present demonstration, that the so-called miracles of Jesus did not specially belong to a dispensation now ended, but that they illustrated an ever-operative divine Principle. The operation of this Principle indicates the eternality of the scientific order and continuity of being.

"In following these leadings of scientific revelation the Bible was my only text-book.

"I know the Principle of all harmonious Mind-action to be God, and that cures were produced in primitive Christian healing by holy, uplifting faith; but I must know the Science of this healing, and I won my way to absolute conclusions through divine revelation, reason, and demonstration."

Mr. McCrackan, Christian Science Lecturer and First Reader of the Mother Church in Boston, writes in his pamphlet "Christian Science, Its Discovery and Development":

"Christian Science teaches and proves by its works that God is knowable through spiritual understanding, and that His relationship to man is wholly normal and natural, and invariably good, and so follows the course of His immutable law of mercy." "God is incorporeal, divine, supreme, infinite Mind, Spirit, Soul, Principle, Life, Truth, Love." * * * "Furthermore, Christian Science by its practice proves that God, Principle, is available in every hour of need, and so places within reach of every one the interpretation of Christianity as a demonstrable religion."

"Now the fact that Life, Truth, and Love act as Principle, and through divine law heal the sick as well as save the sinner—this fact constitutes a discovery. It established spiritual healing as a science, not dependent upon blind belief or upon mere hope or expectation, but as capable of definite, precise, and accurate demonstration."

"Thus Christian Science virtually exists as a continuation of primitive Christianity under modern conditions."

Mr. McCrackan quotes Mrs. Eddy:

"The discovery came to pass this way. During twenty years prior to my discovery I had been trying to trace all physical effects to a mental cause; and in the latter part of 1866 I gained the scientific certainty that all causation is Mind, and every effect a mental phenomenon.

"My immediate recovery from the effects of an injury caused by an accident, an injury that neither medicine nor surgery could reach, was the falling apple that led me to the discovery how to be well myself, and how to make others so."

It may be of interest to trace the life of this remarkable woman. Her life and the movement she built up have been filled with both strife and ever-growing success. We shall, wherever possible, quote the words of Mr. McCrackan from the above named pamphlet:

"Mary Baker Eddy was born July 16, 1821, in Bow, New Hampshire, * * descended from good New England stock, members of the Congregational church. * * She studied with a brother moral science, natural philosophy, Latin, Greek, and Hebrew grammar. At an early age the question of her joining the church presented itself, but she showed opposition to the decree of predestination as taught in the Congregational church. In spite of her stout declaration of disbelief in this, she was nevertheless admitted. She states: 'My connection with this religious body was retained till I founded a church of my own, built on the basis of Christian Science, Jesus Christ himself being the chief corner-stone'."

"In 1843 Mary Baker married George Washington Glover. Mr. Glover had established himself in business in Charlestown, South Carolina, and thither he took his young bride. Mary Baker Glover first came into touch with slavery in the South. Her husband owned some slaves and her sense of right revolted against the practice. Hardly a year had passed since her marriage when her husband died." * * "Mrs. Glover set free her husband's slaves" and returned "to her father's home, which she had so lately left. A boy was born to her not long after her return, and she named him after her husband, George Washington Glover."

"In 1849 Mrs. Glover's mother died, and about a year later her father remarried. There was a re-arrangement of domestic affairs. Mrs. Glover's nurse during her prolonged illness following childbirth was to be married, and it was planned by the family that Mrs. Glover's son George should go and live with the nurse in her new home, as Mrs. Glover's health was precarious, and she was about to move into her sister's house, where her little son might prove too great a charge. Against this plan Mrs. Glover protested vigorously, and only gave up her child when no escape from this necessity presented itself."

"Mrs. Glover continued to write on the subject of slavery, which was daily becoming a more and more burning question and was soon to culminate in the Civil War.* * * Her position of dependence upon her family was at times exceedingly difficult to bear, especially as she found herself moving farther and farther away from their views on the vital questions of the day. Her invalidism made her helpless to resist the drift of her life into almost constant confinement." * *

She gradually won her way to definite convictions concerning spiritualism, mesmerism, and animal magnetism (later called hypnotism), convictions which she has recorded in her writings.

"In 1853 Mrs. Glover, after nine years of widowhood, contracted a second marriage. She married Dr. Daniel Patterson, a dentist." She writes: 'My dominant thought in marrying again was to get back my child, but after our marriage his stepfather was not willing he should have a home with me.'

"* * Shortly after this, Mrs. Patterson's former nurse and her husband moved to the west, taking the boy with them. The bereaved mother writes: * * "A plot was consummated for keeping us apart. The family to whose care he was committed very soon removed to what was then regarded as the Far West. After his removal a letter was read to my little son, informing him that his mother was dead and buried. Without my knowledge a guardian was appointed him and I was then informed that my son was lost. Every means within my power was employed to find him, but without success. We never met again until he had reached the age of thirty-four." * * *

"In the endeavor to regain her health, Mrs. Patterson tried many experiments and followed many systems. She strictly observed the laws of hygiene, as then understood, subjecting herself to a strict diet and to a regular system of bathing. She likewise began the study of homeopathy, but the acts of spiritual healing recorded in the Scriptures were never altogether absent from her thought."

About this time she became the patient and pupil of a magnetic healer and teacher, Phineas P. Quimby, of Portland, Maine. "Mrs. Patterson was cured of physical ills of long standing by Quimby's method." * *

"For some years, from the time of her relief from invalidism until her discovery of Christian Science in 1866, she was apparently under the impression that the solution of true mental healing long sought by her was represented by Quimby's method. In 1862 and in 1864 Mrs. Patterson wrote down her impressions of his system and turned over the manuscripts to him. In view of their collaboration Mr. Patterson signed Quimby's name to these manuscripts, and this gave rise in later times to the report of Quimby manuscripts being in existence from which Mrs. Patterson was assumed to have derived Christian Science."

A heated controversy later arose as to whom the honor of being the founder of Christian Science really belonged, Mrs. Patterson, or Mr. Quimby, and Christian Scientists are still quite touchy on this subject and most eager to claim the honor for Mrs. Eddy.

In 1864, "Mrs. Patterson was returning home one evening from a meeting * * when she sustained an accident which was to become memorable by reason of its immediate results. * * * Of this accident and her recovery Mrs. Eddy herself afterward published the following * * :

"St. Paul writes: 'For to be carnally minded is death; but to be spiritually minded is life and peace.' This knowledge came to me in an hour of great need: and I give it to you as death-bed testimony to the day-star that dawned on the night of material sense. This knowledge is practical, for it wrought my immediate recovery from an injury caused by an accident, and pronounced fatal by the physicians. On the third day thereafter, I called for my Bible and opened it at Matthew, lx. 2. As I read, the healing Truth dawned upon my senses: and the result was that I rose, dressed myself and ever after was in better health than I had before enjoyed. That short experience included a glimpse of the great fact that I have since tried to make plain to others, namely, Life in and of spirit; this Life being the sole reality of existence."

"Here indeed was the healing for which she had always striven, which she felt must be at hand did one only know how to realize its presence. Here at last was the ideal towards which her whole life had tended from her childhood's experiences, her stout refusal to believe in a cruel God, her insistent conviction that love is the liberator of mankind from all woe. * * * Thereafter she could never be deceived again, never in doubt as to what constituted the healing of Bible times. Nor from the moment of her discovery does she ever seem to have hesitated about her manifest mission to give this truth to the world and become the Founder as well as the Discoverer of Christian Science." * * *

"Her experiences for the next ten years proved inexpressibly hard" * * * there "followed Dr. Patterson's desertion of his wife, and Mrs. Patterson was obliged to secure a decree of divorce from him. Her father and mother having passed away, she might naturally have gone to the home of her sister * * but the sister made it a condition that she should forsake her unconventional religious convictions, and this Mary Baker was determined not to do. * * * She chose poverty rather than ease, and now began a life of involuntary wandering from one home to another, from one boarding place to another, the life of a student searching the Scripturism, nourishing her glorious discovery, applying it where she was welcomed; sometimes loved and appreciated, more often misunderstood and even traduced; healing the sick, transforming character, and always writing, writing that mankind at large might gain the spiritual revelation which had come to her. * * * As time went on she began to teach little classes of students. * * * In 1875, while residing in Lynn, Massachusetts, Mary Baker finished her book "Science and Health" with "Key to the Scriptures" (the text book of Christian Science). * * * In that year also was made the first beginning of a Christian Science church, when a number of her students united in inviting her to hold meetings and preach to them every Sunday, and subscribed a weekly salary for her."

"In 1887 Mary Baker Glover was married to Mr. Asa G. Eddy, who, being in bad health, had been sent to her for treatment. She had healed him, had taken him through one of her classes, and had learned to trust him so thoroughly that she had placed many of her affairs in his charge. Some of Mrs. Eddy's students took umbrage at this transfer of her interests and a period of singular unrest ensued, culminating in mutual recriminations among themselves and even in lawsuits, and finally blossomed forth into a veritable conspiracy against Mr. Eddy. Her home with Mr. Eddy provided her an atmosphere of peace and security for her teaching and healing work."

"The beginning of a Christian Science Church made in 1875 had not survived the disaffections of some of her students, but in 1876 the Christian Science Association was formed, which fulfilled the needs of the times. * * * In the spring of 1879, a little band of earnest seekers after truth went into deliberations over forming a church without creeds, to be called the 'Church of Christ, Scientist.' They were members of evangelical churches and students of Mrs. Mary Baker Eddy in Christian Science, and were known as Christian Scientists. Mrs. Eddy was appointed on the committee to draw up the tenets of this Mother Church, a charter was obtained, and Mrs. Eddy accepted the call to become pastor of the new church. * * * In 1881 Mrs. Eddy opened the Massachusetts Metaphysical College in Boston. 'Under the seal of the Commonwealth,' a law relative to colleges having been passed which enabled her to get this institution chartered for medical purposes. No charters were granted to Christian Scientists for such institutions after 1883."

Every three years a course is given to a limited number of thirty students in Metaphysical College, and graduates may receive the degree of C.S.B., Bachelor of Christian Science, or that of C.S.D., Doctor of Christian Science. "This degree followed by the word teacher designates one who has received a certificate and is authorized to teach." "Authorized teachers hold but one class each year, with not more than thirty pupils in a class." Students so taught may then go out as Christian Science "Healers", treating patients of all descriptions. Their usual charge for a visit to and a "treatment" of a patient is $ 2 (6 rupees). They also give "absent treatments," in which case the patient may be miles away, but is thought to receive the healing waves as if present. There are also Christian Science nurses, who attend the patient day or night or both according to need. These nurses usually receive the ordinary medical nurses' pay of $ 25 a week, (75 rupees) or more. Thus Christian Science healing constitutes a quite well-paid profession.

Very early, Mrs. Eddy found herself opposed by a strong public opinion against her doctrines and her treatment of disease, and found herself also involved in other personal quarrels. During the year 1883 "Mrs. Eddy found herself constrained to sue a former student for the infringement of her copyright." She edited many writings and started the Christian Science Journal, the official organ. The copyrighted books are expensively bound in leather and are sold everywhere at high, uniform rates. Every member is in possession of her writings. Mrs. Eddy realized a huge fortune from the return of her works,—over $ 2,000,000, (60 lakhs of rupees).

"In 1879 Mrs. Eddy's son, George Glover had been located by her in Minnesota and upon her request had come to Boston to visit her, but he did not seem open to the reception of Christian Science teaching. * * * Mrs. Eddy conceived the idea of adopting as her son Dr. Ebenezer J. Foster, a former physician, who had become interested in Christian Science, had received instruction in the college, and who resided with other students in Mrs. Eddy's household." These two sons later attacked her in a suit to have her adjudged incapable of managing her own affairs. This suit, intended to keep her fortune from going entirely to the church, dragged in the courts for almost a year. After settling on each of them $ 200,000, the suit was withdrawn by the complainants.

"From 1892 to 1908 Mrs. Eddy resided at Pleasant view, * * * New Hampshire, * * * perfecting the organization of the Christian Science church, supervising the various means * * * by which Christian Science is placed before the public. She founded the periodicals of the denomination," including the Christian Science Monitor, a daily newspaper.

"Outrageous misrepresentations" became current concerning her private life at Pleasant View and "it was necessary for Mrs. Eddy to have a mass of affidavits collected refuting these misrepresentations, and to submit to an interview with some fifteen newspaper men and women in the presence of her banker, her lawyer, the Mayor of Concord, and some members of the Mother Church. The newspaper men were then taken all over the house and were shown the evidences of her simple home life.

Mrs. Eddy died in the winter of 1910, perhaps the most influential woman in America at the time. The "deification" of Mrs. Eddy among her followers is a matter of constant ridicule on the side of the opponents of Christian Science, the bitterest of whom are to be found among medical men. Suits for "malpractice" against Christian Science Healers are nothing uncommon. In spite of this, the number of adherents is on a steady, strong increase.

"The services of the Christian Science Church are strikingly simple. Instead of a personal sermon, a lesson-sermon is read which consists of verses from the Scriptures, and correlative passages from the Christian Science text-book, the pastor of the Christian Science church being the Bible and Science and Health. There are two readers in every church. Every branch church is self-governing and self-supporting... One of the distinctive features of the Christian Science church is its Wednesday evening meetings. * * * They give an opportunity for testimonies and experiences as to the works of Christian Science, * * * the overcoming of all manner of sin, sickness, calamity, and incapacity" out of the lives of attending members. * * * Each church maintains a Christian Science reading room, where "the Bible and Mrs. Eddy's works may be read free of charge, or purchased if desired." Mrs. Eddy instituted a committee of publication in connection with the Mother Church. Committees on publication exist in the different states and in foreign countries, also a board of lectureship, providing excellent speakers.

"New Thought."

It is not easy to give an accurate description of the extent or even the principles of the new strong movement of "New Thought" which has swept over the continent of America during the last half century, especially the last twenty-five years, and is steadily gaining in strength and adherence. A great number of separate organizations, such as the "Divine Science," "Home of Truth," "Truth Center," "College of Divine Science," "Church of the Unknown Disciple," "Essene Circle," "Practical Christianity," "Unity Center," "Higher Thought Center," "Progressive Brotherhood Center," "Church of the New Civilization" and others are the offshoots of this movement, which started everywhere and nowhere.

Mrs. Annie Rix Militz, one of the leaders of The Home of Truth, in "The Master Mind" for March 1915, makes the following statement which comprises the essence of the New Thought movement:

"A thought increases the heart-beats, stops or gives great volume to the breath, jerks the muscles, throws the body into strenuous activities, that may be communicated to hordes of people who then proceed to change the face of the earth, who can measure the influence of a single thought?

"These are some of the ideas that have received the name New Thought:—that disease is of mental origin instead of material: that right thinking brings health to the body and prosperity to one's affairs; that right thoughts about oneself heal perverted appetites, like drunkeness, and sinful living; that knowledge can conquer death; that self-mastery gives one power to control the elements; that God-love in the heart will destroy all enmity on the part of people, animals and other creatures; that there is no limit to thought and its power except what thought puts upon itself.

"New thought is the forerunner of the New Age educating humanity to be fit citizens for the kingdom of heaven that is coming to the earth—that is really here now but veiled to the eyes whose seeing is not "single" to the All-God."

Members of this movement usually, if at all, label themselves merely "Truth-Students" or "New Thought Students." They build no churches, and have no rigidly established organizations and no recognized heads or leaders whose authority they accept. They base most of their teaching upon the Bible; although they accept in part the wisdom and inspiration of the scriptures of all races and nations.

The different New Thought bodies meet in reading rooms, lecture rooms and in private homes. There they listen to special lecturers or to any member who may be able to speak. A great feature of their work is the healing of mental and physical disease. Once a week or oftener, they hold healing meetings, and at all times during the week healers will give individual treatment, present or absent, to patients applying for them. "Healers" do not derive their authority to heal from any college or school, but claim to derive it from the source of all power and wisdom, from God, directly. The proof of anyone's possessing healing power lies in the mere fact of some one's turning to them successfully for help. In this and in the fact that they demand no charge for these treatments lies the great difference between these "healers" and the "Christian Science Practitioners."

In the *Master Mind* for July 1914, not less than 131 separate New Thought centers are listed. This is the nearest indication of the size of the movement. How many members belong to each center it is impossible even to guess. A great many persons who avail themselves of the healing powers of the New Thought healers never break their old church affiliations, as there is nothing compelling them to do so, but all of them refuse any longer to put their confidence in medical science for the healing of physical ills.

As a sample of the beliefs, and the method of healing, and loose but nevertheless powerful, organization of these New Thought bodies, we shall quote from the following brief account of "*The Home of Truth*" publications :

"A presentation of Jesus Christ's teachings and practice is offered to the world here that is believed to be the primitive ministry of Christianity, which was given to the world for man's healing or salvation—body, mind, soul, and estate.

"The chief teacher and founder is Jesus Christ; the great authority for our belief is the Holy Spirit within each one ; and the church is the whole body of divine Humanity everywhere ; the text-books are : Firstly, the four Gospels of Matthew, Mark, Luke, and John, especially the words of Jesus Christ ;

second, the remaining books of the Bible ; and, third, all other Scriptures and writings that have blessed humanity visible and invisible, and we are all brothers and sisters, with one Father and one Mother whose name is God.

"Realizing that the church of Christ is that perfect body of humanity that does not need to be organized or held together by rules and strictures, the workers of this presentation have formed no new Church or creed, but have seen that the homes of the nation are the spiritually natural places for worship and the healing and teaching ministry. The true home is the representation of heaven.

"Two or three souls consecrated with all the love of heart, soul, mind, and strength to God the Good, have been the starters of each of the Homes of Truth. They believe that God the Good is All in All, and that there is none to love or to be, to know or to work for but this one in our neighbor, in our self, or in the world, this being their interpretation of the greatest of all the commandments.—Mark xii, 29, 30, 31.

"They believe that every good gift has been conferred upon us freely by our heavenly Father, and that knowledge of Truth and its application will reveal to us eternal health, unchanging prosperity, age-lasting life, and all the bliss of omniscient, omnipresent, and omnipotent Love.

"They believe that all men and women are innately good, and that all are alive whether visible or invisible, and under the care and guidance of the loving Father, who knows no failure but will present Truth in all ways to His children until every one shall come to himself and to the joy for which his heart has been yearning.

"The public ministration has three departments : healing, teaching, and worship.

"The healing ministry is the same as that of Jesus Christ, who healed through knowledge and by speaking the word of truth, both silently and audibly. The Lord is the great physician with whom all things are possible and to whom no disease is incurable. "I am the Lord that healeth thee."

"No charge is made for any of the ministrations, for all the gifts of God are free and we are all one family, whose members in the heavenly state are under the law of the realm of the Spirit. Love always expresses itself in gifts, and in loving our neighbor as ourselves we give freely even as the Spirit has given to us freely. Therefore, nothing of the healing and teaching is priced or sold, but all are love gifts. The same privilege of free giving is accorded to those who come to the Home or love its ministry, and many give richly and generously to the work in the form of money or other expressions of value.

"The support of the Home and its workers seems unique in the eyes of the world, since there is no subscription list, no fund, no charge for services, no solicitations—all contributions being voluntary in the truest sense of the word.

"The first of these Homes has been in existence over twenty years, and the second almost as long, and thousands can testify to the benefits in healing, both physical and spiritual, conferred upon them by the workers and healers there. Since their beginning certain meetings have never ceased, such as the Healing Meetings and the Sunday Services. Classes in the first principles and for students more advanced are held continually, also Bible lessons, and every evening there is a half hour of silent prayer and meditation.

"The Sunday school for the children is an important feature, and every principle is given to the young that will defend them from the false suggestions of mortality and encourage their individual expressions of the true spiritual self that dwells within.

"Each Home is independent of all the others financially and in methods of ministry, and yet are in perfect harmony as to the main ideas. The desire and aim of the workers is to maintain equality among themselves and to esteem all the work equally honorable, and this is accomplished by working for God alone, and being unmoved by the opinions, criticisms, and ingratitude of people. The Lord within the people knows, and will finally be the only one to speak and act in response to the love and faith extended by the workers.

"There is a guest room in the Home where any one in sympathy with its ministry and not an invalid can reside for a time, according to the good judgment of the household. Also any one who desires to read or meditate in chapel or sitting-room is most welcome to come in at any time that these rooms are not being used for other purposes."

"INQUIRIES AND BRIEF REPLIES ABOUT HEALING."

"How do you Heal? By a certain knowledge of man and his true being and its application in prayer, either silent or audible; the same methods that Jesus Christ used.

"Do you use Means? Nothing but the word of truth. No material means or application of hands, unless especially led to do so by the Holy Spirit.

"Is faith necessary? Enough faith to come for treatment and to obey the directions of the healer.

"Can any disease be healed? God is the real Healer in every case, and nothing is incurable with Him."

DIRECTIONS FOR THOSE DESIRING HELP.

1. Look to the Supreme Mind only for help.
2. Put aside medicine and other material aids.
3. Take no treatment from other practitioners or doctors.
4. Stop talking about disease and troubles, symptoms and pains.

5. Be grateful for all improvement and tell of it, for that hastens the healing.
6. Do not hesitate to confess your faults or errors of the past. Put "confidential" on the envelope.
7. Keep your thoughts on pleasant things. Think as little as possible of your condition.
8. Give everyone good kind thoughts. Carry no bitterness in your heart.
9. Have no anxiety about anything.
10. Take lessons in the Science of Christ Healing as soon as possible. Have at hand good reading on these subjects all the time.
11. Have no doubt of your final restoration to health, even though your case seems slow in yielding.
12. Make your love-offering as though you were giving it directly to Christ.

The Master Mind, a monthly publication, is their official organ. The number for August, 1914, opens with a quotation from the teachings of Buddha. Mrs. Annie Rix Militz is one of the leaders of this school and the editor of its official organ. The following sentences from the opening article of the magazine for August, 1915, read like Buddhism or Vedanta in the English garb:

"It is one of the conclusions of science that matter and energy are not things in themselves, that they are but modes of thinking, a view of the universe. This view is changeable according to our viewpoint and matter has no fixed qualities to one who knows the real substance, which is changeless, and determined in its qualities, which are altogether good; whereas the qualities that are ascribed to matter are mixed, sometimes good and sometimes evil, at times desirable and at others undesirable.

"It is possible for us to give to this appearance called materiality what qualities we choose, for we give those qualities by reflection and not as actually belonging to the appearance. We see all materiality as we would look in a mirror; we know that the image in the mirror can be governed by our knowledge of and power over the thing reflected."

Or:—

"Spirit is the one substance, omnipresent, in and through all things, changeless, perfect, good. Space, limitations, forms, and dimensions are concepts of this divine substance, and they are movable as we know the Truth, and abide by it even in the face of our senses."

The principal thing in connection with this school which is attracting much attention is their healing work. The two noted cases which are being advertized freely are those of one Miss Dorothy Kerin of Herne Hill, London, and of Miss Edith Ballard of Cillingham, Kent. In the first case the patient was said to be in the last stage of consumption and is said to have been healed by the force of spiritual faith. The particulars of the other case may be gathered from the following statement of the patient in *The Master Mind* for August 1914:—

"I was five years in bed and my limbs were bound hard and fast like iron!

"On Sunday morning, the 2nd of November, 1911, when I had come nigh to gates of death, a beautiful light appeared over my head, and I heard someone distinctly say to me, 'Edith, you have borne your suffering with great patience and fortitude! Now arise and walk three times around your bed, for five days, for the five years you have lain upon it. And at the hour of six and nine you shall walk again, after which you shall pass through another fire (the fires were the frightful fits she was subject to), then you shall be healed, for your time is not yet.' Then my two hands were taken and folded upon my breast, and then in this helpless position, my legs were lifted gently out of bed, and then my body lifted up and I stood upright, and then my hand was lifted up above my head and grasped in a warm and soft hand, and thus I was gently led around my bed three times! I was then laid upon my bed again and all my limbs became hard and fast as before!

"My mother, who was present, of course spread the wonderful story among our neighbours, and as the time for the next walk was stated, a company of them came in to witness the marvel. At the appointed time the same Light appeared, and the same walk was taken in the presence of them all. These "walks" were continued for twenty days and witnessed by hundreds of all classes. In my last "walk" the Light on this occasion was like the sun, while the time before it was like moon, and overhead there was a most beautiful rainbow, and this time my two hands were taken and held above my head while I walked, and this time all my limbs were set free and I was made whole.""

How much reliance can be placed on these statements, I am not in a position to say. Evidently there are numerous centers of this school in England as well as in America. Mr. Thomas Troward, once a Divisional Judge in the Panjab, is said to be connected with this school, and Swami Vivekananda spent seven weeks in the Home of Truth, Alameda, California, during one of his visits to the United States. The New Thought Movement is considered by many to be the most spiritual and promising movement in America.

CHARITY AND SOCIAL SERVICE ORGANIZATIONS

Whatever else may be said of the people of America, it cannot be said of them that they are not charitable. It rarely happens in the world that those who have most, give most. America is, however, an exception. Individuals and corporations have made colossal fortunes. Some of the wealthiest families and persons in the world belong to America. A good many of them started with nothing except their brains and are multi-millionaires today.

But if they have made millions and millions, they have also given away millions in charity. The universities of America and the various charity organizations are standing monuments of their generosity, wisdom, and patriotism. In most cases these benefactions combine in them the desire for name and fame, or the perpetuation of the memory of some one dear or near to the benefactor, with highly useful and commendable objects of humanitarian or national value. The country which gave them a chance has every reason to be proud of them. They have repaid what the country gave them, sometimes with double or even treble interest.

But what is most instructive about the charities of America is their thorough organization and the scientific spirit which underlies them. The extent and the scope of these charities is indeed very large, but what is most interesting is the spirit in which they are administered. Perhaps nowhere was the need of organized charity so great as in the United States of America. Perhaps nowhere was the problem so complex and intricate as here. With the never-ending fluctuation in its population, the result of the never-ceasing waves of immigration sweeping over the land from year's end to year's end; with the millions of people coming to its shores just for a chance, among whom there is a large percentage of those who are either moral or social wrecks, victims of their own misdeeds or those of the society in which they were born; with its thousands of refugees who have run from tyranny and oppression of those monsters in human form who rule over the destinies of their native lands; with an ever-increasing army of those who do not know who is responsible for having brought them into this world, who have not known the love of mother or father or the company of brother or sister; hundreds of thousands of such as have left father and mother behind and have no one to think of them in times of distress or trouble; with millions of such as have no home in the proper sense of the term and who have simply to live on chance employment, America did really need the system of charity and social help which has been organized in the interests of humanity, in the interests of national efficiency and in the interests of social welfare, by its sons and daughters, acting in the true spirit of Christ, and in harmony with each other.

If some have given their money ungrudgingly; others have given their lives, their time, their energies and their talents. This is a land of extremes. While you find here perhaps the biggest crowd of sharpers, cheats and scoundrels in the world, men who have no scruples to rob or cheat even the orphan, the widow and the helpless, you come across perhaps the largest number of men and women who have dedicated their lives to the service of the Lord and Humanity. While the credal chains are loosening, the broader interests of true charity and true humanity are being strengthened. All this is very creditable, stimulating and refreshing. But what is even of greater value is the evolving of a scientific spirit in the administering of charity and the application of scientific methods in preventing misery and removing poverty and distress. Business methods and humanitarian instincts are combined in making charity effective, not only in the immediate relief of the sufferers, but also in providing a normal and a healthy future for him. The object is immediate relief as well as future prevention —individual help as well as national efficiency. The thoroughness with which charity and social service work is conducted in this country is amazing. It is one of the biggest departments of human activity in which the National government, the State, the City, the Church, the private benefactor, the scientific investigator, the scholar, and the business expert, all co-operate. Its ramifications are widespread and the persons engaged in this work constitute an army which is larger in size than the United States army or perhaps the army and navy combined. The amount of money that is handled by these organizations must be many times more than the money that is spent on the United States army and navy, and the kind of service they do is surely better than the other.

The bye-products are perhaps even more valuable than the immediate results. The work of these organizations, the investigations made by their agency, the facts brought to light by them, the experiments made by them in relieving and preventing distress, the knowledge gained by a study of the needs of the different strata of society covered by their activities, throw such a flood of light on human problems and on social science as to form a material help in the advance of civilization and in the intelligent progress of humanity.

It is a poor world where there should be such great need of charity ; that there should be so much distress, disease, suffering, privation, and poverty ; that there should be so many inequalities arising from an unequal and unjust distribution of wealth and denial of social and economic opportunities ; that there should be resources of charity and dispensers of charity. Yes, it is a poor world that inflicts so many wounds and then tries to heal them, that first strikes and then consoles. Yet however we may wish that society were so constituted as to delete the idea and the necessity of charity, however noble it may be to give charity, it is anything but honorable to receive it or to be considered as deserving of it. While it perhaps raises the giver, if he acts in a spirit of duty, it certainly lowers the one who receives it. If men are brothers, sons of the same father, there should be none who are forced to be the recipients of other people's charity and the objectives of other people's pity. Yes, all that is true, but so long as the world is what it is, it is next best that charity should be administered, not by individuals, but by organizations; that it should be administered as a social obligation and a part of national duty rather than simply as an outcome of pity and sympathy; that the causes which make it necessary for people to apply for relief should receive a scientific probing into; and that steps should be taken to remove those causes so that the repetition of such applications either by the same individual or by others becomes impossible or at any rate rare. A study of the charity and social organizations of America shows that the directors and leaders of these organizations are alive to these principles and that they are acting accordingly.

II.

I will now let them speak for themselves and in giving an account of the charity organization of America, profusely quote from their literature. But before I start giving an account of the methods and the work and the extent of organized charity in America, I would like to give a brief account of a charity foundation which has materially helped in the evolution of the scientific methods spoken of above.

The foundation known by the name of Russell Sage Foundation, owes its origin to the generosity of Mrs. Sage, who gave away ten million dollars i.e., three crores of rupees, for the Foundation in 1907. It began its work in two small offices in New York, but is now occupying its own nine storied building (absolutely fire-proof and made of solid stone and iron)—a noble structure devoted to a noble purpose. The purpose of the Foundation is "the improvement of social and living conditions in the United States by any means which shall seem expedient, including research, publication, education, and the establishment, aid, or maintenance of charitable or benevolent activities or institutions. In her letter of April 19, 1907, which is her deed of gift, Mrs. Sage further defines the scope of the Foundation, and makes plain the wide vision of its usefulness that lay behind her gift. In that letter she wrote :

"The scope of the foundation is not only national but it is broad. It should, however, preferably not undertake to do that which is now being done or is likely to be effectively done by other individuals or other agencies. It should be its aim to take up the larger and more difficult problems, and to take them up so far as possible in such a manner as to secure co-operation and aid in their solution. In some instances it may wisely initiate movements, in the expectation of having them maintain themselves unaided after once being started. In other instances it may start movements with the expectation of carrying them on itself."

The trustees at one of their earliest meetings decided not to attempt to relieve individual or family need, partly because the trustees did not wish to free the philanthropic public of its responsibilities toward unfortunate members, and partly because they believed that the foundation could accomplish more by attacking evil at its root and attempting to remove the causes of poverty, pain, and suffering, than in undertaking mere individual relief. It was decided that grants should not be made to universities and colleges, because these institutions were already provided for to a certain extent by Mr. Rockefeller's General Education Board, and incidentally through pensions by Mr. Carnegie's Foundation for the Advancement of Teaching. Aid to churches of all denominations was also eliminated from the purposes of the Foundation. "The Foundation" has ten direct divisions, each with a department head and staff of workers apart from its indirect work in co-operation with a score of other altruistic movements. It is in touch with 250 charity organization societies, 900 libraries, 900 mayors, and 800 school superintendents in the forty-eight states; it distributes between 200,000 and 300,000 pieces of its own printed matter annually, an average of a thousand every working day in the year.

The ten direct agencies of the foundation are the Charity Organization Department, the Department of Child Helping, the Department of Recreation, the Division of Education, the Division of Remedial Loans, the Committee of Women's Work, the Department of Surveys and Exhibits, the Division of Statistics, the Southern Highland Division and the library. As is entirely logical in the scheme of an institution seeking permanent results, a great part of the work of the Foundation is among children—the men and women of the next generation.

As interesting and as important as any of the

work of the foundation is that of the Charity Organization Department, directed by Miss Mary E. Richmond. This department studies the work of charity organizations in all parts of the country, digests the information it obtains, and acts as a clearing house of this information with the purpose of raising the standards of charity work everywhere it can. It seeks to eliminate duplications of expenditure and time. It makes special studies in field work on its own account and publishes its findings on them. It makes a special effort to get the best workers into the fields where they can be most useful. Its labors and purposes and methods are really at the root of all the work of the other departments of the Foundation. It is teaching thousands of people that the causes of dependency are preventable ills, and how they may be prevented.

The Department of Surveys and Exhibits is doing some of the most interesting and suggestive work of recent years to bring about better conditions in American cities. "For example a survey of the City of Newburgh showed that the city had a typhoid death rate twice that of the whole state. This led to an immediate investigation of the watershed." The pamphlet containing the report of the Newburgh survey, each of its hundred pages crowded with concrete suggestion, without one instance of personal or bitter criticism, indicates that the undertaking was wholly constructive. The needs of Newburgh are summarized thus: reorganization of financial methods; a housing code; better financial and better organized health work; more emphasis upon reformation, less upon humiliation of prisoners; the employment of a paid probation officer; more investigation and further co-operation in charity work, with emphasis upon prevention of dependency and family rehabilitation rather than the giving of alms; permanent public playgrounds and recreation use of school buildings; better enforcement of child labor laws and a better understanding of the wage problem, better physical conditions in older schools, better provision for securing teaching efficiency; provision for abnormal children and more attention to physical training.

The Department of Recreation originated in an undertaking entered into by the Foundation, under the name of the Playgrounds Extension Committee, to further the establishment of children's playgrounds and to give temporary aid to what has now become a national movement—the Playground and Recreation Association of America. One of the leading phases of the work of this department is in the arousing of public sentiment to the demand that playgrounds and breathing places for children shall be established throughout the cities of the United States. Careful playground work on a properly organized, supervised, and directed playground is as educational as going to school. When the Foundation began to push the playground movement five years ago, there were 90 American cities which had playgrounds: to-day there are more than 800. The Foundation has investigated playgrounds and recreation undertakings in every part of the United States and also in Europe; and this information having been accumulated and digested, the resulting conclusions are put at the service of any individuals or committees that desire to know the best way, under local conditions, to start and conduct any form of public recreation. And this information is kept up to date, new pamphlets and books on the subject being issued whenever new ideas or new accomplishments make their publication worth while. In all this work the Department, although not giving financial assistance, is co-operating with the Playground and Recreation Association of America.

Another division of the work of the Department of Recreation, to which Mr. Clarence Arthur Perry, the assistant director, devotes a great deal of attention, is the development of the idea of using the schoolhouse as a social centre for adults as well as children. Mr. Perry's books and pamphlets on the wider use of the school plant (buildings, equipment, and yards) are the result of five years of study on the subject, and they describe all the activities and how they are carried on after regular school hours, from evening schools to social centres, in the public school buildings of the entire country.

A movement that has been greatly extended by this department of the Foundation is the "Safe and Sane Fourth." The campaign was begun in 1909, the number killed and wounded in fourth of July celebrations in American cities in the preceeding year being 5,623. Last year the killed and wounded numbered only 988, a reduction of 4,635. The Department of Recreation writes directly to anyone asking for information in any of its divisions, and gives advice suitable to particular cases in different parts of the country. Representatives of the Foundation make personal visits whenever they can to cities, towns and villages where the playground or social centre situation may be under discussion, and give talks and lectures and general assistance in perfecting the scheme best adapted to local resources and needs.

The sister division or the Department of Recreation is the Division of Education. This division serves as a laboratory for the study of educational problems. Its fundamental purpose is to discover, formulate, and apply methods for illuminating and clarifying the questions which confront workers in the field of public education. The division takes the difficulties which confront the school superintendent and brings to bear upon them its fund of special knowledge, the educational experience and scientific training of its workers, the powerful organization of its office machinery, and the solid financial backing of the Foundation. Questions too large to be handled by one city or one superintendent are taken over by the division as its contribution towards the progress of education in the United States. A few of the special problems studied by the Division of Education during the last few years are the medical inspection of school children, open-air schools, the backward child, the measurement of educational processes and products, psychological tests in vocational guidance, the effect of promotion rates on school efficiency, and a comparative study of public schools systems in the forty-eight states. The division aims not only to discover facts, but to bring them to the attention of educators in such a form and manner that they can neither be misunderstood nor disregarded.

Both the Department of Recreation and the Division of Education lend lantern slides illustrative of the various phases of their work. They also publish bulletins from time to time, in which the results of their studies are reported.

In the Division of Remedial Loans, conducted by Mr. Arthur H. Ham, concrete results are perhaps more definitely shown than in any other department of the Foundation. When, in 1909, Mr. Ham began his crusade against the extortionate lenders on salaries and chattel mortgages, they were at the height of their prosperity. It was estimated that in every city of the United States of more than 25,000 population, containing any appreciable number of citizens dependent on fixed salaries or wages, there were loan sharks in the proportion ot one to 5,000, and that one in every 20 voters was discounting two days' labor for the price of one. To-day in 28 of the states the people have risen against the sharks and are driving them out of business by legislation that permits the small loans traffic to be done on a reputable basis. In 1909 the statute books of only ninc states contained laws tending to restrain the rapacity of the loan sharks ; to-day in 23 states their teeth are being drawn, and in five more states legislation is in progress for similar results. The rapidity with which the movement for driving out the extortioner has grown throughout the country may not be better shown than in the records of the National Federation of Remedial Loan Associations which was organized in 1909. At that time semi-philanthropic societies for the assistance of the small borrower existed in twelve cities of the United States. Since the organization of the National Federation it has been joined by 17 new remedial loan societies, and 8 more such societies are in process of formation. The semi-philanthropic Chattel Loan Society of New York, that was organized last year and has already demonstrated the economic proposition that money may be lent at a profit on household goods at 2 per cent. a month plus a small investigation fee, is one of the results of the work of the Division of Remedial Loans.

The province of the Committee of Women's Work is the gathering of data about the conditions of the employment of women in New York City, and to make the facts known as a basis for sound, constructive legislation. Miss Van Kleek has already published intensive studies of the book-binding and artificial flower making trades.

The Southern Highland Division, whose headquarters are at Asheville, N. C., and whose secretary is Mr. John C. Campbell, has made careful studies of social and living conditions in the Southern mountains. It aims to promote co-operation and co-ordination among all the forces of advance in the mountain country. It aims also to stimulate in other parts of the United States intelligent and sympathetic understanding of the mountain people, their problems and their needs. The division began its studies in 1908 and has carried them steadily forward. Extensive journeys have been made in the mountains in Tennessee, Kentucky, the Virginias, the Carolinas, and Georgia, the more remote sections being reached by horseback or wagon. Interviews have been held with teachers, physicians, ministers, social workers, farmers, and other mountain citizens, and the people and their life have been sympathetically studied at first hand. Conferences have been held with representatives of private organizations and public departments that do mountain work, not only to become familiar with what is being done but to promote co-operation and harmonious effort. Special studies have been made of the racial characteristics of the mountaineers, problems of sanitation and health, the influence and needs of schools and churches and the best ways of developing industrial and agricultural resources.

The Russel Sage Foundation Library is one of the best working collections on sociological subjects in the country. It contains about 10,000 volumes and 15,000 pamphlets. Special classes of books in which the library is particularly strong are city problems, charities and corrections, housing, recreation, health and disease, vocational training, vagrancy, church socialization, and labor conditions, with special collections on child labor and women in industry. Serial publications received include reports of federal, state, and local institutions and associations, and are in many cases complete from the beginning. There are specially valuable files of the proceedings of national and international conferences. The library receives 250 periodicals, and articles of value on social subjects are clipped from the popular magazines, filed, and indexed.

The library aims to serve the staff of Russel Sage Foundation, the student of the New York School of Philanthropy, and other social workers and investigators. However, it is not content simply with those who seek its help, but, like a business house, endeavors to create demands for its services from new sources. The Foundation is also a large publisher of authoritative books on social problems, written from the original researches of its staff and of other experts commissioned by it. These publications are among the foremost agencies in the Foundation's work to give the widest publicity to the most authentic date for the use of students of social questions.

Among many other movements in which the Foundation has taken an indirect part—that is, wholly or in part outside of its own departments, may be mentioned campaigns for the study and prevention of tuberculosis, of blindness, and of infant mortality, and movements for child welfare, better schools, prevention of child labor, "placing out" dependent children in homes, better organization of juvenile court work, higher standards of probation, children's school gardens, open-air schools, better housing, town and city planning, more efficient hospitals, better facilities for public recreation, and better labor laws. The Foundation aided the re-organization of the American Red Cross and the development of better methods of relief work in great disasters. It has aided schools of philanthropy in New York, Chicago, Boston and St. Louis to conduct departments of social research and give more thorough training to those preparing for social work. It has aided financially in the preparations for such important conferences at Washington as the International Tuberculosis Congress in 1908, the White House Conference on Dependent Children in 1909, the International Prison Congress in 1910, and the International Congress of Hygiene and Demography last year.

Through these movements, through the development of the exhibit idea as a means of reaching the people, through publicity bureaus and newspapers, through *The Survey* magazine, through its own publications, and in a hundred other ways, the Foundation has for six years been bringing social facts to the attention of the people of the whole country, awakening intelligent interest and enlightened opinion, and leading to serious study, discussion, and effort toward national improvement.

I have given a detailed account of the activities of the Russel Sage Foundation in order to give our social reformers an idea of the work that is needed for an effective social reform programme. Mere paper resolutions passed once a year in social conferences are not sufficient.

III.

WHAT IS AN "ASSOCIATED CHARITIES" ?

There are societies in the United States known by the name of "Associated Charities" or "Charity Organizations." The following account of the Charity Organization Society of New York will explain the objects and scope of these societies. I copy below the first two sections of the written constitution of the society. The society is a legal corporation incorporated by an act of the Legislature.

Section 1. This society shall be conducted upon the following fundamental principles :

1. Every department of its work shall be completely severed from all questions of religious belief, politics and nationality.

2. No person representing the Society in any capacity whatsoever shall use his or her position for the purpose of proselytism.

3. The Society shall not give relief from its own general funds, but may hold and apply any property or money received by it for relief or special purposes.

Section 2. The objects of the Society shall be :

1. To be a center of intercommunication between the various churches and charitable agencies in the city. To foster harmonious co-operation between them, and to check the evils of the overlapping of relief.

2. To investigate thoroughly, and without charge, the cases of all applicants for relief which are referred to the society for inquiry, and to send the persons having a legitimate interest in such cases full reports of the result of investigations. To provide visitors, who shall personally attend cases needing counsel and advice.

JOSEPHINE SHAW LOWELL

From the bas-relief by Augustus Saint Gaudens.

3. To obtain from the proper charities and charitable individuals adequate relief for suitable cases.

4. To procure work for poor persons who are capable of being wholly or partially self-supporting.

5. To repress mendicancy by the above means and by the prosecution of impostors.

6. To promote the general welfare of the poor by social and sanitary reforms, by the inculcation of habits of providence and self-dependence, and by the establishment and maintenance of any activities to these ends.

7. To provide philanthropic education and to promote the training of practical workers in charity.

In every state in the Union there is a State Board of Charities having representatives of the different cities and other local areas in the State. In October 1881, one Mrs. Lowell, acting on behalf of the new York City members of this Board, made a special report to the Board "in relation to outdoor relief societies in New York City." This report giving all the information about the work of charity in the city of New York which could be gathered, was the basis of the action which resulted in the formation of the Charity Organization Society of New York, with the objects stated above.

For about four years the society carried on its operations having charitable objects until in 1890 it was realized what an advantage it would be to have a "charity building" for all the societies engaged in the work of charity. In that year the scheme was made possible by an offer of a lakh and a half of rupees by one Mr. James Scrymser toward such a building to be erected under the joint auspices of

the Charity Organization Society and the Association for Improving the Condition of the Poor, but it was not materialized because the requisite amount of 6 lakhs more, required for the building, could not be raised at once. It fell short of a little over 3 lakhs. The immediate need, however, was met by a capitalist offering to erect a United Charities Building with a beneficial interest in favor of the Charity Organization Society and the other societies interested in the project.

It is in this building that the offices of the numerous charitable societies and social service organizations in New York are located. The very first glance shows what a wise thing it was to do, viz., to have all the charity societies in one building. No wonder that the society's twenty-five years' report issued in 1907 calls it one of the wisest and most far-reaching benefactions of the period. The "very lively personal intercourse among the leaders in the different organizations which has sprung up could hardly have developed to such proportions without it; nor except for it could there be such effective formal co-operation as there is in many ways. The advantage it is to the poor, the discouragement it is to the impostor, and the convenience it is to all the social workers and contributors of the City and to those of other cities in their visits to New York" are obvious.

The United Charities Building in New York was one of the first buildings visited by the writer on this his second visit to that great city. Since then he has seen similar buildings in the other cities of

the United States. It is a typical American Institution well worthy of being copied by other countries.

The following summary of the activities and achievements of the Charity Organization Society of New York is taken from the 25 years' report of the society issued in 1907:

SUMMARY OF 25 YEARS' WORK.

"The twenty-five years within which lies the history of the Charity Organization Society have been throughout the country a period of unprecedented progress in charitable methods, in resources available for relief, and in the improvement of social conditions.

"In 1882 almshouses and orphan asylums were the principal relief agencies in the state of New York. There were private homes for the aged, but then, as now, more of the aged and infirm were in almshouses and with them were insane, feeble-minded (called "idiots"), epileptic, blind, deafmute, and children. There was in them little provision for the sick, even for contagious diseases. Sanitary arrangements were frequently unspeakable. Two-thirds of the known insane of the state were in country and city almshouses, and stocks, fetters, and other restraining appliances were utllized, at least in New York City, as attendants on the sick. There was a large and increasing number of children in institutions and no definite means of supervising expenditures from the public treasury for their support. Fresh-air work was only beginning. Hospitals and dispensaries were as yet only slightly specialized. Such social and educational work as is now carried on by clubs, settlements and other agencies in infinite variety was represented only by a number of "industrial schools" for poor children, and the work of church visitors and missions. The relief of poor families in their homes was accomplished by the city's distribution of coal and by a number of relief societies giving out doles indepe-

dently of one another. The State Board of Charities and the State Charities Aid Association had brought about important improvements, but their reports indicate the feeling that their work was only begun.

"In the quarter of a century that has passed since 1882 the almshouse has become a home for the friendless aged and infirm; the defective classes have been much better provided for in specialized institutions, the care of the insane has been concentrated under state management, and has become more nearly adequate, more humane, and more remedial; the administration of public charities has been divorced from correction in New York City; and the city no longer distributes coal. A uniform system of accounting has been established in state institutions, and the subsidies to private institutions have been systematized on a basis of payment for services. Contract prison labor has been abolished; matrons have been supplied in the police stations; reformatory methods have to a considerable extent displaced punishment in correctional institutions; and a decent probation system is being worked out. Police station lodgings have disappeared, and in their stead in New York City is a well conducted municipal lodging house. All the progress that has been made in protecting working women and children, and in controlling the evils of the workshop, has been made in this period. Provision for the sick has increased enormously, and has become greatly diversified; medical attendance and nursing for the poor in their homes have developed, as well as the educational and preventive work carried on by the Department of Health. The improvement of the dispensary and the increase of voluntary public service by physicians have supplemented with great social advantage the work of the hospitals and Health Department. Dependent children are provided for in more natural ways; many are kept with their own families; for others homes are found in other families; and among the institutions there is a tendency to re-organize on the cottage plan in a

country location, and greatly to improve the curriculum. A separate bureau has been created for dependent children in the Department of Public Charities, and juvenile delinquents are treated in a children's court. Families dependent on private charity are cared for with no less sympathy, but with more thoroughness, and resources are not only more plentiful but are also better organized in their behalf. The administrative, financial, and relief methods of many private relief agencies have improved so enormously as to amount to a revolution.

"There has been also marked improvement in the environment of the poor, brought about by governmental activity and private interest. Unchecked competition in the building of tenements with its abuses has been brought under control; playgrounds and small parks have been opened in congested districts, and on the water-front have been built pavillion-piers for recreation and refreshment; public baths have come into existence; recreation centers, vacation schools and lectures are evidence of the socializing of the public schools, which has but recently begun. The settlement movement has developed entirely within this period, and has made its contribution of sweetness and light, as have the many independant clubs and the 'institutional work' of the churches, to the lives of working men and women and boys and girls. Certain efforts for improving conditions have assumed such proportions and such definite organization that they have become 'movements', of which the most conspicuous examples are the movements to protect children from premature and excessive employment and to diminish tuberculosis. Others, which may develop similarly, are now in their incipiency—for the control of all kinds of preventable disease whose persistence depends on social causes, for the mitigation of the evils of congested population, for the protection of purchasers of food, drugs, life insurance, and other commodities, for the equitable adjustment of the burden of industrial accidents.

"There has come about also during the twenty-five years a change in the conception of social work. It has become a profession, with a literature, defined standards, training schools, and powers of attracting an increasing number of men and women in their choice of a life work, and of retaining the most competent. In the general characteristics of social work the most notable development has been the popularization of the method which has always been pre-requisite to efficiency, the method which bases action on a knowledge of facts. This method may be said to have become the standard in the treatment of social conditions. 'Investigation' of families has lost its terror and is generally accepted as an essential preliminary to real assistance. The necessity for research into working and living conditions has made itself felt by everyone who tries to bring about any social improvement. The Russel Sage Foundation, established this year, is not only 'the most nobly conceived benefaction of an age in which many benefactions have been generously conceived and executed'; it is also a response to the insistent demand for knowledge which many charitable organizations, settlements, universities, governmental departments, and private citizens have been trying in fragmentary but earnest ways to meet.

"These are advances which have been brought about by conscious social effort, as distinguished from the action of economic forces, and as distinguished from the action of the awakening social spirit of the organization of industry and the conduct of government.

"The specific help which the Charity Organization Society has given in bringing about this advance has been outlined in the foregoing pages. In indirect or intangible ways it has been of perhaps greater service. Through the successful accomplishment of certain tasks; through the collection and presentation of facts about social conditions; through vigilant interest in the action of the legislature and other branches of government as it bears on the welfare of the poor; through the participation of its officers and members of its staff in national, state, and special conferences, and in the emergency relief work occasioned by great disasters; through its own employes who have gone to social work in other cities; through its cordial relations with public officials and with other charitable agencies; through its pioneer work in developing a course of instruction for the training of social workers; and, above all, through its publications, notably charities, it has exerted an influence on the social work of the city and the entire country.

"It has not been an easy path through these twenty-five years, though the apparently obvious course of this history may give that impression. The next step has not always been clear to all. Long, earnest, even heated discussions have occured in the councils of the Society, and years of untired effort have sometimes been necessary to convince an opponent on the outside of the wisdom of the Society's position and the disinterestedness of its motives. Prejudice, false sentiment, the clash of selfish interests, and the inherent difficulties of many of the problems encountered, have taxed the judgment and the patience of directors and workers.

"In spite of the evils of increased congestion, the physical strain of overwork, and the numerous forms of exploitation from which the poor suffer, there has come about, through increased efficiency of educational and philanthropic agencies, through the adoption of better administrative methods, and above all through the deepening sense of social responsibility, a more just and more adequate discharge of the obligations of charity. And yet these obligations have not been fully met. Of the work to be done not very much has as yet been accomplished. An advance has been made, but there is now the vision of far greater things, and there is justified a confidence that is not an unattainable vision, which comes from the success of past efforts and from the sense of strength given by sympathy and unity of purpose among the forces working for the common welfare."

The constitution of the society :—The affairs of the society are managed by a central council consisting of 33 members, one-third retiring each year, elected by the Society at its annual meeting, one delegate member for each district committee and certain ex-officio members. The ex-officio members are the New York City Commissioner of the State Board of Charities, a representative of the State Charities Aid Association and of Columbia University, the United States Commissioner of Immigration, the Mayor of the City and the heads of those departments most closely connected with the welfare of the poor.

Then there are district committees and standing committees. The district committees, which are charged with the care of needy families in their homes within their respective districts, in contradistinction from the standing committees of the Council, are independent and autonomous, electing their members on their own initiative, subject only to the approval of the Council, and conducting their affairs in many respects independently.

The standing committees and the district committees have an aggregate membership at present of over three hundred. The original members of the district committees, one in each of the ten sections into which the city is divided for the Society's purposes, are appointed by the Council, but after that each committee is self-perpetuating, its choice to fill vacancies being, however, subject to the approval of the Council.

It is the function of the district committees to "manage the work of the Society" within their own boundaries, "subject to the control of the Council." They "establish" the district offices; decide on the treatment of the cases applying for assistance in their part of the city; carry the responsibility for developing co-operation with the Society by churches, other charitable agencies and residents of the district; and take part, more or less actively as their interests lead them, in carrying on the general educational work of the Society. They have no responsibility, as committees, in raising money for their expenses. The finances of the society have been centralized from the beginning. The paid employes for the district work are appointed by authority of the Central Council, subject to the approval of the district committee to which they are assigned.

Through the standing committees, now numbering twenty, the Central Council carries on the rest of the Society's work, and supervises the work of the district committees. The Executive Committee, consisting of not less than five members, all of whom must be members of the Council, acts for the Council in the interim of its sessions, and has charge of the work of the Central Office. It holds weekly meetings and it is the most important of all the committees. For the convenient transaction of business it may meet in two sections. The president and the vice-president of the Council are *ex-officio* members of all committees.

There is a standing committee in charge of each distinctive branch of the work. Six of the nine original standing committees are still continued, and new ones have been added as the diversification of the work has called for them. The chairman of each is a member of the Council but the rest of the committee need not be. This freedom of choice has been a source of strength, enabling the Society to unite varied interests in a much more efficient prosecution of new undertakings than would otherwise have been possible.

The officers of the Central Council, elected by the Council, are the officers of the Society. The executive officer of the Council, the general secretary, is responsible to the Council for the management of the Central Office, and for exercising a general supervision over all departments and districts, and is an advisory member of both sections of the Executive Committee and of all standing committees. The director of the Department for the Improvment of Social Conditions is responsible to the Council for the conduct of that Department, with which has been consolidated the established work of the Committees on Mendicancy and the Prevention of Tuberculosis and the Tenement House Committee.

The work is organized in bureaus each with an executive head designated by a variety of titles and responsible directly to the general secretary or the director of the Department for the Improvement of Social Conditions. The School of Philanthropy, Charities, the Wood Yard, the Laundry, and the

Penny Provident Fund, are conducted by standing committees responsible to the Council.

The Society is supported entirely by voluntary contributions. It has never received appropriations from the state or city. On one occasion an offer of a thousand dollars made by the Board of Estimate and Apportionment was declined. The contributions during the past year, amounting in the aggregate to ninety-nine thousand dollars, i.e., three lakhs ot rupees, represented twenty-six hundred contributors.

THE CLASSIFICATION OF WORK.

It is as difficult to classify satisfactorily the work which is now being carried on by the Charity Organization Society as it is to divide the twenty-five years into sharply demarcated periods, and for the same reason. In each part of the work are found the characteristics of the others. The care of individual families is educational; the development of co-operation is in the interests of the individual poor; the industrial agencies give immediate help to men and women in need, and also train some of them to greater efficiency and promote the social welfare by employing persons who would otherwise be idle; the Tuberculosis Committee, primarily educational, directs the application of a relief fund, maintains a "day camp," secures more sanitary conditions in lodging-houses, and does many other things both for individual consumptives and for social conditions: the School and all the publications are means for securing better relief methods and promoting "social and sanitary reforms."

According to their predominating characteristics, however, the different features of the work may be classified in five groups, described in the language of the constitution; (1) those which serve to establish "a center of intercommunication" for charitable agencies and individuals of the city and "to foster harmonious co-operation between them"; (2) those which deal directly with persons in need of help; (3) the agencies designed "to procure work for poor persons who are capable of being wholly or partially self-supporting"; (4) the various specific undertakings "to promote the general welfare of the poor"; (5) the educational activities for the training of social workers and the diffusion of general information about social work and social conditions.

The departments of the Society's work which are primarily and specifically directed toward securing the first object for which the Society was organized are the Registration Bureau, the Reception Bureau, and the Bureau of Advice and Information. In addition to this a series of monthly conferences with charity workers is held during the winter; the heads of departments act, to an ever-increasing extent, as bureaus of information about their particular work; and the district offices are, in varying degrees, centres of consultation in their neighbourhoods. For the poor themselves the Joint Application Bureau and the district offices serve as bureaus of information; and "harmonious co-operation" of all the social forces of the city is fostered by the methods and the policy of every department of the work.

The Registration Bureau.

Registration of dependent families and exchange of reports regarding them was naturally the first work undertaken by the Society, whose organization it may be of interest to recall, was promptly hailed by a morning newspaper as the outcome of its own "advocacy of a sort of clearing house for the various charitable societies of this city."

In the first year 53,886 reports were recorded, relating, as nearly as could be ascertained, to 39,617 different cases.

The Bureau of Advice and Information.

One particular kind of inquiry has been so frequent and persistent that it has led to the development of an organized bureau. As early as June 30, 1882, the organizing secretary stated that it was hoped "to make this office a bureau of accurate intelligence regarding the history, scope and conduct of all the charities of the city"; and the first annual report of the Society stated that inquiries were already frequently made of it "concerning the standing and work of the various charitable enterprises of the city by those from whom they solicit contributions."

The need thus indicated was met in part by the publication of the Charities Directory ; but for many purposes its necessarily formal and limited statements were inadequate, and it contained no mention of the pseudo-charitable and embryonic enterprises which are the greatest embarrassment and the greatest danger to the benevolent individuals of the city.

Soliciting contributions for a charity which does not exist at all or exists only for the benefit of its promoters, was a recognized form of mendicancy when the Society was organized, and the suppression of such fraudulent enterprises and the exposure of the methods of the individuals concerned was undertaken whenever the occasion demanded. Fraudulent charities were, from the first, included with individual impostors in the Cautionary Bulletin. Threats of libel suits were not infrequently incurred in the earlier years, but none was ever brought to an issue, and many spurious collectors have been forced to retire from their business in New York. This year a a man who has obtained thousands of dollars in the name of charity was arrested on the basis of discoveries of his methods made by this bureau, and he is now in the Tombs awaiting trial.

Public exposure of flagrant instances of deception or mismanagement is a relatively small part of the work of the Bureau of Advice and Information. A special bulletin is now issued, at intervals, of enterprises concerning which members of the Society are urged to inquire before contributing to them, on account of some well-founded criticism that their methods have received. The Bureau is also ready to put at the disposal of members facts about charitable enterprises whose methods are not at all questionable, such facts as put the possible contributor in a position to decide intelligently whether or not the undertaking is one which he wishes to support, or which of several he prefers to help. Advice is frequently sought, also, by charitable organizations themselves, and the Bureau is thus able to bring about improvements in their methods and ideals. Still another kind of work done by this Bureau is the investigation, at the request of members, of problems connected with the charitable resources of the city such as the studies made during the last year of the adequacy of the provision for the aged and for crippled children.

By influencing the direction which contributions shall take, diverting them entirely from fraudulent schemes, by improving the methods of existing organizations, and by suggesting the best form for new undertakings, the Bureau of Advice and Information is an important factor in determining the character of the charitable provision for the poor.

There are now on file records of investigations that have been made in regard to 2,090 charitable organizations. A thorough investigation is made of the standing and methods of any institution or society about which an inquiry is received, and supplementary information is added from time to time. During the year 1032 reports, of which 911 were written, were made on 425 of these organizations. The report is not a statement of the Society's impression of the organization with a recommendtion as to whether the solicited contribution should be granted or withheld; it is a statement, as long as the circumstances may require, but as concise as possible, of the facts which a business man needs as a basis for forming his own judgment. The relatively large number of organizations represented in the inquiries indicate that the Bureau is used systematically by many members and not merely on the occasion of a widely-circulated suspicious appeal.

MONTHLY CONFERENCES OF SOCIAL WORKERS.

Since 1888 the Central Auxiliary Committee of Women has conducted annually a series of conferences for the social workers of the city. Topics of common interest are discussed and the meetings are pleasant and profitable to all who attend. The general subject of these conferences is the Evils of Pauperism; the possibilities of religious and charitable organizations to overcome them. The program in 1907 was as follows:

January 15. Causes of truancy: Clarence E. Meleney, assistant superintendent of public schools; Edgar S. Barney, principal of the Hebrew Technical Institute; Mrs. P. J. O'Connell, superintendent of the Alliance Employment Bureau.

February 19. Opportunities for the blind: Miss Winifred Holt, secretary of the New York Association for the Blind; Edgar P. Morford, state commissioner for the blind, 1906, superintendent of the Industrial Home for Blind Men in Brooklyn.

March 19. Club work among boys and girls: Ludwig B. Bernstein, superintendent of the Hebrew Sheltering Guardian Society. The work of the National Plant, Fruit and Flower Guild: Miss A. L. Fairfield, secretary of the Guild.

April 16. Penny lunches for school children: Mrs. A. D. Farnum, of Milwaukee. Playgrounds and recreation centers: George B. Markham, principal of one of the New York centers.

CASE WORK.

Direct service to individuals and families in need of help is now, as it has always been, the foundation of the Society's work. It engages the exclusive attention of nearly half of the Society's employes and a corresponding proportion of the time of the administrative officers, and is the primary interest of some two-thirds of all the committee members. If it has been less conspicuously before the public in recent years this is not because it has in any way been declining in importance, but because the new features of the Society's work have attracted attention by their novelty and because they have been of such a nature that the degree of their success has depended largely on the publicity they could gain.

The work for individuals and the work for improving social conditions have had a close interrelation. The impulse for each new undertaking has come from a realization of some definite need, gained from intimate acquaintance with the circumstances of the poor; and in carrying it on this intimate knowledge of the poor and access to them has been of great value. The new undertakings, on the other hand, have in each case added resources to be used in behalf of the individual families with whom we come in contact; have broadened the view of those who deal directly with the poor; and have probably been more effective in both these directions for the reason that district agents and visitors have contributed to the success of the educational work and sanitary improvements and have felt them to be the work of their own organization.

The work for the individual poor has, at any rate, improved, with the expansion of the Society's activities, with the development of the city's resources, and with the experience of the years. It is true beyond a doubt that mistakes are more rarely made because of inadequate knowledge of facts; that possible sources of assistance are more thoroughly organized in the family's behalf; that the aid given is better suited to the family's need and more often adequate in amount, than at any previous period in the twenty-five years.

The case-work is carried on by the Joint Application Bureau, the Investigation Bureau and the Districts. There are also several accessories, with varied functions: the Committee on District Work, the Committee on Appeals, the Provident Relief Funds, and the Bureau of Statistics.

During 1906-07 the total number of cases under care was 9456, distributed as follows:

In addition to these 9,456 who were actually under care for a period of time, reports were made or information received in regard to 1,898 others, making a total of 11,354 cases to whom the Society rendered service of some sort during the year. The number of different persons or families, not "cases," who were assisted by advice in the various offices during the year, cannot be ascertained, but such advice was given in 4,797 instances in the Joint Application Bureau alone.

THE SPECIAL EMPLOYMENT BUREAU FOR THE HANDICAPPED

To study the abilities of persons handicapped physically, mentally, or socially; to find work adapted to their powers which would enable them to be "wholly or partially self-supporting;" to persuade employers to accept a responsibility toward them, were the tasks which had to be faced in establishing this Employment Bureau. There were no precedents for method, as this was the first attempt of the kind ever made, and the early months were necessarily experimental.

Efforts were made at first to secure publicity, through the daily papers and the trade magazines, and to gain the co-operation of large employers, but gradually it became clear that this was not the most profitable way to work. Attention was then centered on the smaller employers, who have been found more ready to give the time and thought which co-operation requires. Gradually, too, the agencies which refer applicants have learned to distinguish better than they did at first between those who are only handicapped and those who are incapacitated for any kind of remunerative work. The methods which are now being pursued by the Bureau include keeping an accurate record of each applicants's qualifications, frequently with a physician's opinion as to what kinds of work are permissible, and of the Bureau's experience with him; patiently building up a list of employers whose assistance can be counted on; finding among the applicants persons who can fill positions offered, actively seeking positions for the others; providing training for some, and medical assistance for others in order that they may become qnalified for new tasks.

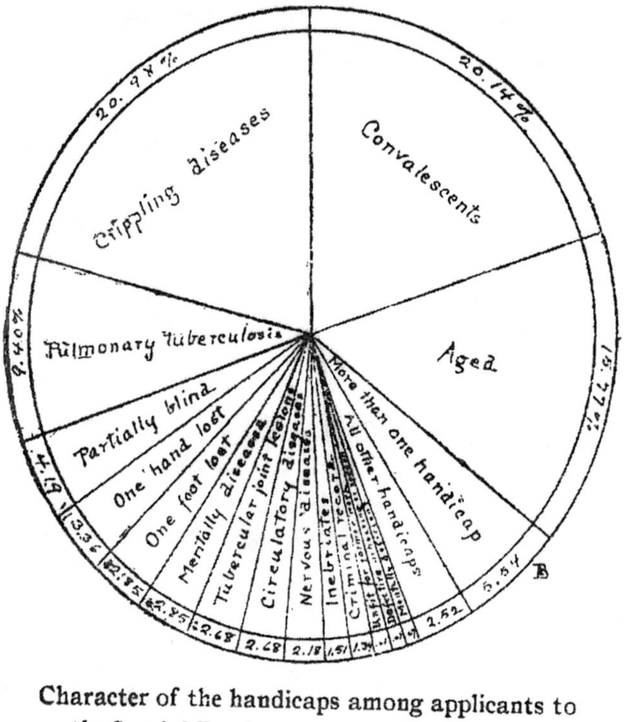

Character of the handicaps among applicants to the Special Employment Bureau.

During the winter an inspection was made of 107 recently installed out-door water-closets, at times when the temperature was below freezing point. The conditions which were found demonstrated clearly the advisability of embodying in the law a requirement that all toilet accommodations hereafter constructed for old tenement houses as well as new be within the buildings. Another investigation made during the year, of 200 two-family houses erected since the passage of the Tenement House Act, showed that thirty-six per cent of them were subsequently occupied as tenements in spite of such conditions as dark, interior bed-rooms, and inadequately lighted and ventilated toilets, and points to the urgent necessity for action to prevent the continuance of this state of affairs.

In October 1906, a special number of Charities, on the progress of the housing movement in America and Europe, edited by the secretary of the Committee, was widely distributed. The Committee acts as a bureau of information for those interested in housing reform, placing at their service for consultation its collection of literature on the housing question, its photographs and investigation schedules, and other reference material of all kinds.

THE COMMITTEE ON THE PREVENTION OF TUBERCULOSIS

The efforts of the Society to check the spread of tuberculosis and to improve the condition of individual consumptives cover a period which again tempts to retrospect and review. At the end of five years the Committee on the Prevention of Tuberculosis counts as its important achievements the program it has worked out for an effective educational propaganda and the opportunity it has given to dispensaries to develop a comprehensive district plan of dispensary treatment for poor patients and to standardize such treatment.

The contributions to educational work have been of two kinds. The Handbook and the Directory, together with several pamphlet publications, are a reference library of facts and principles which has been of the greatest assistance to the pioneers in tuberculosis work in other places, and has had a direct influence in informing public opinion and creating a general interest in preventive measures all over the country. While in this way educating the educators, the Committee has also been trying out various plans for getting the essential information before the general public and has arrived at a fairly definite idea of the relative productivity of different methods, and a fairly well crystallized equipment for general educational work at the present time. The "Don't card," evolved by much attrition from the long circulars in unintelligible language which used to be the principal instrument for imparting information, has become the standard form of literature for general use; the use of the daily newspaper has been developed; and the travelling exhibit, administering instruction in the guise of entertainment, has been adopted as the best educational device, not only a new method but also a means for enhancing the efficacy of lecture and literature.

At the beginning of last year the Committee's exhibit was being shown in Brooklyn by the Brooklyn Committee on the Prevention of Tuberculosis, to whom it had been loaned in June. On its return in January it was again put in circulation in Manhattan, and was exhibited at fifteen places in the nine months, to an aggregate audience of 70,495 persons. The fifteen places were five public libraries, four public schools, one parochial school, one immigrant school, two settlements, and two branches of the Young Men's Christian Association. The exhibit consists of 249 framed photographs and charts, thirteen models, and ten pathological specimens, all packed and mounted in such a way that the exhibition can be set up or knocked down in a day. It is widely advertised by hand-bills and local newspaper notices, and once even in theater programs. Thousands of circulars are distributed to the visitors, evening lectures are arranged for adults; and the children from the neighboring schools are sent to it in charge of their teachers, as a part of their regular work. The intelligent interest expressed by the school children, and the knowledge they gain as shown in the compositions they write about it, is one of the most encouraging features.

Lectures were given at 12 places last year in addition to those in connection with the exhibition. Six of these were to factory-workers, in their factories, and 62 at labor union meetings ; the other 61 at settlements, churches, lodges, and clubs. The lectures given under the auspices of the Committee during the five years have reached an audience of nearly 150,000 persons. The growth of the audiences in number and diversity is shown in the following table :

Lectures, 1902-07.

Year.	Number of Lectures.		Attendance.
1902-03	70		7,373
1903-04	75*		7,100*
1904-05	52		8,842
1905-06	49 at exhibitions 26 at other places		40,264
1906-07	46 to adults at exhibitions	14,913	
	250 talks to school children at exhibitions	45,077	
	6 in factories	352	
	62 at labour union meetings	10,781	
	61 at other places	7,736	78,859
Aggregate audience 1902-1907			142,438

About 60,000 of the "Don't cards" have been distributed during the year in the ordinary ways. The distribution of 400,000 supplied by the Board of Health is now under way. Every member of the police force and of the National Guard in New York City, and every employe of the Street Cleaning Department and the Metropolitan Street Railway Company has been given one, and orders for large numbers of them have been received from merchants and manufacturers to whom they have been offered through the medium of a reply postal card. The Board of Health is now preparing a catechism for

* This figure, and those for the following years, do not include Board of Education lectures for which lecturers were recommended by the Committee.

school children, modelled on the "Don't card," which the Board of Education has given the Committee permission to place in the hands of each of the 600,000 school children of the city. This is a typical illustration of the amount of co-operation involved in the Committee's work.

There have been several novel features in the educational work of the past year. A press service has been maintained by which newspaper copy has been sent once a week, from January 1 to September 30, to newspapers and magazines all over the state. Starting with a list of 1,600 papers, those which did not use the material were quickly eliminated and the number reduced to about 250. The country papers and several of the large city dailies are especially appreciative of this service. It will be kept up until January, 1908, when the State Charities Aid Association will take it over as part of its educational work through the state. Every Sunday since January 1, 1907, the back of the transfer slips on all the surface car lines of the city have been used for short printed notices about tuberculosis. This has been possible through the courtesy of the Siegel Cooper Company, which has the advertising rights on these transfer slips. It is estimated that the circulation of each one of these issues reaches a million.

The district dispensary system is an out-growth of the special fund for the relief of consumptives. The administration of the fund was placed in the hands of a sub-committee composed of the chiefs of the tuberculosis clinics of the city and several persons familiar with the relief work of the Society.

Research and Education.

It has been a cardinal principle of the Charity Organization Society since its beginning that knowledge of its own work, based on a study of facts rather than unverified impressions, is essential to progress. Monthly reports have always been made to the general secretary by all the departments, showing statistically the amount and to a certain extent the character of the work done, and the general secretary has kept the Central Council informed of the facts contained in them. The annual reports of the Society have given to the public rather more specific information about its work than is usual in annual reports. The Society took part vigorously in the movement to study characteristics of dependent families, for the purposes of discovering the causes of poverty, which originated in the National Conference twenty years ago and took form in the "national statistical blank."

SOCIAL RESEARCH.

A Committee on Statistics was appointed in 1893 to have charge of the studies of the Society's records which should be made by Columbia students, and it was succeeded by the Committee on Social Research, appointed in January, 1905, whose primary object is the interpretation of the Society's case-work. Under this committee a Bureau of Statistics was organized in the Central Office.

In the Bureau of Statistics is centralized information about the current case-work of the Society.

Besides the continuous and systematic review of the Society's work from year to year there have also been made, from time to time, special studies of certain social problems and of selected groups of cases. The most important studies that have been made, aside from the investigations undertaken by CHARITIES and the School of Philanthropy, which will be mentioned in their proper connection, are the following :

Analysis of the records of five hundred homeless cases, by the Committee on Statistics, Professor Richmond Mayo-Smith chairman. Published in the Fourteenth Annual Report.

Analysis of five hundred records of dependent families, by the same Committee.

Dispossessed tenants, by Harold K. Estabrook, special agent employed to make this investigation.

Results of the investigation of twenty-five hundred applications for city coal in 1898.

Lack of employment as a cause of distress, by the Committee on Statistics.

Industrial displacement and unemployment: a study of seven hundred and twenty case records by Francis H. McLean.

Tenement house conditions and allied subjects.

Characteristics of beggars: much descriptive statistical material in the annual reports of the Reports of the Committees on Dependent Children.

Families under care of the Society during 1904-05 and 1905-06, by the Committee on Social Research.

Investigation in regard to the purchase and management of food by one hundred tenement house families, by Caroline Goodyear.

Five hundred and seventy four deserting husbands and their families, by Lilian Brandt.

Social aspects of tuberculosis, by Lilian Brandt.

Tuberculosis among Negroes in New York,
Report to the Hospital Commission on tuberculosis,

Careful study of conditions, treatment, and results in the two hundred and thirty cases treated in 1906 by the sub-committee on relief of the Committee on the Prevention of Tuberculosis.

THE NEW YORK SCHOOL OF PHILANTHROPY

Not least among the Charity Organization Society's contributions to social work is its pioneer service in providing professional and technical training to those who wish to enter upon any form of charitable or other social work.

It is no longer necessary to argue for the acceptance of the position that persons charged with the delicate task of assisting in the difficulties of complex human lives need all the knowledge they can gain of the resources at their command and of the accumulated experience of the years already spent in attempts to solve the very problems with which they are confronted. The advantage of professional training to every one concerned, above all, to the poor—a novel, and to some a distasteful idea ten years ago—is now a commonplace.

The School aims to prepare its students to become expert visitors for charity organization societies; investigators of social conditions, factories, and tenement houses; matrons and administrators in institutions; financial secretaries for charitable societies; executive officers of educational and philanthropic societies; private almoners; probation officers; head-workers and assistants in social settlements, institutional churches, welfare departments of manufacturing and mercantile establishments; friendly visitors; members of boards of managers and of committees; employes of the state and municipal departments which deal especially with public health, charities and correction; and to fill many other highly specialized positions.

The full course requires the entire time of the student for the academic year, October to May, inclusive. The summer session, designed especially for those already engaged in social work, lasts six weeks, beginning the middle of June. Lectures, class-room discussions, assigned reading, field work in the way of visiting institutions and poor families, original investigation, practice in office work, and the preparation of a thesis, constitute the year's work. The lecturers are in nearly every case men and women who are doing or have done, the work they discuss, and are recognized to be experts.

The reference library of applied sociology, which the Society has been accumulating since the first year of its existence, is now housed in rooms adjoining the class-rooms of the School, and is administered primarily for the School's convenience. It contains now about five thousand bound volumes, an equal number of pamphlets, and several hundred periodicals. Students have free access also to the rich libraries of Columbia University and to the many special libraries in the city.

Students of the School of Philanthropy are admitted without tuition fee to courses in Columbia University including Columbia, Barnard, and Teachers' Colleges and the graduate schools, and students of the University are given reciprocal privileges in the School of Philanthropy. The work of the School is accepted by the University as the equivalent of one minor subject for an advanced degree.

I have given copious extracts from the 25 years' report of the Society in order to make clear to my readers the methods of organized charity in the United States. From another report (from 1882 to 1913) I make the following extracts showing the nature of the Society's work for the improvement of social conditions. This work was mainly done by

THE COMMITTEE ON CRIMINAL COURTS:

The tendency has been to lessen the chasm between society and the criminal; to see him as an integral part of the community and to recognize the economy of restoring him to social usefulness. In dealing with the minor offender, the trend is towards special courts and judges as trained specialists; reformation by the probation system, rather than deformation through prison incarceration. The probation office is attaining the dignity of a profession and high grade men and women are being attracted to it by prospects of better compensation, and the elimination of political appointments. The first offender is coming into his own. Means of identification have been provided for distinguishing the new or casual offender from the "rounder." A separate court and detention home for the use of all women offenders for which the plans are now being drawn will permit an insight into social problems heretofore impossible. But the great advance of the year has been in the treatment of the woman offender, in the steps taken towards an intelligent grappling with the difficult problem of the Social Evil.

The investigations of the Committee have resulted in many improvements being effected in the personnel, constitutions and powers of the courts; in alteration of laws, and in the awakening of the national conscience resulting in new and reformed institutions being founded to meet the evils pointed out by social investigators.

I have given a rather full account of the history, constitution, methods and scope of work of the New York Charity Organization Society, as the society is typical of other similar organizations throughout the States. If the numerous charitable and social organizations in a city be compared with a body, the Central or Charity Organization Society, sometimes also called by the name of "Associated Charities" is the heart of the system. In some cities, however, the work of the Information Bureau is done by an organization called "The Confidential Exchange," organized quite independently of an "Organized Charity Association", but closely allied with the same.

The Confidential Exchange is a card index; but, far from being a mere device, it grows out of and is dependent upon a living spirit not often associated with indexes. Skilfully manipulated by a group of people believing profoundly in the principle of of social co-operation, it can win gradually the working together of a large group of social agencies. Through its aid no one of these agencies need take a step in any direction to benefit a human being without being assured of the advice and experience of all the others that have ever known the the same person or any of his kindred.

The Exchange that is the oldest in point of time, though one of the youngest in spirit, is that conducted by the Boston Associated Charities, and the story of its development throws an interesting light on the present status of the movement for Exchanges.

Thirty-five years ago even Boston had few of the modern types of philanthropic agencies now so generally established. There were no children's aid societies, no charity organization society, no medical social service, no settlements. A few large relief agencies existed, including the city out-door relief department, and, in addition, there were sewing circles and other small groups giving relief with informal and kindly service to the poor. With the increase in their number and with the beginning of the foreign immigration, these agencies found it more and more difficult to know the people they helped and to know what the others were doing. So, in 1876, a group of volunteer workers decided to start a Registration bureau in which they could enter the names of all the families being aided by charity and the amount of relief that they were receiving. Delegates from the various agencies came together to discuss the plan and, after expressing their approval, elected a committee to carry on the work. A small amount of money was raised and one of the volunteers interested undertook to do the work for a nominal salary.

At first, the emphasis was largely on preventing duplication of relief, and only secondarily on combining knowledge of individual families. In the first annual report of the Associated Charities in 1880 the objects were given as follow:

Registration aims to accomplish Four Great Aims by gathering up a Full True Record of Every Family Receiving Relief.

1. To aid every private person to give alms only to the worthy poor, or rather to give with knowledge.

2. To lesson the labors of relieving agencies, by giving to each the knowledge of the others.

3 To stop imposture, so that the occupation of living on alms may cease. Registration notifies every lazy tramp to quit Boston or go to work.

4. The main object is to make sure that relief is adapted to the real needs. This will lessen relief for the unworthy. But for the really worthy and most suffering poor it should make relief, more full and prompt and tender.

Or again, its object is "to secure an interchange of information and thereby to detect imposture, discourge begging, distinguish the worthy from the unworthy, and promote economy and efficiency in the distribution of relief."

The Confidential Exchange, as it is now called, is no longer an office where you record your knowledge of a person or family for the benefit of some one else; it is rather a source through which you may secure information that will be of definite value to you in your own service to that particular client. Societies now do not "register their cases with the Associated Charities", but "inquire of the Confidental Exchange." When an agency telephones or otherwise refers the names of all the new families applying to it that day, these are recorded in the office as so many "inquiries," even though the family may not previously have been registered in the Exchange. Sometimes there is a good deal in a name, especially as in this case, where a change of name expressed a definite change in policy. The Registration Bureau of other days is now a Confidential Exchange of information among the societies of Boston, for which the Associated Charities acts as an agent. The history of its growth marks the direction of social service development in the last thirty years.

The mechanism of the Exchange is an alphabetical index with a card for each family or unattached person known to any of the inquiring agencies. This card gives the "identifying information," the names, ages and occupations of the members of the family group, names and addresses of relatives, and the names of agencies interested, with the date on which each inquired. No facts about family history or treatment are included. When a co-operating society becomes interested in a new family, or in any of its members, it inquires at once whether the Confidential Exchange knows the family or person. This inquiry is made either by telephone or by mail on printed slips furnished by the Exchange. The Exchange looks up the family in the index, and then reports to the inquiring agency the names of any societies that have been previously interested and the dates on which they have inquired. If the information given by the inquirer is not sufficient to make identification possible, the agency is so notified with the request that it inform Exchange when further facts are secured. The Children's Aid Society, for example, inquires about Mrs. Mary Jones, and is informed that the North End Mission "inquired" in January, 1910, the S. P. C. C. in December, 1910, and the Social Service Department of the Massachusetts General Hospital in March, 1911. The Children's Aid Society then calls up, or, better still, personally interviews all these agencies, and secures directly from them what data they have about Mrs. Jones and the story of their relation with her. Experience has indicated that it is wiser to have no information in regard to the family pass through the office of the Exchange; that it should give only the names of interested societies.

On the next two pages we give two sample cards of the filing system used in the work of the Exchange. While its mechanism is simple, the success of the Boston Exchange has depended in a measure on an admirablea rrangement of cards and a filing system which have made accurate and rapid identification possible.

THE PRESENT INTEREST IN EXCHANGES:

As we contrast the present situation in social work with 1879, when the first Registration Bureau was started, we see a marked increase in the number of agencies dealing with the family either directly or through some one member whose

Surname	Wom's first name		Names of Agencies
Harrington,	Amanda		
	Man's first name		Legal Aid 5-1-08
	Arthur		Mass. Gen. S.S. 4-6-09
Alias			School Vis. 2-1-11
		S.W.	Milk Fund 2-10-11
Previous Marriages, Husb. or Wife			
Stewart, John			Dist. Nurse 3-6-11

Birthplace	Date	Occupation
1. England	1860	Waiter
2. Boston	1870	Laundress

Mental and Physical Defects

John blind in one eye.

Children	Date	Birthplace
Mary	1890	Dedham
John	1905	Boston
Edw.	1909	Brookline
Emma	1911	Boston

Date	Address	Date	Address
1908	1819 Washington		
1909	135 Tremont		
1911	1627 Roxbury		

Relatives	Address	Kin	No.
Jameson, Amanda	1627 Roxbury St.	mo.	2

Surname	Wom's first name
Cohen	Bessie
	Man's first name
	Abraham

Alias

S. W.

Previous Marriages, Husb. or Wife

Birthplace	Date	Occupation
1. Russia	1874	
2. Russia	1878	

Mental and physical defects

Children	Date	Birthplace
Benjamin	1900	New York
Morris	1903	,,
Bessie	1904	Boston
Abraham	1907	,,
Mary	1907	,,
Jacob	1910	,,

Names or Agencies

Hebrew Ass'n 5-28-08
Mass. Inf. Asy. 6-27-08
St. Minor Wds. 10-16-08
Gwynne Home 3-3-09
Bos. Disp. SS. 11-17-08
Mass. Inf. Asy. 7-25-10
Chdns. Mis'n 7-25-10
Chdns. Friend 8-5-19
Mass. Gen. SS. 8-5-10
Dist. Nurse 11-10-10

Date	address
	Everett
1903	1920 Dover
1908	1650 Washington
1908	1307 Warren Ave.
1908	1432 Dover

Date	address
1910	6010 Charter St.

Relatives **address** **Kin** **No.**

Identification Card (With names changed) of family described in the Annual report of the Social Service Department of the Mass. General Hospital of 1910. (see over) problem is nevertheless bound up with that of the whole family group. Children's agencies are now realizing the desirablility of keeping children in their own homes whenever this is possible. Social service departments of hospitals are seeking to remove social handicaps to physical recovery. These are but two instances of the general recognition of home conditions to the welfare of individuals. This interest in home life means that many more people are visiting homes, and that the investigation of home conditions is becoming more and more extensive. It therefore follows that the Confidential Exchange is growing to become more and more necessary; that the experience of any given agency with a family is going to be utilized by an increasing number of others. The constant interchange of information, moreover, leads to a better understanding of one another's point of view.

1. MORE INTELLIGENT WORK WITH FAMILIES.—As our standards of investigation are raised, we must see to it that a family shall not have to answer the necessary questions more than once. In justifying a careful investigation, the charity organization society has always claimed that a family need never be so investigated more than once, since records keep the most important facts of family history permanently. But when a number of agencies in one city have quite as high a standard of investigation as the charity organization society, or a better one, we can never be assured unless we have a Confidential Exchange, that the family may not have to tell its story repeatedly.

This is not only true of past history. Each agency now dealing with a family sees the present situation from a different angle and makes its own contribution toward the complete picture which is often needed. The success of future treatment depends, however, upon joint plans, in which each agency has a definite part assigned to it. The Confidential Exchange is the center through which such co-ordination is most easily effected.

2. HELP IN MEDICAL DIAGNOSIS.—Especially are physicians coming to realize the value of social evidence in the diagnosis and treatment of disease. The following story shows how the accumulated experiences of several non-medical societies in dealing with a case finally pointed the way to a mental diagnosis:

A Mrs. W. applied to the Associated Charities, saying that she had been married a year before, and that, as her husband was now ill and she was soon to be confined, she needed help. Through the Confidential Exchange the visitor learned that a reform school for girls had inquired about her some years earlier. The school stated that the girl was below par mentally, had been unruly and untruthful, and had already had one illegitimate child. Every effort was made by the Associated Charities to keep the girl straight, but without success. During the next two years six agencies inquired of the Exchange in regard to her, the last a hospital to which she was applying for care during confinement. It had intended to admit her, but, on hearing her record, decided to send her to the almshouse infirmary, with the request that she be placed under observation for commitment to an institution for the feeble-minded. Each agency that had known her contributed some facts that helped to reveal her mental condition. She is now under careful medical supervision.

3. FINANCIAL SAVING.—Lastly, we may refer to an important argument for the Exchange—to its saving of time for each society using it. A children's society in a large city estimated that by eliminating unnecessary investigations the Exchage had saved them the equivalent of one worker's time—no mean item in a crowded budget. In addition, the knowledge secured from other agencies had reduced the time and money expended in trying out wrong plans for bettering family situations.

SUMMARY OF ONE YEAR'S WORK OF A CITY EXCHANGE:

June 1, 1010 to May 31, 1911.

Number of Agencies	Inquiries & Reports recieved	Reports sent
38 Children's Agencies	8,367	4,698
33 Medical ,,	8,944	4,113
27 Relief ,,	21,153	4,959
58 Miscellaneous ,,	25,794	17,650
37 Religious ,,	356	162
(267 private individuals)	343	76
95 Agencies in other cities	...479	135
Total 288	65,436	31,793

Total number of NEW NAMES during the year 13,440

Total ,, ,, names previously indexed upon which a report or inquiry has been received during the year 6,321

19,761

SETTLEMENTS.

Another agency for social service are the settlements, which are to be found in almost all the large cities in the States. Every Settlement has a habitation of its own consisting of a big building or a group of buildings. Often the buildings have been specially erected for the settlement by subscriptions or donations raised by the settlement workers. In some cases the work of the settlement is done in ordinary residential houses either gifted or rented for the purpose. I had the privilege of visiting two such settlements in New York. Both had been founded and are governed by ladies.

The settlements are "centres for social, educational and civic improvements". The object is to render social service to the neighborhood by (a) persons resident in the settlement, and (b) such as are employed for the purpose or are occasional visitors. Permanent residents are called members of the household ; others as resident visitors or co-operating members.

The following extracts from the report of the Director of one of these settlements, an American lady married to a Russian who is a professor in the Local University, should give my readers an idea of the work of the settlement. The settlement is called Greenwich House and is situated in one of the Italian quarters of the city.

"Our work is naturally divided into two parts : the activities of the House and our social work in the neighborhood. Among the activities of the House foremost place must be given to our clubs. The purpose of our CLUBS, which are organized together in a self-governing Club Council, is to develop sociability and self-government. These clubs are an important factor in building up that community consciousness without which the realization of democracy is impossible. Each group has a loyalty of its own, but this is subordinate to the loyalty to the House and through it to the larger unities, the City, the State, and the Nation. The purpose of the CLASSES is to prepare for life and to enrich its content; to attempt in a small way to offer to the young people of this neighborhood the same cultural and artistic advantages which are open to groups with more money at their command. The result of the club and class work are dependent for their success upon an intimate knowledge of the home life of their members, and this NEIGHBOURHOOD VISITING lies at the foundation of all work of the settlement. It is an essential part of the life of every resident worker. As an ever-increasing number of Italians is coming into the neighbourhood, knowledge of the Italian language is essential.

The socical work of the House finds its outward expression in PLAYS, pageants, concerts, entertainments of many kinds and in DANCING. To keep these entertainments on a high level, and yet to make them entirely acceptable, is the problem. Local life expressing itself without outside suggestion in social forms has in it many values, but it is well to have a constant interplay of suggestion which can come only from a combination of local talents and ideas with those from the larger life of the whole community. It is indeed in this constant interplay of local life with the life of the city that those mutual advantages are obtained which make the settlement an important force.

Personal help is also an integral part of the life of the Settlement. SCHOLARSHIPS are granted to enable gifted children to continue in school who would otherwise have to enter industry too early. Temporary RELIEF is often furnished, but never without consultation with others for whom this is a primary task.

A District Nurse and an Obstetrical Nurse from the Nurses' Settlement are stationed at Greenwich

House. As in past years, we have sent away to the country during the summer many of our neighbours. We take children to dispensary and hospital. During the past summer we maintained a CAMP at King's Park, Long Island, where our boys for a small sum could enjoy a short outing. We co-operated with the New York World and the Babies' Welfare Association in holding a BETTER BABIES CONTEST at Greenwich House, offering prizes for the best baby. The real value of these contests, of course, will come later when the Improvement Contest takes place.

THR NEIGHBORHOOD.—A report of progress in the neighborhood ought to begin with a recognition of the facts that an ever larger spirit of co-operation exists in the district. The library authorities have been most numerous in their use of the hall in Hudson Park Library. Many of the Association of Neighborhood Workers' Conferences were held there during the past winter; meetings of the Schools and Civic League, organized by Greenwich House, often take place in the library hall; our Christmas play was held there. We have used the public gymnasium for many of our larger social dances.

The class for anaemic school children on the roof of the Carmine Street Bath was made happy by the presentation by the city, at our request, of an awning for the roof. On the petition of Greenwich House a late class for delinquents was established by the Department of Education in Public School No. 95. This PROBATION CLASS was started in June as an experiment. It has worked out successfully, and the idea could be profitably applied, we believe, to other parts of the city.

The needs of the LONGSHOREMEN of this district have been the special subject of attention during the past season by the civic and charitable societies of this neighbourhood. Meetings have been held at Greenwich House during the summer for the purpose of organizing an additional longshoremen's Rest for this section.

A very interesting and successful social center was

developed during the year at Public School No. 41, under the fostering care of Ascension Forum. It is now, however, an entirely local, self-governing group which is in the charge of the Center co-operating with the Department of Education. With this Social Centre idea the Settlements are in full accord. For years the settlements have been engaged in opening the schools for an ever wider use. With every effort for the introduction of recreation centres, vacation schools, school lunches, visiting teachers, the introduction of special classes, the better working out of the truancy problem, and the after-school care of school children, the Settlements have been identified. The special relationships which Greenwich House has had with the schools in the district have centred around the Downing Street School now consolidated with the Clarkson Street School and Public School No. 3; with the work of the School and Civic League in this district we are intimately associated. The teachers of these schools have helped us quite as much if not more than we have helped them, and our joint enterprises have worked out most smoothly. As a development of this work, we have now been granted the use by the Department of Education of Public School No. 95 to be developed as a social centre as fast as sufficient means and a local demand render advisable."

The other settlement which I visited is the Henry Street Settlement, situated in the Hebrew quarter of the city. It has this year celebrated its twentieth anniversary. The following extract from the founder director, Miss Lilian D. Wald, will give some idea of the origin, development and activities of the settlement :

"The sight of a woman in a rear tenement, under unspeakably distressing conditions, was the starting point of the Settlement. The story, and its effect upon the present Head Worker, told to Mrs. Betty

Loeb and to Mr. Jacob H. Schiff, brought immediate ways and means to create the Settlement. Miss Mary Brewster and I, both graduates of the New York Hospital Training School, established ourselves on the top floor of a tenement house near by. We charged ourselves with creating a visiting nursing service, on the terms most considerate of the dignity and independence of the patients, free from denominational or political influence, and under any doctor, paid or unpaid, who might be treating them, and also with contributing our citizenship in an industrial neighborhood.

Laying the Foundation.

The first two years were experimental, and the founders on their top floor had many opportunities of becoming acquainted with the problems of their neighborhood. In quick succession they were invited into conference by trade unionists, by workers in philanthropy, by the clergymen and the orthodox rabbis. The unemployed, the anxious parents, the girls in distress, the troublesome boys, came as individuals to see them, but no formal organization was effected until they moved into the first house, No. 265 Henry Street, which was purchased for their use by Mr. Schiff in 1895.

We believed that we possessed an organic relationship to the neighborhood, which was of importance for opening up a deeper knowledge of the social conditions about us, and from the first we asserted our desire to be identified in every way with the neighborhood which we selected as our own. Gradually an organized program of activities has been developed, related to the social, philanthropic and educational needs of the community, and fashioned out of the experiences of the men and women who have been a part of the Settlement during the twenty years of its existence.

The Nursing Service.

The maps and charts indicate the progress of the nurses' work. In 1913, 22,168 patients were treated, to whom, in round numbers, 200,000 visits were paid. A comparison of the numbers of patients brought to the hospitals and to the visiting nursing service is not entirely fair, since the character of the diseases is not comparable, but it would indicate the growth of the dependance upon the visiting nurse. Mt. Sinai, Presbyterian and New York Hospitals combined, admitted 21,120 patients during the year, 1,048 less than the number who called for the settlement nurses. Children, concerning whose treatment at home or in hospitals there has been much discussion, lend themselves to home treatment, particularly those suffering from pneumonia. The figures give the patients with this disease in the three hospitals as totalling 590. The number of pneumonias cared for in the year by the visiting nurses was 3,909 and of these 3,377 were children.

There have been so many "campaigns of education" upon questions of public health, that perhaps the public is better informed than at any other period of history, and the charts and statistics given will be significant. The service of the visiting nurse, though covering so wide a range, has been capable of control and supervision. The division of it in the city can be compared to a well organized and administered hospital, with the classification of wards, a system of bedside notes, observance of etiquette among doctors, and, in addition, the enormous value of strengthening the home, working there with such tools and such equipment as the homes themselves afford. Cases that can best be cared for in the hospitals are sent there, the sifting process being accomplished by the doctors and the nurses working together. During the last year, 1,442 were dismissed to hospitals.

Out of their experience with the sick, the nurses organized for themselves a system of care for tuberculosis patients and instruction for their families, long before the great work was started for the municipality by Dr. Biggs. From their knowledge of the children kept out of school because of sickness has come the Settlement's share in the medical inspection of the public schools, first the appointment of the doctors, and then, some years later, the inauguration of the school nurse under municipal control. Under Major Low's administration, Dr. Lederle and Mr. Burlingham, combining with the Settlement for children, municipalized the school nurse, the first in the world so far as known.

Training for Service.

The Settlement has also been a training place for other communities, both in this country and abroad, where interest has been roused in the care of sick people in their homes, and in forms of public health nursing. As a natural corollary to the demands upon the Settlement, educational opportunities under academic auspices became necessary, and Mrs. Helen Hartley Jenkins, one of the friends of the Settlement, upon our advice, endowed at Teacher's College a department to give this special postgraduate training. More recently, at the suggestion of the Settlement, the National Red Cross Society has taken up the nursing of people in rural communities and small towns.

I mention these things as illustrating the community use of the experiences of the Settlement and their application. When the nursing service was first established, it was impossible to find any tools that could be used, and the bag was invented for the Settlement by Miss May Brown. It is a matter of congratulation to us that in that way also we have served the cause both here and abroad. If you are familiar with it, you might recognize the bag in China, Japan, Hawaii and places nearer home.

Milk Station.

Side by side with the treatment of the sick in their homes is the preventive work. The milk station was established in 1903, when Mr. V. Everit Macy began sending, from his private dairy, milk to be used for convalescents and infants. From the first, the Settlement, following its principle of building up in the homes, has taught the modification there. The milk is of extraordinary quality. Children under two, and particularly those who show lowered vitality, are given the preference. Drs. Tunick and Bakst have from the first been the consulting physicians, and conferences are held with the mothers and babies twice a week. Out of 400 babies taken care of during the year 1913, only two have died. The money made from the sale of the milk is used to put nurses in the field. The quantity sent is not always the same, but the net profit from this source provides from two to four nurses.

Stillman House.

Though the Settlement has from its beginning shown no discrimination between color, race or religion, it has developed a special piece of work for the colored people, and that has grown out of a request from a trained nurse, who wanted an opportunity to serve her own people. This, told to Mrs. Edward Harkness, brought about the establishment of the Stillman House, named to memorialize her father, Mr. Thomas Stillman. A staff of four or five nurses work acceptably and by preference with their own race, giving an unusual quality of devotion and capacity. Boys and girls are enrolled here in 27 clubs and classes and there is a monthly attendance at the House of over 1,200 people.

Educational and Social Activities.

It is an irresistible temptation to dwell upon the nursing work, because upon it has focussed much attention and effort, and to it has been given both money and unpaid service of priceless value.

But as the nursing work has rooted so deeply and securely in the neighborhood, so also has the educational and social work of the Settlement. The rooms of the Settlement have been freely given for neighbourhood uses. Three kindergartens and a Montessori class have possession in the morning, the latter under the guidance of two gifted young women, (one of them specially prepared by Dr. Montessori herself,) who, in the true settlement spirit, are giving their services to demonstrate, first for the neighbourhood and later for the community, the value of the latest word in education. The carpentry shop, sewing classes and art classes are referred to everywhere. Parties and dancing classes have been conducted under Settlement auspices for many years. We used to say that next to nursing a typhoid we liked to give a ball!

Boys and young men to the number of 1,368 have membership in the clubs and classes in the Henry Street Houses, and children, girls and young women to the number of 1,275. Last December there was a total attendance of 25,000. The Men's Club, composed of young men who have graduated into it from the boys' clubs, is selft-supporting, and contributes valuable leadership to the Settlement. Its members are responsible for the weekly forum, where present-day problems are presented by distinguished speakers and discussed by the audience. The mothers and other women have distinctive groups. One club has a membership of one hundred and fifty, all of them mothers, all interested in questions, public and private, related to the welfare of their homes and their families. A loan fund, underwritten by the members of the club and the Settlement, is ably administered. Other groups of people, both women and men, come together for social purposes and to consider the problems of their children and the neighborhood.

I can give no picture of the life of the Settlement and the spirit that animates it unless I can make clear the part that the original group of club leaders has played. They came first to the Settlement with youth and courage. We have grown together and I think we have kept young together. This contribution is definite, continuous and inspiring. The club and class work, interpreted in another place, is taken seriously. The club leaders' meetings resemble faculty meetings, where the problems of the groups and the difficulties of the individual are seriouly discussed, always with the realization that in the Settlement, because of its elasticity, we can do the things that are not possible to more conventionalized forms of education."

CONCLUSION.

I cannot close this chapter without once more laying emphasis on the idea briefly mentioned in the opening paragraphs, that the world would be richer and nobler if society could be so constituted and organized as to make charity unnecessary.

In a society in which people are born rich or poor, without any reference to their personal merits or demerits; in which so much depends on opportunities, which some get and some do not get; in which the rich grow richer and the poor poorer; in which the rich have numerous opportunities, organised and legalized, of exploiting the poor, however abler and worthier the latter may be as compared with the former; in which force, organized, unorgainsed, plays such a decisive part; in which merit, ability, hard work and high character sometimes fail even to bring competence to the possessors of these virtues; it is really adding insult to injury for people possessed of wealth acquired under such conditions to pose as dispensers of charity. It is only a shade different from the conduct of a robber who robs and then gives.

The Hindus explain these differences in the pecuniary and social positions of people by the doctrine of Karma, and whether that idea be right or wrong, it is to their credit that they so organized society as to make charitable institutions unnecessary. According to the basic ideas of Hindu religion, a possession is a trust. Every one possessed of more than he needs is a master or a debtor. In giving away or in feeding or clothing or helping others, he confers no obligations on the latter; he simply discharges a debt which he owes to society at large by taking more than his share. I do not know if there is any word in Sanskrit which exactly covers the same meaning which the word charity carries in the English language, or its equivalents in other languages of the West. "DHARMA ARTHA" is the expression used for a charitable gift. Literally it means "for dharma," i.e., in the performance of one's duty or one's religion (though Dharma implies much more than religion). Charity is a social duty. Social duties according to the Hindus are debts to be discharged or obligations to be fulfilled. The giving for name or fame or for perpetuating one's name or memory is entirely foreign to ancient Hinduism. Consequently we find little or no mention of organised charity in the history of ancient Hinduism. Feeding the hungry, clothing the needy, the care of the orphan, the crippled, the blind, the aged, and the afflicted, was a part of every Hindu householder's daily duties. He owed this as a debt to the society and he considered himself fortunate and privileged if he could pay off this debt during his period of householdership. By doing so he expected no return in gratitude; nor was this any special merit. It was merit to deprive himself to meet the wants of another; but to give out of the fulness of one's possessions what was beyond one's own needs was no merit. It was an act of duty.

The Hindus too, alas! have lost that idea, and long before the need of organised charity was felt under the altered conditions of society in India, they had adopted the semitic conception of charity. With the breaking up of the joint family system, with the influx of Western ideas, with the stimulus which capitalism has received under Western domination, with the displacement of cottage and home industries by organized industries and with the growth of huge cities with their unequal distribution of wealth and collossal disparities of life, organized charity has become a necessity. In the world as it is, with its present social conditions, the American method seems to be the best and the most effective.

Not that every one in America who gives millions is moved by the true spirit of Christ. Some are undoubtedly moved by that spirit. But there are others who give because they think that is the best way of keeping out socialism. They would give doles to those whom they want to keep down, as price of their silence and their acquiescence in the existing order of things. Only the other day I was told how in certain privately endowed universities, socialistic ideas were tabooed and professors had to keep within limits in discussing modern problems of liberty. Yet this is the narrowness of human character that even in dispensing charity it is actuated by class considerations and class prejudices. The word charity has some very beautiful associations with it, but personally I would see the word and idea swept away. Let every human being stand on his right and let every person do his duty. The only right charity consists in not sitting in judgment over others and in making allowances for human weakness. Charity in the shape of doles (whether of money, of food, or of clothes or any other benefits) is a most degrading element which deserves to be uprooted. But no long as it is not uprooted, the method of dispensing it should be that developed in America, and the spirit which should impel one to acts of charity is the old Hindu conception of discharging one's debt thereby.

THE PHILIPPINE ISLANDS

The Philippine islands are a group of islands in the Asiatic waters of the Pacific coast. They have a total land area of 127,853 square miles and a population (according to the Census figures of 1910) of about 9 million people. For a long time these islands were included in the Spanish empire and were under Spanish administration up to 1895. About that time came the American-Spanish war resulting in the success of the United States Government and the occupation of the islands by the Americans in 1898. It took the American Government two years to establish order and during that period the country was in charge of the Military. Civil Government in the Philippine islands under American sovereignty as distinguished from military administration dates from the appointment by President Mckinley, in March, 1900, of the Taft Commission.

From the very first there was a great difference of opinion among the American politicians about the advisability of taking possession of and occupying the Philippine islands. The thinking and far-seeing portions of the community saw in it the beginning of an Imperial policy—a policy which inevitably leads to the development of a ruling class, of social jealousies, of international quarrels and of eventual curtailment of the democratic spirit at home. The very idea of democracy excludes the idea of empires including dependencies and possessions. All growing and

KITCHEN AND COOKING CLASS, PHILIPPINE NORMAL SCHOOL, MANILA.

Photograph by
Bureau of Education, Manila.

prosperous nations have a tendency to become Imperial and it requires a constant and vigorous vigilance on the part of the people opposed to Imperialism to keep the nation out of it. The first step of the United States Government towards Imperialism, was the occupation of Cuba ; then came the occupation of the Phillipine Islands and this led to the starting of an organised agitation against Imperialism. In 1905, when I visited the United States for the first time, I had a letter of introduction to the Secretary of the Anti-Imperial League of America at Boston and consequently came in touch with people who felt very strongly in the matter. The organisation had not been started in 1905. It had existed before and it was due to the efforts of those anti-Imperial citizens that Cuba was given her independence. Those anti-Imperialists could not prevent the occupation of the Philippine Islands by the United States Government, but they have maintained a continuous agitation for the release of the islands from American control. Their opposition to the United States developing an Imperial policy is based on broad humanitarian principles as well as self-interest. In their opinion the adoption of an Imperial policy by the United States is opposed to the letter as well as the spirit of the Republic. In a deviation from those principles and in the adoption of a policy of empire-making they see a menace to their own liberties and the eventual and sure involving of the Republic in international wars. The general feeling of the American people is opposed to Imperialism, but there are ambitious persons among them, too, who are in favour of extension of territories for purposes of trade. So a constant agitation has to be kept up against the United States Government embarking on Imperial enterprise. As a result of that agitation we find that within less than fifteen years, the Philippine Islands have made wonderful progress politically and educationally. The policy which the American Administration is following in the Island has "for its *sole* object *the preparation of the Philippine peoples for popular Self-Government in their own interests and not in the interests of the United States.*" The capitals and italics are mine. Only recently this object was repeated in the most emphatic language in a bill that was introduced in the Congress of 1914-15 relating to the Government of the Philippines. The Preamble lays down the object of the measure:

> To declare the purpose of the people of the United States as to the future political status of the people of the Philippine Islands, and to provide a more autonomous government for those Islands.
>
> Whereas it was never the intention of the people of the United States in the incipiency of War with Spain to make it a war of conquest or for territorial aggrandizement; and
>
> Whereas *it is, as it has always been, the purpose of the people of the United States to withdraw their sovereignity over the Philippine Islands and to recognise their independence as soon as a stabler Government can be established therein* : and
>
> Whereas for the speedy accomplishment of such purpose it is desirable to place in the hands of the Philippines as large a control of their domestic affairs as can be given them without, in the meantime, impairing the exercise of the rights of sovereignity by

the people of the United States, in order that, by the use and exercise of popular franchise and governmental powers, they may be the better prepared to fully assume the responsibilities and enjoy all the privileges of complete independence :

Therefore be it enacted," and so on.

In the discussion that followed the introduction of the measure in the Congress as well as in the Press, the principles underlying the Bill were universally accepted. The only difference that existed among the political parties of the United States was as to the fixing of the time when the United States should withdraw from the islands. The consensus of opinion among the Democrats was in favour of an early withdrawal and also in favour of fixing a time limit within which the withdrawal must take place. The Republicans are opposed to this.

We will now briefly describe the constitution of the Philippine Government as it now exists and will start from the bottom. In order to enable the reader to have a clear idea of the political progress made by the Philippines under the United States within the last fifteen years, it is necessary to compare the existing conditions with those that existed before the occupation of the islands by the Federal Government. We will therefore first describe the condition of things as they existed before the American occupation.

The term "municipality" in the Philippines is used to designate not only a town but the surrounding rural territory. Thus there is no part of the country not included in a municipality. The rural Filipinos as a rule live in villages, and these subdivisions of a municipality are called "barrios," the central one, ordinarily bearing the name of the municipality, being termed the "poblacion."

Municipal Government under the Spanish Regime.

The Maura Law promulgated in 1893 reorganized the municipal governments excepting Manila, Iloilo, and Cebu, in Luzon, and the Visayan Islands, in towns where more than a thousand cedulas personales (poll taxes) were paid. Each municipal tribunal consisted of a captain and four lieutenants, one called mayor, and the others having charge of the police, cemeteries, and live stock. These municipal officers and two substitutes were elected behind closed doors by 12 electors belonging to the privileged classes and selected by the principalia at a meeting presided over by the Civil Governor, the parish priest, and the municipal captain. As representatives of the principalia, these 12 electors attended the sessions and joined in the discussion of measures coming before the municipal council. Municipal officers were elected for four years, their services being obligatory and without compensation.

For the purpose of imposing taxes, holding elections, school inspection, and the preparation of the budgets the presence of the parish priest was necessary at the sitting of the board.

The Governor General and, in his absence, his representative, the governor of the province, was

CALISTHENIC DRILL BY 3000 PUPILS FROM THE MANILA SCHOOLS, PLAYGROUND DAY, CARNIVAL OF 1915.

Photograph by
Bureau of Education, Manila.

honorary or ex-officio president of each and every municipal council.

Article 7 of the law' provided: "By principalia shall be understood the group of persons formed in each town, of indeterminate number, consisting of those formerly called petty governors (gobernadorcillos), lieutenants of justice, of the cabezas de baranguay in active service or who may have filled the office for 10 consecutive years without any unfavorable mention, of the past captains, the municipal lieutenants who may have filled their offices during the legal term without unfavourable mention, and of the residents paying 50 pesos as territorial tax."

Municipal Government under the American Occupation.

From the first, emphasis has been laid by the American authorities upon extending to the municipalities the fullest extent of local self-government compatible with securing even fairly good results for the people themselves.

Under the military Government one of the most important acts was the advance toward the inauguration of civil government in the municipalities where the people were prepared for control over their own local affairs.

The announcement prefixed to this order stated:

For the first time the Philippine people are to exercise the right of suffrage in the election of municipal officers, a right only slightly restricted by conditions which have been imposed for the purpose of rewarding as well as encouraging the people in . . . their aspirations to become educated.

Naturally it is impossible to frame legal provisions which are perfect, but these are susceptible of future improvement in order that they may meet the future necessities and keep pace with the development in political knowledge of the Philippine people, with whom now rests the creation of municipalities which shall faithfully administer their interests and protect their rights and liberties.

In line with this policy the instructions of President McKinley to the Philippine Commission directed :

Without hampering them by too specific instructions, they should in general be enjoined, after making themselves familiar with the conditions and needs of the country, to devote their attention in the first instance to the establishment of municipal governments, in which the natives of the islands, both in the cities and the rural communities, shall be afforded the opportunities to manage their own local affairs to the fullest extent of which they are capable, and subject to the least degree of supervision and control which a careful study of their capacities and observation of the workings of native control show to be consistent with the maintenance of law, order, and loyalty. . . .

In the distribution of powers among the governments organized by the Commission, the presumption is always to be in favor of the smaller subdivision, so that all the powers which can properly be exercised by the municipal government shall be vested in that government, and all the departmental government shall be vested in that government, and so that in the governmental system, which is the result of the process, the central government of the islands, following the example of the distribution of the powers between the States and the National Government of the United States, shall have no direct administration except of matters of purely general concern, and shall have only such supervision and control over local governments as may be necessary to secure and enforce faithful and efficient administration by local officers.

In accordance with these instructions, there was enacted the Municipal Code, providing that the powers of each municipality were to be exercised by a president, vice-president, and council, whose members serve without pay for four years and are ineligible to re-election until another four years have elapsed.

Qualification of Voters.

Every male person of twenty-three years of age or over who has had a legal residence for a period of six months immediately preceding the election in the municipality in which he exercised the suffrage, and who is not a citizen or subject of any foreign power, and who is comprised within one of the following three classes,

(a) Those, who, prior to the thirteenth of August, eighteen hundred and ninety-eight, held the office of municipal captain, gobernadorcillo, alcalde, lieutenant, cabeza de barangay, or member of any ayuntamiento;

(b) Those who own real property to the value of five hundred pesos or who annually pay thirty pesos or more of the established taxes;

(c) Those who speak, read, and write English or Spanish shall be entitled to vote at all elections: Provided, That officers, soldiers, sailors, or marines of the Army or Navy of the United States shall not be considered as having acquired legal residence within the meaning of this section by reason of their having been stationed in the municipalities for the required six months.

The organized cities and towns of the Philippine Islands, with the exception of the city of Manila, the Moro Province, the settlements of the non-Christian tribes, and such other exceptions as may be made by special-territory acts, are all governed by this general law.

The municipalities are divided into four classes, according to population, as follows :

First class, those having not less than 25,000 inhabitants.

Second class, those having 18,000 and less than 25,000.

Third class, those having 10,000 and less than 18,000.

Fourth class, those having less than 10,000 inhabitants.

They are entitled, respectively, to 18, 14, 10, and 8 councillors.

The municipalities are divided into barrios or wards, and these for administrative purposes are grouped into as many districts as there are councillors, including the vice-president, each under the supervision of the councillors.

On July 1, 1912, there were 725 such local self-governments.

General Powers of the Municipalities.

The general powers of the municipalities in the Philippines are substantially those which are exercised by cities, towns, and villages in the several

SEWING CLASS AT WORK, PHILIPPINE NORMAL SCHOOL, TAFT AVENUE, MANILA.

Photograph by
Bureau of Education, Manila.

States, which have like population and income. The limitations and restrictions imposed by the municipal code relate principally to the amount of taxes and to the severity of punishments which may be imposed for violation of local ordinances.

Provincial Government.

Under the Spanish regime there was a great diversity in the form of Government provided for the numerous administrative divisions. Civil Provincial Governments were found only in the island of Luzon. In the Visayan islands no civil government was established by the Spaniards.

Civil Governors of Provinces were of course always Spaniards named and removed by virtue of royal decrees.

In 1893 a royal decree sanctioned the formation of provincial councils consisting of nine members, five of whom, including the Provincial Governor, were ex-officio members, and four others, who must be residents of capitals of provinces, elected by the captains of the various municipal tribunals of the provinces.

The duties of the council consisted mainly of inspection of the administration of the treasuries of the pueblos, keeping accounts, and of consultation by acting as advisory board to the provincial governor and to the tribunals in the matters of approval of elections, taxes, public works, suspension of members, and filling vacancies of municipal tribunals, questions of territorial or jurisdictional limits, consolidation of towns, and in other cases where the governor deemed it wise. The Governor General exercised jurisdiction over all provincial councils.

UNDER THE AMERICAN SYSTEM.

In each of the so-called Christian provinces there is a provincial board, which determines the rates of local taxes, makes appropriations for roads, schools, etc., besides having some supervision over the administration of the municipalities included in the province. The boards are each composed of the governor of the province, the treasurer, and a third member. The governor and third member are elected for four years, by qualified voters of the province. The office of treasurer is a civil-service position, he being appointed by the Governor General. In the majority of the provinces the treasurer is an American, but in those where it has been possible to secure a Filipino possessing the requisite qualifications, he has been given preference and appointed. The duties of the treasurer pertain chiefly to the collection of the revenues, both municipal and provincial, their safe handling, disbursement, and the necessary accounting. There is also, except as otherwise specially provided, a provincial fiscal or district attorney, appointed by the Governor General. The fiscal acts as the attorney and legal adviser of the governor and other officials of the province and of municipal officials, and he also performs the duties of the register of deeds. In these provinces, outside of Manila, none of the fiscals are Americans.

The plan of provincial government has been, in its scope, increasingly of a popular nature. Under the original provisions of the provincial code of 1901, the government of the province—legislative and executive—was under a provincial board, consisting of a governor and treasurer and a supervisor of roads and buildings. Other appointed officers were provided, as the prosecuting attorney and the secretary of the province, who did not sit on the provincial board. The governor was originally elected by the councilmen of all the towns of the province assembled in convention, they themselves having previously been elected by the people. The treasurer and supervisor were each selected and appointed under the rules adopted in accordance with the merit system provided in a civil-service law, which was among the first passed by the Commission.

One of the early difficulties in the maintenance of an efficient government in the provinces was the poverty of the provinces and the lack of taxable resources to support any kind of a government at all. It was soon found that the provincial supervisor, who, it was hoped, might be an American engineer, was too expensive a burden for the province to carry. For a time the district superintendent of education of the province was made the third member of the provincial board instead of the supervisor, whose office was abolished. This, however, did not work well, because the time of the superintendent was needed for his educational duties. Subsequently, therefore, it was thought wise to provide a third member of the board, who served with but little compensation and who was elected as the governor was elected. The system of electing the governor by convention of councilmen of all the towns of the province was changed, so that now the governor and the third member of the board are elected by direct popular vote.

In provinces inhabited by wild and primitive tribes the form of government is more or less patriarchal. All are alike in having an appointed governor who in combination with one or more of the other appointive officers forms the Provincial Board. In some instances the organisation is based on tribal organisations.

The Central Government.

The insular government is composed of the legislative, executive, and judicial branches. The Governor General and heads of the four executive departments are also members of the Commission, which is the upper house of the Legislature and is the exclusive legislative authority over the territory inhabited chiefly by Moros and other non-Christians.

The Governor General as the executive head is assisted by four secretaries of departments, each of which has a number of bureaus, 21 in all, and four minor offices or divisions.

Aside from these the City of Manila, not being a part of any province, is considered as being under the Governor General as are also the three executive bureaus.

THE PHILIPPINE LEGISLATURE.

The Philippine Legislature consists of two houses, the Philippine Commission and the Philippine Assembly. The Philippine Commission (equivalent to the executive council of India) consists of 4 Americans and 4 Filipinos. The members are appointed by the President of the United States with the advice and consent of the Senate. The Assembly membership must be at least 50 and not exceeding 100, apportioned according to population, but no province to have less than one member. It is now composed of 81 members.

The qualifications of electors voting for delegates to the Assembly are the same as prescribed for municipal electors.

The new Bill referred to above provides:

Sec. 12. That general legislative powers in the Philippines, except as herein otherwise provided, shall be vested in a legislature which shall consist of two houses, one the senate and the other the house of representatives, and the two houses shall be designated "The Philippine Legislature": Provided, That, until the Philippine Legislature as herein provided shall have been organized, the existing Philippine Legislature shall have all legislative authority herein granted to the Government of the Philippine Islands, except such as may now be within the exclusive jurisdiction of the Philippine Commission, which is so continued until the organization of the legislature herein provided for the Philippines.

Sec. 13. That the members of the Senate of the Philippines, except as herein provided, shall be elected for terms of six and three years, as hereinafter provided, by the qualified electors of the Philippines. Each of the senatorial districts defined as hereinafter provided shall have the right to elect two senators. No person shall be an elective member of the senate of the Philippines who is not a qualified elector and over thirty years of age, and who is not able to read and write either the Spanish or English language, and who has not been a resident of the Philippines for at least two consecutive years and an actual resident of the senatorial district from which chosen for a period of at least one year immediately prior to his election.

Sec. 14. That the members of the house of representatives shall, except as herein provided, be elected triennially by the qualified electors of the Philippines. Each of the representative districts hereinafter provided for shall have the right to elect one representative. No person shall be an elective member of the house of representatives who is not a qualified elector and over twenty-five years of age, and who is not able to read and write the Spanish or English language.

Sec. 15. That until otherwise provided by the Philippine legislature herein provided for, the qualifications of voters for senators and representatives in the Philippines and all officers elected by the people shall be as follows:

Every male citizen of the Philippines twenty-one years of age or over (except insane and feeble-minded persons and those convicted in a court of competent jurisdiction of an infamous offence since the thirteenth day of August, eighteen hundred and ninety-eight), who shall have been a resident of the Philippines for one year and of the municipality in which he shall offer to vote for six months next preceding the day of voting, and who is comprised within one of the following classes:

(a) Those who prior to the thirteenth day of August, eighteen hundred and ninety-eight, held the office of captain municipal, gobernadorcillo, alcalde, tenientes, cabeza de barangay, or member of any ayuntamiento.

(b) Those who own real property to the value of five hundred pesos, or who annually pay thirty pesos or more of the established taxes.

(c) Those who are able to read and write either Spanish, English or a native language.

Section 16 divides the islands into twelve Senate and ninety Representative districts for the purposes of the first election. The section also provides that in the territory not now represented in the Philippine Assembly (equivalent to certain non-Regulation Districts of India) there shall be established one Senate and nine representative districts, thus giving complete representation in both houses to all parts of the Islands. Section 18 lays down that the Senate and the House of Representatives respectively shall be the sole judges of the elections, returns and qualifications of their elective members; each house to determine the rules of its proceedings, punish its members for disorderly behaviour and with the concurrence of two-thirds expel a member. Both houses are authorised to elect their own speakers, clerks and sergeants at arms and such other officers and assistants as may be required.

The restrictions on the power of the Legislature are contained in section 3 which should be read with interest in India, particularly the provisions italicised by me :

Sec. 3. That no law shall be enacted in said islands which shall deprive any person of life, liberty, or property without due process of law, or deny to any person therein the equal protection of the laws. Private property shall not be taken for public use without just compensation.

That in all criminal prosecutions the accused shall enjoy the right to be heard by himself and counsel, to demand the nature and cause of the accusation against him, to have a speedy and public trial, to meet the witnesses face to face, and to have compulsory process to compel the attendance of witnesses in his behalf.

That no person shall be held to answer for a criminal offence without due process of law ; and no person for the same offence shall be twice put in jeopardy of punishment, nor shall be compelled in any criminal case to be a witness against himself.

That all persons shall before conviction be bailable by sufficient sureties, except for capital offences.

That no law impairing the obligation of contracts shall be enacted.

That no person shall be imprisoned for debt.

That the privilege of the writ of habeas corpus shall not be suspended, unless when in cases of rebellion, insurrection, or invasion the public safety may require it, in either of which events the same may be suspended by the President, or by the governor general, wherever during such period the necessity for such suspension shall exist.

That no ex post facto law or bill of attainder shall be enacted nor shall the law of primogeniture ever be in force in the Philippines.

That no law granting a title of nobility shall be enacted, and no person holding any office of profit or trust in said islands, shall, without the consent of the Congress of the United States, accept any present, emolument, office, or title of any kind whatever from any king, queen, prince, or foreign state.

That excessive bail shall not be required, nor excessive fines imposed, nor cruel and unusual punishment inflicted.

That the right to be secure against unreasonable searches and seizures shall not be violated.

That slavery shall not exist in said islands; nor shall involuntary servitude exist therein, except as a punishment for crime whereof the party shall have been duly convicted.

That no law shall be passed abridging the freedom of speech or the right of the people peaceably to assemble and petition the government for redress of grievances.

That no law shall be made respecting an establishment of religion or prohibiting the free exercise thereof, and that the free exercise and enjoyment of religious profession and worship, without discrimination or preference, shall forever be allowed; and no religious test shall be required for the exercise of civil or political rights. No public money or property shall ever be appropriated, applied, donated, or used, directly or indirectly, for the use, benefit, or support of any sect, church, denomination, or system of religion, or for the use, benefit or support of any priest, preacher, minister, or other religious teacher or dignitary or sectarian institution as such. Polygamous or plural marriages are forever prohibited.

That no money shall be paid out of the treasury except in pursuance of an appropriation by law.

That the rule of taxation in said islands shall be uniform.

That no bill which may be enacted into law shall embrace more than one subject, and that subject shall be expressed in the title of the bill.

That no warrant shall issue but upon probable cause, supported by oath or affirmation, and particularly describing *the place to be searched and the persons or things to be seized.*

That all money collected on any tax levied or as-

INTERIOR OF MACHINE SHOP, PHILIPPINE SCHOOL OF ARTS AND TRADES, MANILA.

Photograph by
Bureau of Education, Manila.

sessed for a special purpose shall be treated as a special fund in the treasury and paid out for such purpose only.

Judicial.

Coming to the judicial side three of the 7 Supreme Court Justices have been and are Filipinos, and one-half of the judges of the First Instance are natives. Justices of Peace are all Filipinos.

The Attorney General of the Islands has for several years been a Filipino.

At present the judges of the Supreme Court are appointed by the President of the United States by the advice and with the consent of the Senate of the United States. According to the proposed law they shall be appointed by the Governor-General by the advice and with the consent of the elected Senate of the Philippine Islands.

The Executive.

The Executive of the Islands consists of a Governor General and nine Commissioners all appointed by the President of the United States by the advice and with the consent of the Senate of the said States. For several years five members of the commission have been Americans and four Filipinos. At present, due to a vacancy, there are 4 Americans and 4 Filipinos. Under the proposed law the only officer to be appointed by the President of the United States shall be the Governor General. All the other executive heads of Departments shall be appointed as provided for by the proposed Philippine Legislature.

Conclusion.

Under the circumstances, the claim made by the Chief of the Bureau of the Insular Affairs corresponding to the Secretary of State for the Colonies in England that "the Filipino as distinguished from a small class has been given more power in his government than is exercised by any oriental people and all the agencies which are supposed to work for the advancement of a people in popular self-government are being used to the greatest possible extent for the Filipino," seems to be perfectly valid.

II.

Having described the constitution of the Government of the Philippine Islands in the previous pages it remains now to take a bird's eye view of the general condition of things in the country.

Army & Police :—In connection with the United States troops stationed in the islands, the most important fact to be noted is, that not a single cent of the expenses of their maintenance or their salaries or any incidental expenses in connection therewith is paid out of the Revenues of the Islands. The only military organisation maintained and paid for by the Government of the Islands is the Police force. The Director and four of the Assistants are officers of the United States Army detailed for this duty. While in detail, they have increased rank, the United States paying only the salaries of their grades in the Army and the difference being paid from the Revenues of the Islands.

On June 30, 1912, the actual strength of the constabulary was 323 officers and 4157 men. Three times each year local examinations are held to determine the fitness of natives for appointment as officers. Equal opportunities are offered within the organisation for Americans and Filipinos and the same standard of efficiency is required of both.

Taxation:—The Revenue of the Central Government is derived from three general sources:

(a) Customs duties.

(b) Internal Revenue.

(c) Miscellaneous, including interest, rents, sales of public lands, &c.

The land taxes accrue wholly to the provincial and municipal governments. The provinces are required to levy a land tax of ⅛th of one per cent of the assessed valuation, for roads and bridges, and municipalities to levy ¼th of one per cent for schools, in addition each may lay a further tax of ¼th of one per cent for general purposes, the maximum that may be imposed being ⅞ths of one per cent.

The income in 1912 from taxation was about 7½ Rupees per capita including customs duties.

Agricultural Bank:—The islands have an "Agricultural Bank of the Philippine Government" for which a capital of 15 lakhs (in Rupees) was provided from the general funds of the treasury. Loans are made only for agricultural purposes and to persons and corporations engaged in agricultural pursuits. 50 per cent of the capital is reserved exclusively for small loans.

Trade:—The total value of imports in 1912 was

roughly about 18½ crores (in Rupees) in value and that of exports of about 16½ crores.

In 1891 the exports were in excess of the imports, but in 1912 the imports exceeded the exports by about 2 crores of rupees.

III

EDUCATION.

Before the American Government took possession of the Islands there were 2143 schools in the country, about equally divided between boys and girls. But, in the words of a great Spaniard himself, this was "superficial only." While Schools were nominally maintained for purposes of show, "at the same time measures of all kinds were adopted to keep the people submerged in ignorance."

This was, however, completely changed under the American Government. The general purpose was well indicated by one of the first reports of the General Superintendent of Education.

"In reviewing the history of the islands for the past three years, one is immediately struck by the great emphasis placed upon public schools, first, by officers of every rank of the United Sates Army who administered this archipelago during the first two years of American sovereignty, and subsequently by the United States Philippine Commission and the civil government of the islands. This emphasis upon the public schools is undoubtedly the result of the primary importance which they play in American civilization and the supreme confidence which Americans feel in the necessity to this and to every aspiring people, of a democratic, secular and free school system supported and directed by the State. It has resulted that the school system of these islands is the most typically American institution which our Government has here established."

In 1901, i.e., within 3 years of the occupation of the islands by the American Government, one thousand Americans were selected from the United States to organise the public schools in the Philippines. What has been accomplished educationally in a dozen years may well give just ground for statisfaction and pride to the Americans.

In 1912 there were about 700 American teachers and 8500 Filipino teachers in the service of the Bureau of Education.

The work includes the organization and conduct of—

(1) Primary schools, which offer a four-year course, providing instruction in English, simple arithmetic, geography, and at least the rudiments of some useful occupation.

(2) Intermediate schools, which give three years' additional instruction, and which throughout the course lay great emphasis upon vocational training, including a general course, a course as a preparation for teaching primary grades, a course in farming, a course in housekeeping and household arts, a trade course, and a course for business.

(3) High schools, offering a regular secondary course of four years, modified in outline in certain special schools to conform to the aims of such institutions as the Philippine Normal School, the Philippine School of Commerce, and the Philippine School of Arts and Trades.

All instruction is given in the English language.

The bureau of education is devoting itself to the problem of formulating and putting into operation a program of industrial instruction which will be at once logical in its sequence from grade to grade and in close harmony with the industrial needs of the community and which will prepare boys and girls in a practical way for the industrial, commercial, and domestic activities in which they are later to have a part.

General statistics.

Population, excluding the Moro Province, census of 1903	7,293,997
School population, one-sixth of total population	1,215,666
Average monthly enrollment, 1911-12	395,075

The average monthly enrollment is 33 per cent of the school population, or 5 per cent of the total population.

Annual expenditures.

Fiscal year.	Expenditures.	Fiscal year.	Expenditures.
1901......	* $233,411	1907......	$2,390,011
1902......	* 1,194,381	1908......	2,563,558
1903......	* 1,732,483	1909......	2,913,833
1904......	* 1,752,247	1910......	3,256,418
1905......	2,140,099	1911......	3,258,964
1906......	2,234,668	1912......	3,176,617

* Figures incomplete or uncertain.

During the 12 years the number of schools has risen from 2000 to 3685, that of teachers from 3928 to 8363 and that of scholars according to monthly enrolment figures from 150,000 to 629,380.

Industrial Education.

Every pupil in the Primary and Intermediate

grade has to take an industrial course. The following facts taken from the report of 1912, must prove very interesting:

Pupils engaged in industrial work, primary and intermediate courses.

Hand weaving	... 221,618
Loom weaving	... 11,926
Housekeeping and household arts	... 79,382
Manual training (wood) ...	... 13,210
Gardening and farming ...	... 111,652
Miscellaneous	... 25,002
Actual number of pupils engaged	... 341,493
Enrollment for February, 1912 ...	... 371,187

Thirteen trade schools are maintained in various provinces; manual-training classes are conducted in all provincial schools, in 150 intermediate schools, and in 400 central primary schools. These schools manufactured during the school year 1911-12 products to the value of $71,508.22. There are over 2,000 school gardens and nearly 25,000 home gardens supervised by school authorities. Eighty-three school nurseries have been established, and during the year 1911-12 school children planted 363,183 trees, of which number 201,868 were living at the close of the year. Five school farms are operated.

At the Philippine Exposition held in February, 1913, the bureau of education placed on display 23,305 articles, the product of the industrial classes of the public schools, valued at $28,591.62, of which $20,056.76 worth were sold, or 70 per cent of the exhibit. Of the amount sold, pupils received $17,802.79 as their share, while the balance was returned to the schools to pay for the material used.

Cost of public instruction per capita of total population in the Philippine Islands as compared with other countries.

Philippine Islands	$0.475
United States	4.45
Average in Europe	1.235
Japan	.275
Russia	.15
British India	.02

The annual expenditure for each pupil based on average monthly enrolment for the school year 1910-11 was $7.73 in the Philippine Islands.

Certain features have received emphasis.

Industrial Instruction.

The figures as to industrial instruction, given elsewhere in the statement, show that most favorable progress is being made. These figures must stand for what they are worth. However, there is one criterion by which the success of a system can be judged and which can not find adequate place in a summary of this kind, i.e., the place which the industrial instruction of the public schools has in the estimation ot the people. The annual exhibits of industrial work of the public schools for the past few years have been a succession of surprises. The last one, held during February, 1913, was successful to such an extent as to guarantee the approval of the public, official and non-official, both American and Filipino.

As plans along these lines develop, the problems to be solved assume more definite and tangible form. The industrial product of the schools is not

MANILA SCHOOL GARDEN.

Photograph by
Bureau of Education, Manila.

the ultimate result of the work, not the end to be attained, its scope is much broader. In industrial instruction, as in every other subject, the schools must serve as a medium of instruction only, and the great problem now is to extend to the homes of the people the industries now taught in the islands.

In line with this problem, and closely related to it, are several others, viz., acquainting the producers with the most profitable markets and prices their handiwork should command; keeping those who engage in such work in touch with demands of the markets as to style, quality, etc., and the securing of a uniform and standard production from all parts of the islands. The bureau is now in a position to undertake this solution intelligently.

The School of Household Industries.

In furtherance of the bureau's purpose to extend industries to the home, the School of Household Industries has been organized for the purpose of training adult women in certain selected home industries. At the end of the first six months' period after this school was opened it was the opinion of those who were familiar with its work and had seen the variety and excellence of the handwork which the students did, that the school will be instrumental in stimulating throughout the Philippine Islands a widespread interest in and appreciation of hand industries and lead to their introduction into thousands of Filipino homes. The physical and mental adaptability of the Filipino women to work of this sort is universally recognized and this institution is certain to have a very great influence in its effect upon the economic welfare of every community in the Islands.

EDUCATIONAL STATISTICS, PHILIPPINE ISLANDS.
School year, 1911-1912.

University: College of liberal arts (with a course in pharmacy), college of medicine and surgery, college of agriculture (with a school of forestry), college of engineering, school of fine arts, college of veterinary science, college of law	...	1
Normal school	...	1
Insular trade school	...	1
School of commerce	...	1
School for deaf and blind	...	1
Provincial trade and manual training schools	...	35
Municipal manual training shops	...	200
High schools	...	38
Intermediate schools	...	283
Primary schools	...	3,364
Total number of schools	...	3,685
Secondary students	...	*3,599
Intermediate-school pupils	...	*24,458
Primary-school pupils	...	*367,018
		395,075
Director of education	...	1
Assistant directors	...	2
Division superintendents	...	40
Supervising teachers	...	444
American teachers	...	664
Filipino teachers	...	7,699

* Average monthly enrolment for the year.

Expenditure for schools during fiscal year 1911-12; insular, provincial and municipal, exclusive of special building appropriations ...	$3,176,617.04
Appropriation from insular sources for secondary, intermediate and primary buildings, and for trade and other special school buildings since Dec. 6, 1904 ...	2,121,500.00

Nearly 253,000 school pupils are engaged in some kind of industrial work.

What is being done educationally in the Philippines is well summarised by a noted teacher and student of social conditions, who, on returning from a trip around the world, told President Taft that the Government is "doing the most interesting and most promising piece of original work in education now in progress anywhere in the world."

The Language Question.

The American Government lays great stress on the teaching of the English language, because in their opinion the use of a common language is one of the essential steps in the preparation of the Flipino people for self-government.

At least 3,000,000 children have had instruction in English. For many years English has been the official language in all branches of the government except the courts. This, however, does not mean that the business of the government has not been very largely conducted in Spanish and in the various dialects. A recent executive order requires the use of English, so far as possible, in the conduct of administrative business in provinces and municipalities. The purpose of this order was to encourage its use by all who understand it; and provision was made that officials affected might, upon request, be granted permission to defer its use. Various requests to this effect have been in every case granted; while, on the other hand, various indorsements of the order have been received from Filipino organizations of one kind or another throughout the Archipelago. The aim, of course, is not to impose a burden upon any, but rather to encourage the use of English.

Until this time Spanish has been the official language of the courts of the Philippines, under the law English replacing it in January of this year. Spanish has not been used universally; in fact, scores of languages are used in the courts.

Acting Governor Gilbert said in his message to the Legislature, in October, 1912:

I myself had the experience, while sitting on the bench, of having six languages used in the trial of one case. I think this is not unusual. It is not possible, of course, to use English or Spanish or any other language exclusively in the courts. Many lawyers of the Philippines are not able to use English. Large numbers of justices of the peace and a few judges of the courts can not speak English. Younger men who are being appointed to these positions now, as a rule, can do so. The Filipino has a genius for languages and readily acquires a new one when he chooses.

I therefore recommend, as earnestly as I may, not that the law be repealed which makes English the language of the courts and thereby postpone the achievement of Philippine desire for more complete nationalization (if I did this I should regard my action as contrary to the desires of the majority of

Filipinos and should proclaim myself as an enemy of *Philippine autonomy*), but that the law be amended so that all safeguards may be provided so as to permit the judge or lawyer or litigant to elect whether in the particular case that is to be tried, the proceedings, or any part thereof, shall be conducted in Spanish. If this recommendation be adopted, the steps already taken toward acquiring a common tongue will not be useless; young men, educated in the public and private schools of the Islands, will not be disheartened: those who by reason of age or disinclination have not acquired the new tongue will not be discriminated against; justice will be served in every particular, and the gradual adjustment of the lauguage used in the courts will take place of its own force as fast and as fast only as the people who have business to transact in the courts are ready to adopt it.

In the account given by me of the Government of the Philippines and of the progress made by the Islands under the United States, I have made no comparison with India. That I leave to my readers, but there is one note which I would like to add, viz., that in the Philippines as in India there is a distinction between "advanced" and "backward" provinces. The backward parts of the Philippines, comparatively very small in population as compared with the advanced provinces, are, of course, treated differently, though the proposed law contemplates to give them ample and popular representations in the new Legislature.

POLITICS AND GOVERNMENT IN THE UNITED STATES

Politics is the very breath of modern life in Europe and America. Rich and poor, aged and young, man and woman, even children are interested in it. Nothing sways men and women so much, nothing moves them so profoundly, nothing agitates them so markedly, nothing interests them so thoroughly, as politics. Every problem of life, domestic, social or national, has its political aspect. Even religion is not altogether outside the pale. Politics in this country is all-covering and all-comprehensive and as such every citizen is intimately interested in it. In practice, if not in theory, life is one compact whole and it is impossible to divide it into water-tight compartments. In theory, the nature of politics is much circumscribed, but when it comes to the practical handling of problems professedly outside politics, it is found that they are profoundly affected by politics.

It follows therefrom that government and the machinery of government, the constitution and the laws, are the concern of the whole nation and not of one particular class or of classes. Comparatively speaking, people are so keen over politics that they would risk their liberty, their property, and even their life in the dissemination of their political propaganda and in the furtherance of what they consider their cause.

It would evoke a contemptuous laughter if any-one were to say that religion and education have nothing to do with politics and men engaged in religious propaganda or in educational work should not dabble in politics. What is the ultimate good of a purely academic atmosphere if it does not help people in solving the vital problems that immediately affect them and their society? Learning is judged by its value both immediate and ultimate. Every ultimate value has its immediate counterpart. Ideals and theories are good or bad according as they affect life. Consequently everything taught and learned has an immediate value and what better use of it could be made than by enabling men and women to apply it to the improvement of their condition and to the bringing about of desirable changes in their environment ?

Politics are thus of paramount interest to every human being already living or to be born. The generations to be born are perhaps even more vitally affected by political conditions existing at the time of their birth. That is the Hindu idea of law (of dharma shastra) and that is coming to be the modern idea of law in the West.

The European critics of American politics and American government speak very disparagingly of both and even the most loyal American nationalist cannot and does not deny that there is a great deal of truth in their criticism. The American government is perhaps the most complex government existing in the world to-day. At one time it was claimed that it was the last word in democracy. If by a popular government is meant a government elected by the votes of the people, then surely there is hardly any other government in the world which is better entitled to that designation than the American government. In no other republic on the face of the earth are so many offices elected as in the United States. No other country or constitution can show so many checks designated to keep the different parts of the governmental machinery independent of one another and dependent on the will of the electorate. Nowhere perhaps does the constitution provide for so many safeguards against the monopoly or misuse of authority by the component parts of the government. The American constitution provides for a complete separation between the executive, the legislative, and the judicial. It professes to make each independent of the other. The legislatures are of course elected and so are the judges from the highest to the lowest; but even the executive are elected. It often happens that the president belongs to one party and the majority in either house to another. The same is true of the governors and legislatures of the different states in the Union. In the states, not only the governor is elected by the people, but also the secretary of state, the state treasurer, auditor, attorney general, and similarly the city and county governments are independently elected by the people and work independently of the state and the federal government.

All these governments are no doubt co-related, but no one exercises anything like an effective control over the other.

Under these circumstances it would rather seem paradoxical that the constitution of the United States should be considered by some Americans to be "a reactionary document" framed by men "with financial interests to subserve." Even President Woodrow Wilson says that "the federal government was not by intention a democratic government; that in plan and structure it had been meant to check the sweep and power of popular majorities"; and that it had "in fact been originated upon the initiative and primarily in the interest of the mercantile and wealthy classes."

That as a fact it is in the hands of the mercantile and wealthy classes no one who knows America doubts. "The fact is notorious," says Mr. Haworth, "that in many states and often in the national government itself, public opinion and the officials in power are not in accord and that the actual ruling force is an oligarchy known as 'the invisibe government' standing behind the political machine." Persons who want to know exactly what this invisible government is, how it works, and what influence it has over the machinery of government, should read the proceedings of the libel suit Barnes *vs* Roosevelt, only lately decided by the supreme court of New York. Winston Churchill, the great American novelist, gives a graphic picture of it in his new story called "The Far Country." This invisible government is sometimes bossed by financial and industrial magnates. Its methods and procedure are often of the most corrupt kind.

It is this invisible government, this boss system,

which is the curse of the American government and which brings about corruption in governmental machinery. To this is ascribed the success which is attained by the mediocrities in securing government offices and in entering the congresses. The following description of the government officials and the senators and the representatives of the congress is taken from a book by an American writer:

"Any one who comes in contact with public men is often destined to a sad disillusionment. Many are poorly educated, often are narrow in their views, some are brutally vulgar in language and manners and the proportion of efficient, broad-spirited statesmen among them is much too small."

Mr. James Bryce (now Lord Bryce) has remarked in one of his books that "great men are rare in politics" and Mr. Leland Haworth supports him by saying that "few of the able men, we have, enter politics." One of the chief reasons assigned by him and which is quite true is that no self-respecting man can stoop to getting his nomination for public offices "by cultivating the favour of a boss and, in many localities, this is virtually the only thoroughfare by which a man may reach in public life." Once there, his constant and never-failing concern is to stay there and get re-elected. Hence the necessity of his keeping himself well with "bosses" and "Tamany Halls." It is not the purpose of this book to describe the political system of the United States in detail nor to discuss it. This much, however, may be said in fairness to the Americans, that in my humblejudgment, everythin gconsidered, the American system has been a great success. Success is after all a relative term and does not imply perfection. The American system is defective in many respects, yet its defects are the defects of its peculiar conditions of life. Considering the constituent elements of the American democracy—the races, the nations and the countries from which it has been recruited, and the circumstances under which a large number of its would-be citizens come and stay at first only to make money for a few years and go back to their native homes, and last, but not the least, the social strata from which they come, the success of the American democracy is marvellous. The success of a nation in these days is estimated by the material prospects of its component parts. Judged by that standard the American democracy has been most successful. Even tested by intellectual standards, by the spread of education, by the progress of ideals of freedom, by the amount of security of person and property enjoyed by the general mass of the people, America is behind no other nation on the face of the globe. It is absurd to compare the United States of America with Great Britain or Germany or France. The circumstances which complicate American politics do not exist in any of these countries. Their population is more or less homogeneous, fixed and determinate. The cross currents in their social life are comparatively fewer. Their institutions and their history give them a fixity of standards and of life which go towards stability and harmony. Looked at in this light democracy has succeeded remarkably well in the United States and deserves the admiration of the world. It is an old weakness of mankind that every one can discover the mote in another person's eye, but can not see the beam in his own. It may be that American public life is perhaps more corrupt than public life in Great Britain or in Germany or in France, but, when judged in the light of the considerations set forth above, it would appear to an impartial observer that public life in the best and the most civilized countries of Europe is by no means better than in America. The white are very fond of criticising adversely and strongly the want of public morality among the Asiatics, but when such criticism is examined in the light of what is happening in the most advanced countries of Europe and America most of it loses its force. The truth is that under democratic forms of Government a certain amount of corruption is inevitable. The functions of the Government being distributed over a wide area, it is impossible to expect an equally high standard of morality and purity from all. There are greater chances of honest and pure government under an efficient and well-controlled bureaucracy than in the case of a Government chosen by democratic forms, but bureaucracy is a machine which takes the life out of a nation. When the heads of a bureaucracy are inclined to be corrupt and dishonest then the whole system follows them to such an extent and degree as to make life under that Government intolerable. Under bureaucratic forms of Government corruption and dishonesty reign for long periods unless the patience of the people is exhausted and they take the law into their own hands. This is well illustrated by the history of Russia. But under democratic forms of government corruption and dishonesty are soon found out and checked. A certain amount of curruption and dishonesty is inherent in the very institution of Government, but under despotic and bureaucratic Governments the governed lose their soul, which is a much greater loss than is inflicted by the corruption and dishonesty of a few public officers however appointed.

A discussion of the defects of the American Government will not be of much use to my countrymen for whom this book is principally meant, as they are yet far from democracy ; but this much I may say now that a comparison of the morality and purity of public life in India, such as is allowed under the present conditions, with similar institutions in England, France, the United States of America, and Japan has convinced me that, man to man, the elected members of the municipal institutions of India and of the councils do not compare unfavourably with similar public men in the west and in Japan. Perhaps they are a little backward when compared with men in the best of these countries, i.e., Great Britain, but they are in no way inferior to the generality of men of similar standing in the other countries named. My travels have enabled me to take a more sensible view of the faults of my countrymen in public offices than I was disposed to do when at home. Most of their faults and shortcomings are the faults of the system than of themselves.

SOME OBSERVATIONS ON CIVILIZATION

Five hundred and ninety-three days ago I left my home and my people on my way to England. Two days later I sailed from Bombay and looked for the last time on the shore, the trees, and the buildings of my dear country. Since, I have travelled a good deal in Great Britain, crossed the great Atlantic and seen the United States. I have seen and lived at times for months in some of the biggest cities of the world, I have witnessed the highest achievements and the biggest glories of what passes under the name of modern civilization, I have met numerous men, good, bad and indifferent—some of them the cream of the modern world, its intellectual and political leaders, professors, scholars, students, ministers, cabinet ministers, secretaries of state, newspaper editors, journalists, members of parliament, politicians, authors of books, thinkers, lecturers, teachers, merchants, bankers, poets, artists, orators, philanthropists, charity organizers, educationists, and others; I have met many women, most of them good women, leaders in their respective spheres; I have read many books on all sorts of subjects—politics, religion, sociology, history, economics, art, fiction, and many a magazine and paper; I have gazed at the achievements of modern science and modern man with wonder and admiration. Yet all the time the ruling note of my thoughts has been one of sadness and helplessness. Looked at superficially and from outside, the world (I mean the world I have seen in this period) seems to be very happy, very gay, light-hearted, cheerful and hopeful. The theaters, the moving picture palaces, the concerts and fairs are all crowded, ringing with the laughter of men, women and children; so are the saloons and restaurants, dancing halls and billiard table places. In short, there is no lack of play and pleasure. The resorts of pleasure are always overcrowded, where men and women, boys and girls, of all ages and of all classes, from the richest to the poorest, jostle each other in their pursuit of pleasure and in their desire to have a "good time" and make the best of their lives. All do their alloted work in their respective spheres of activities in all earnestness and seriousness. The idea of doing their duty and doing it well, seems to be fairly common among modern men and women, though the objective all the time is the pleasure that is to follow, after the work is finished. At times I have felt a sort of bewilderment at what the genius of man has achieved in the West. I have admiringly studied democracy and democratic institutions and have made myself conversant with all the currents, undercurrents, and cross currents of social and political life in the great cities of the United States. The wealthy classes, the gentry, the nobility and the rich among the middle classes live in a constant whirlpool of pleasure and gaiety. The social functions they organise and attend; the pleasure engagements they make and keep; the time they spend on personal adornments and on shopping, hardly leave them any moments to devote to the serious side of life. This they avoid as they would avoid a ferocious, man-devouring beast. The generality of them have neither time nor inclination for the serious questions of life and death, of sin and virtue, of duty and religion. They read a lot and some even noble books. But the desire all the time is to be able to amuse themselves as well as others; to show off; to keep up and carry on interesting talk; to entertain and be entertained. The poorer middle classes and the workmen spend most of their time in making the two ends meet, in earning sufficient to live decently and to support those that depend on them. But even in their case the desire for pleasure and the hankering after the good things of the world is the ruling passion of life. They are discontented because they believe that the wealthy classes enjoy at their cost and because they have not sufficient opportunities of doing so. The standard of general intelligence is fairly high. The number of those engaged in intellectual work and in stimulating thought is fairly large. Yet the desire for pleasure and power is the dominating passion of the western man and woman. Serious thought and serious work is only a means to an end—the acquisition and the accumulation of power, power to possess, power to enjoy, power to do good, power to serve. The desire for power and pleasure absorbs the best thought and the best life of the west and no one can deny that the western people have had wonderful success in tapping all the resources of humanity, physical and intellectual, to gain these ends and that they are at the present moment the masters of the world. The world rolls at their feet. Even the elements obey their commands and do their behest. Land, water and air are all at their service. They make and unmake heat and cold. They yoke and unyoke all material forces to meet their wants and contribute to their pleasure and power. Yes, I have seen all that, but at the same time I have not been able to free myself from the feeling that all is not well with the world. I have found myself going in and going out, thinking and trying to find a reply to the questions, "Are they really happy"? "Has the modern civilization really added substantially to the sum total of the happiness of humanity"? "Has it brought humanity nearer to perfection"? "Has it drawn the hearts of mankind nearer to each other"? "Has it spread contentment"? "Has it reduced misery and wretchedness"? "Is the majority of mankind really happier and better today than it was before the discovery of the steam-power and the printing press?" "Is the lot of the toiler, the unfortunate drawer of water and hewer of wood, the miner, the farm labourer, the factory man and the factory woman, the working boy and the working girl, better and more endurable than it was before?" "Does the pleasure that men and women, boys and girls, derive from saloons, picture-shows, and pleasure-resorts, sufficiently compensate for the misery and the squalor that attend their labor in the factory or the mine?" Even in the West in these richest countries, which own the mines of the world, which possess most of its gold and silver, and which control the destinies and the labours of the rest of mankind, the number of those that have to live from hand to mouth, that have to toil and labour, without the compensation of having the ordinary decencies, not to speak of the finer pleasures, of life is enormously large. The majority only live to provide for the pleasures of the few, however large the number of these few may be. But if to their numbers one were to add the vast masses of humanity that are kept down and exploited for the benefit of the fortunate few in the ancient and the most populous countries of the world, in Asia, and in Africa, one can not but feel extremely uneasy about the real nature of the modern civilization. These vast masses of Europe and America, of Asia and Africa form the bulk of humanity. The socialist literature is full of bitterness towards the few. The vast bulk of humanity in the West is at war with the wealthy in possession, and at times even with themselves. They are thoroughly discontented and rebellious. If one were to believe all that is printed and published in their name the majority of men and women in the West must be very miserable and unhappy. They have minds and bodies that require nourishment both mental and physical. They also want happiness and pleasure. What of their lives? Why is theirs an unending struggle without a single ray of joy and happiness in it, subjected to tyranny and oppression of the worst sort, obliged to work under compulsion for their lords and masters, for low wages or for the ebnefit of the latter, constantly abused, insulted, humiliated and sometimes even whipped and lashed ; always spoken of and treated with contempt, and disposed of like chattel ? A legion writers have told us that mankind are equal ; that all men are brothers ; that liberty is the birthright of every son of a mother and so on. I have listened to many a sermon and many a lecture on universal brotherhood, on the philosophy of equality, liberty and fraternity. I have heard of "the rights of man." But so far I have failed to see them in life, in practice, either in the East or in the West. Our respected leader, the late Mr. G. K. Gokhale, used to say that when the Europeans talk of the peace of the world, they mean Europe, and when they talk of humanity they mean "whitemanity"; but even in Europe and even in the midst of whitemanity, one does not find many traces of that equality, and liberty, which the modern civilization boasts to have brought into the world. In what does then lie the superiority of the modern civilization ? If it lies in the conquest of nature, in the subjugation and harnessing of the forces of nature, and in the application of the powers acquired thereby for the benefit of the few, then the claim may be admitted. If civilization consists in making life more complex, in multiplying the needs of man, in adding to the pleasures of the outer man, in concentrating power in the hands of the few, even then the claims of modern civilization may well be conceded.

But if civilization means a reign of truth, honesty, brotherhood, justice, and equality ; then what passes under the name of modern civilization is not a genuine article. If civilization consists in securing peace of mind to the bulk of humanity; or in giving equal opportunities to mankind in general; or in establishing a reign of universal brotherhood, universal justice and universal love all over the world (not the European world only); then the modern civilization has ignominiously failed. The world is still dominated by merit; by power and by force—not even benevolent force but aggressive force. Here in Japan, where I am writing these lines, only 65 years before, simplicity and domesticity held their sway. There was neither a navy nor an army. The people had fewer wants and they were easily satisfied. They were a hermit nation who had practically no intercourse with the outside world. No doubt, they often quarreled among themselves and even then the mighty and the wealthy ruled the weak and the poor. But they were a self-contained people who had no political, military or commercial ambition outside their own island empire. About 60 years ago they were at the point of the bayonet forced to open their doors. They did open their doors and began to learn lessons of modern civilization from those who had thus forced them out of their seclusion. They are good at learning and so they have learnt their lessons well; in fact, so well that to-day they are a source of embarrassment and anxiety and trouble to their former masters and teachers. The progress of Japan in the modern ways of life is remarkable. They have a grand army and a formidable navy. Their ships navigate all seas and their commerce is worldwide.

Yet it remains to be seen if the people are really happier than they were under the old conditions. Life in Japan is more strenuous, more exacting and more agitated to-day than it was in the beginning of the 19th Century. The country is groaning under the millstone of military expenditure, which must go on growing as the importance and the fears and ambitions of the nation grow. They have won their place in the comity of nations, won it with iron and blood, won it honorably; they are proud of it and anxious to increase their prestige; add to their wealth and extend their dominions. Judging from the modern point of view they are justified in their ambition and it does not lie in the mouth of the Western people to find fault with them. They are simply following their example. Nay, they have to do it in self-defence. But for their huge army and their grand navy they might be attacked and deprived of their national existence, any day. In their case it is a choice of evils and if they have chosen the one that is consistent with the current political morality, no one can blame them. Yet the question remains, if Japan is really on the path of happiness and if the bulk of her people would be happier under the altered conditions. We must wait and see.

If on the other hand civilization means the negation of the world, a negation of its reality, a refusal to face it by renouncing it—a contentment which might bring servility, and an idealism which might end in political bondage, humiliation and disgrace, even then I am unable to reconcile myself to it. In fact if a choice were given to me between the two I would rather choose the former than the latter.

The ancient Aryans were a virile people. They conquered the world and spread over and occupied the East and the West. Even to-day the descendants of those who settled in Europe are ruling the world. The Hindus went down, because at a certain stage of their developement they took to the analytic way of looking at things. They proclaimed "*neti, neti*" (neither this nor that). The Far Eastern nations followed the Hindus and they also fell. Now there is a reaction and the materialistic civilization of the West is at their door. The choice lies between extinction and Europeanisation, unless they can find out a mean by which they may be able to retain the best parts of both and evolve a new and a more humane civilization of their own. That is the problem before the East, and on the solution of that problem depends the future happiness of the world. When and how it will be solved is in the womb of the future.

Be that as it may, I see no justification for saying that the world to-day is happier, morally better, more righteous and more God-fearing than it was 2000 years ago. It may be perhaps that the speculations of the Vedic Hindus about the world, about spirit and matter, their solution of the social problems, their ideals of life and society were nearer the truth than those of the modern civilization ; it may be that the moderners are on the right road to the evolution of a perfect ideal and civilization ; or it may be that human affairs move in a circle. In any case I have not yet found a reply to the question "What is real civilization ?"

WOMAN IN THE UNITED STATES

Alexis de Tocqueville, one of the most distinguished and ablest French visitors to the United States of America, wrote: "In the United States men seldom compliment women, but they daily show how much they esteem them. They constantly display an entire confidence in the understanding of a wife, and a profound respect for her freedom." In order to understand this fundamentally true observation, it is necessary to follow closely the development of woman's life in the New World.

The so-called Western "Woman's Movement" in the United States possesses several special features which distinguish it from the development of woman in European countries. It is an openly active force of tremendous importance in every phase of American life, and it is impossible to write justly of anything American if the mention of her connection with it is left out. We find her intimately connected with the education of the youth of the United States; with industry; a wage-earner as well as a home-maker; a religious preacher as well as a politician. In short, there is no large movement on foot in the States with which she is not intimately connected, and there is hardly a gainful occupation listed in the census in which she can not be found.

In order to understand in any degree the present status of woman it is necessary to trace her history from the time the pioneers first landed in New

England to the present. We shall endeavor to do this, wherever possible, in the words of accepted authorities on the subject.

Wherever the early pioneer women went with husband or children, with father or brothers, they had to face the everpresent danger of violent death at the hands of the Indians, the possibility of starvation during the dread isolation of the long hard winters, the great probability of being left without male protection at any time to fight it out as best they could with nature, sickness, and want. No wonder that a strong sense of independence was soon ingrained in these early frontier women and their children by virtue of both inclination and necessity. No wonder that the men beside whom and for whose children they fought, suffered, and worked, did not dream in those times of interfering with the independence of their women, which was a very necessity of life.

The following quotations are taken from H. Addington Bruce, who has written several works on early American history:

"The American pioneer women were able to make the American pioneer home a center from which cheerfulness and sunshine unfailingly radiated. This, it need scarcely be said, meant much to the men, and so did the rugged, virile qualities which their wives and sisters and daughters displayed in times of great emergency."

"The picture of the Pilgrim mothers falling upon their knees on the deck of the *Mayflower* to thank God for a safe journey, and then going ashore to wash clothes, is eloquently descriptive of the spirit shown by all the women of early America. They had come not for a life of ease, but to play their part earnestly in the home-making for the men."

"There was no task, however difficult or unpleasant, from which they shrank. When occasion demanded, they willingly went into the fields to break the ground, sow the seed, or aid in harvesting the ripened grain. They lent a hand in the actual building of the rude log cabins that sheltered them; and . . . in burrowing out the caves in which the Quaker pioneers took refuge along the banks of the Delaware river."

"The severest demands were made on those colonists who pressed forward from the settlements by the sea into the lonely depths of the inland forests. Here they were menaced not only by wild beasts, but by the enmity of the native inhabitants, who, friendly enough at first, soon began to resent any further invasion of their ancestral lands. In face of this double danger, the women showed themselves no less resolute and courageous than the men."

"They learned the art of molding bullets and loading muskets, and how to use all manner of weapons of defence. Many of them became expert shots. And when the Indians at last took the warpath in earnest, and raged along the border with torch and scalping knife, they met a brave resistance from countless heroines. Nor did defeat, the slaughter of their loved ones, and their own captivity break the spirit of the dauntless frontier women."

Many of these women, when bereft of their immediate male protectors, were therewith entirely cut off from relatives, such having remained in the old world or on the settled sea-shore. It is thus easy to understand why we find already at that early time some women who engaged independently in business and as wage-earners. There are records of "acute ingenious gentlewomen" operating plantations and cultivating farms. The founder of the American indigo industry and of a silk industry was a woman.

As society began to become a little more organised, many of the earliest pioneer-life characteristics began to disappear, and in their place old-world methods started rapidly to replace them. With this, men assumed their "sole right" of governing the new society. But these women, feeling themselves and being held solely responsible for the business management of their affairs, felt that it was also their right and privilege to represent such in every way, shape or form; and so we find early "suffrage protests" from some "against all proceedings in this present (town) assembly (of men) unless" they "be present and have a vote." These women felt the attempt to restrict their interest in all affairs of the community, in the up-building of which they had had such a paramount share, as an entirely artificial proceeding, and resented it accordingly. In the Southern States, where the greater part of the white women lived on large plantations in comfort and plenty, and where there was practically no community life, where slaves did most of the hard labor and women had not as intimate a share in the up-building of the new homes, this assertion of political and social equality lay dormant, and European political and economic sex-distinctions easily asserted and fixed themselves. In the North, however, where men and women built their own homes, tilled their own ground, pushed forward shoulder to shoulder on horseback, on foot, in prairie schooners, into the unconquered wilderness, where democracy was the very heart-blood of the intense community life that sprang up at the touch of their hands,—here the women never lost sight of their inherent equality with men and were quick to assert their opposition to the encroachment of the old-world ideas. Through all American history we find the spirit of democracy and the recognition of woman as an equal and most trusted and respected help-mate of man, strongest where the spread of the new civilization was most recent. In the older sections of the country, such as Boston and other Eastern cities, society crystallized more readily under the influence and pressure of old-world ideas. To the women of the colonial times, before the outbreak of the American Revolution, A. Bruce pays the following tribute:

"For all her hardihood and energy, she remained essentially womanly, finding her chief interest in her home, her husband, and her children. It was for these she toiled and sacrificed, directing her every effort to the upbuilding and preservation of a happy home life."

THE WAR OF INDEPENDENCE.

"The truth of this is strikingly shown by the course she pursued during the great struggle which ended with the complete separation of the colonies from the mother country, and the establishment of the free and independent United States of America:

"From the first mutterings of the approaching storm, women were quick to urge their husbands and sons to oppose vigorously the slightest infringement of what they held to be their rights. Women were enthusiastic supporters of the early measures of resistance—non-importation agreements and the like—by which it was hoped to convince the British government of the folly of attempting to impose on the colonists laws not of their own making and contrary to their desire."

"In every colony, matrons and maids resumed the old-fashioned industry of making home-spun clothing, and banded themselves into associations to forego, at no matter what personal inconvenience, the use of imported goods. "Liberty tea," brewed of loosestrife, sage, ribwort, strawberry, currant, raspberry, or plantation leaves, became a popular beverage. No discomfort was too great for the women of America to undergo in their effort to help the men prove that England need not expect to do business with her colonies so long as she dealt with them unjustly and oppressively. And when this usually powerful argument of appeal to their purse failed, when England, instead of yielding gracefully and meeting the colonists in a conciliatory spirit, chose instead to send over troops to dragoon them into submission—the wives and daughters of the "rebels" were zealous as before in counselling resistance, if need be to the death.

"Nor did they falter when the gage of battle was actually thrown down—when the news from Lexington......announced that war had at last become inevitable. With splendid promptness of decision, they hastened to make ready their men for the fray, to send them forth well-armed, well-clothed, and strengthened by the knowledge that they were leaving at home not weeping and despairing women, but women whose greatest hope was that their loved ones would indeed acquit themselves like men.

"Typical of the prevailing spirit is a letter written by a Philladelphia lady in the first year of the war:

" 'I will tell you what I have done. My only brother I have sent to the camp with my prayers and blessings. I hope he will not disgrace me......and had I twenty sons and brothers they should go. I have retrenched every superfluous expense on my table and family; tea I have not drunk since last Christmas, nor bought a new cap or gown......and, what I never did before, have learned to knit, and am now making stockings of American wool for my servants; and this way do I throw in my mite to the public good.

'*I know this—that as free I can die but once, but as a slave I shall not be worthy of life.* I have the pleasure to assure you that those are the sentiments of all my sister Americans. They have sacrificed assemblies, parties of pleasure, tea-drinking and finery, to that great spirit of patriotism, that actuates all degrees of people throughout this extensive continent. If these are the sentiments of females, what must glow in the breasts of our husbands, brothers, and sons! They are as with one heart determined to die or to be free......' "

And truly women of "all degrees" worked in a splendid spirit of unity throughout this whole period. Lady Martha Washington, the wife of the great general, was busy early and late providing comforts for the wounded soldiers. Addington Bruce quotes the interesting experience of a certain Mrs. Troupe, who writes:

"Several of us thought we would visit Lady Washington, and as she was said to be so grand a lady we thought we must put on our best bibs and bands. So we dressed ourselves in our most elegant ruffles and silks and were introduced to her ladyship. And don't you think! We found her knitting and with a specked apron on! She received us very graciously and easily, but after the compliments were over she resumed her knitting. There we were without a stitch of work and sitting in state, but Governor Washington's lady with her own hands was knitting stockings for herself and husband.

"And that was not all. In the afternoon her ladyship took occasion to say in the way that we could not be offended at, that at this time it was very important that American ladies should be patterns of industry to their countrywomen, because the separation from the mother country will dry up the sources whence many of our comforts have been derived. We must become independent by our determination to do without what we can not ourselves make. Whilst our husbands and brothers are examples of patriotism, we must be patterns of industry."

We see thus how the social and national spirit was awake from the beginning in American womanhood and continued steadily on the increase. Women were acquainted with and keenly alive to national problems involved in current events. In the crusade against slavery, women again took an intensely active part. The burning question of slavery brought forth the first public speakers among women in America. Two sisters, Sarah and Angelina Grimke, did remarkable work in speaking and organizing. During the meeting a seething, angry mob waited outside while the splinters of glass from breaking windows flew about the hall, but Angelina calmly and dauntlessly continued her address and carried her audience to the highest pitch of enthusiasm.

Possibly the greatest single woman's achievement during the abolition campaign is Harriet Beecher Stowe's "Uncle Tom's Cabin," that most gripping story of Negro life and suffering. Within three weeks 80,000 copies were sold and 18 editions were out before the close of one year. President Lincoln, meeting her a few years later, remarked :

"So this is the woman who brought on the civil war."

The women organized anti-slavery fairs and soldiers' aid funds through which they raised 50 lakhs of rupees, to be used for the army and the support of sufferers left behind.

Women also did splendid work in caring for the wounded and in making camp-life more bearable. Inspiring stories of heroic service and devotion fill the annals of this war. One of the most active women was known as "Mother Bykerdyke." She did not belong to any organization and had not been sent by any one, but came and worked here and there and everywhere on the battle-fields day and night, administering food to the sick, bandaging their wounds, comforting them. An officer found her working thus and after observing her admiringly, asked her: "Madam, you seem to combine in yourself a sick-diet kitchen and a medical staff. May I inquire under whose authority you are working?"

Never stopping in her work, she replied: "I have received my authority from Lord God Almighty. Have you anything that ranks higher than that?" Mother Bykerdyke was present at nineteen battles.

But by far the most effective work was done through the sudden burst of organizing power which the women developed. They soon realized that separate societies for relief, no matter how successful and efficient in their place, were not sufficient for a speedy answer to the clamoring need of the times. They decided to form a central organization. Bruce writes concerning this movement:

"The woman's Central Association of Relief was organized in New York, to guide and supervise the labors of all local aid societies. After a time this association became subsidiary to the Sanitary Commission, with branches established in all the larger cities and managed almost without exception by women. When it is said that these branches and the different minor organizations collected and distributed money and supplies amounting in value to more than fifty million dollars, the magnitude of woman's work in the Civil War will be better understood."

* * * * * * *

"In the whole course of the war, it has been estimated, the Sanitary Commission furnished four million five hundred thousand meals to sick and wounded soldiers. And all this was rendered possible through the tireless devotion of the women of the Union."

"Even the aged and infirm vied in generrous rivalry with the young and strong. In many barrels of hospital clothing, socks were found having inscriptions like the following: "The fortunate, owner of these socks is secretly informed that they are the one hundred and ninety-first pair knit for our brave boys by Mrs. Abner Bartlett, of Medford, Massachusetts, now aged eighty-five years." A homespun blanket was ticketed: "This blanket was carried by Milly Aldrich, who is ninety-three years old, down-hill and up-hill, one and a half miles, to be given to some soldier."

From the moment that the woman's Central Association of Relief was organized, it was flooded with hundreds of applications from women of all stations of life desiring to serve as nurses in the war. American women of to-day recall with great satisfaction that the task of selecting and sending out the best fitted among these applicants was confided to a woman by the government. This woman, Dorothea

L. Dix, had behind her a very active public life : early intensely interested in the fate of the poor and outcasts of society, she had toured the states, investigated prisons, alms-houses, asylums everywhere, and through her agitation brought about much-needed amelioration in legislation concerning these. But her chief activity was in hospital work, both during her intimate connection with the Sanitary Commission and afterwards. Altogether she founded thirty-two hospitals.

The temporary impoverishment of the war and the death of so many men again threw an increased number of women into the field of wage-earners. Then the steady stream of immigration into the free United States steadily swelled the tide of women workers. Like the early pioneers, these women came usually with one or a few male relatives, leaving all other family connections behind them, and thus were often thrown entirely on their own resources. Most of them entered the country poor, and most of them came from agricultural districts in the old world. While there was still free government land to be had in the Eastern sections of the United States, close to the landing ports of the immigrants, many of the newcomers took up homesteads and made their living in the building up of farms. But as the tide kept on and free land was to be had only further and further West, many of the newcomers possessed no means to reach those distant places, and were therefore forced to make their living as wage-earners near their landing place. The rise of different industries fostered this, and instead of becoming landowners or farmers, the immigrants turned into factory employees, necessity forcing the women to work alongside with the men.

But aside from the compelling hand of necessity, many women, who had tasted the joy of economic independence, preferred, even where there was no immediate need of doing so, to earn some or all of their living expenses to being dependent on the good will of male relatives. Those American women, whom necessity did not compell to accept any kind of work offered, early turned to the acquirement of higher education and professions, charity and public organization work ; the others filled skilled and unskilled trades. Thus the independence acquired in pioneer times was never lost in the ranks of American women. They also retained their sense of unity acquired under the urging need of war times. This sense of common interests soon began to express itself in the formation of Women's Clubs, towards the middle of the nineteenth century.

Women's Clubs.

At first these clubs mainly occupied themselves with cultural interests, art and literature. From the first they met with a great deal of opposition and ridicule. This was mainly due to the steady influx of old-world ideas, and the opposition to club activity was termed, and attacked as, "neglect of the home and a most pernicious tentency," by both men and a number of women. The often quoted writer, Addington Bruce, writes :

"It has been charged that the club movement among women involved neglect of home duties, would increase frivolity, and meant the ultimate disruption of family life. However well-grounded those objections may be in the case of other countries, they are glaringly erroneous when applied to the United States. Here the woman's club has developed into a most valuable and powerful instrument for social betterment."

In 1900, not less than 100 women's clubs formed The General Federation of Women's Clubs, whose watchword is: "The Home, Patriotism, and Good Government,"

The G.F.W.C. alone, not counting the membership of the non-affiliated clubs, has a membership of well beyond one and one-half millions. The President of the G.F.W.C. of Austin, Texas, Mrs. Pennybaker, in an article on "Civic Activities of Women's Clubs" writes in the November (1914) number of the Annals of the Academy of Political and Social Science;

"Very early the club women became unwilling to discuss Dante and Browning over the tea-cups at a meeting of their peers in some lady's drawing-room, while unsightly heaps of rubbish flanked the paths over which they had passed in their journeys thither. They began to realize that the one calling in which they were, as a body, proficient, that of housekeeping and homemaking, had its out-door as well as in-door application. They soon learned that art, in its best and highest sense, was a thing of practical, everyday life, and that wherever there were cleanliness and symmetry and beauty, there was art in its best and highest sense. They learned that well-kept lawns were but the outer setting of well-kept houses, and that back yards and back alleys had their places in the great science of home-making. They learned that tenement house* and factory conditions were but

* Tenement house:—poorly constructed, badly lighted, and unventilated, fearfully overcrowded houses in the slum-sections of

places of the daily lives of other women; and that juvenile courts and playgrounds and eleemosynary institutions were determining factors in the character of another woman's child." * * * "No single address or magazine article can do justice to the civic activities of the club women ; it is a story in which each community has its chapter, for these activities reach from the lecture course of the small club in the rural community to the many-sided work of the great departmental club whose work is interwoven into every good deed which the great city knows.

"Thousands of towns, cities and hamlets can bear testimony to the work of these organized women : there are more sanitary and better ventilated school houses ; there are more numerous parks and more cleanly streets ; there are district nurses who visit the sick poor in their homes and give instruction in the simple rules of wholesome living ; there are sanitary drinking fountains for man and beast; there are vacation schools and playgrounds ; there are juvenile courts and equal guardianship laws ; there are cleaner markets ; there are many free public libraries and thousands of travelling libraries ; there is a lessening of objectionable bill-board ornamentation ; there is a determined campaign, nation-wide, against the housefly ; there is a more intelligent knowledge of the prevention and care of tuberculosis ; in short, there is scarcely any movement for the betterment of living conditions or for the social and moral uplift of the American people that has not received a helping hand from the club woman.,"

In small towns or rural communities the women's clubs usually consist of a study club. The best informed women will hold classes of instruction in civic and social conditions concerning the women of that particular community and the women and children of the nation at large. Where the commu-

the great American cities, where the poorest and most exploited laborers live.

nity is large enough the club also concerns itself with training and organizing workers for actual work on the outside.

In larger towns and cities, where the demands upon women are large and manifold, the clubs are divided into departments, each department devoted to some special subject, for instance, juvenile reform, school conditions, lecturing committee, study class, etc. Each department has its departmental head, its regular committee and committee meetings according to parliamentary rules. Each department has as its aim to do its utmost to fit the woman successfully to fill her place as home-maker, wage-earner, tax-payer, and citizen. The women feel that the more highly organized society imperiously demands that they should no longer confine themselves to their immediate families. In earlier and more primitive times, when agriculture was the sole occupation of the population, and each family lived on land owned by themselves and virtually formed a community by themselves, it was not necessary that women looked beyond their four walls. They could observe there as much as was necessary to control the lives of their children at all times. But in modern times, when the school takes the child away from the home for the greatest part of the day, when at every turn new and powerful influences surround it, mothers feel that it is not only their privilege, but a part of their duty of motherhood to look into all conditions affecting the life of children, and to leave no effort untried to keep such conditions on a high level or to better them where necessary. But aside from their actual or potential motherhood, modern life makes it essentially necessary for woman to consider herself, and train herself to be, a responsible citizen.

As Addington Bruce puts it: "They began to attack problems of importance to them not only as women and mothers, but as residents of the cities and towns in which they made their homes."

When their interest broadened to include "municipal housekeeping and housecleaning", the women soon found it essential to inquire into the industrial system under which thousands of their sisters were slowly being crushed through unhealthy conditions, low wages and fierce competition. Therefore, in the last number of years club-women have been active in visiting and reporting conditions of women workers in mills, factories, stores. Their aim is the protection of women wage-earners and the ultimate abolition of all child labor.

The industrial pressure and economic greed of big interests has caused grave conditions of overwork and underpay in most gainful occupations, and women workers suffer under these equally with, if not more than, the men. There is therefore great need of energetic protest and organization among wage-earning women, and aside from the work done by club women, the women workers are organizing themselves into strong labor organizations, and as such, are more and more able to make their demands concerning shorter hours, a living wage, and sanitary conditions heard and heeded. These working women enjoy a great deal of the result of the work of the organized club women.

The women's clubs have created many travelling libraries and art galleries. They have also banded together for special purposes in clubs solely devoted to such, for instance, the National Woman's Christian Temperance Union concerns itself solely with the aim of suppressing the liqor traffic and with educating the children in the effects of alcoholic beverages on body and morals. They have succeeded in introducing instruction of an anti-alcoholic character into most public schools and as an effect of their effort 18,000,000 children now receive such instruction. They have also succeeded in causing many states to "go dry", that is, in making all forms of liquor traffic unlawful in such states.

Since their work extends over the whole length and breadth of this continent, it is easily seen that women's clubs have a very unifying effect. They tend to an abolition of distinctions of place, station, and religion among members, and have added their generous share in making the South and the North forget the bitter feelings that still lingered as an aftermath from the civil war. "There is no East and West, or North and South. We stand for a united people", is their watchword.

We shall quote the opinions of two prominent public men of the present day concerning women's clubs and their work in the United States. Josiah Strong, president of the American Institute for Social Service announces the following conviction:

"Except in the United States Congress, I know of

no body of men or women representing so much of intellect and heart, so much of culture and influence, and so many of the highest hopes and noblest possibilities of the American people as the General Federation of Women's Clubs."

Judge Ben Lindsey of Colorado, who has acquired a nation-wide reputation and a nation's gratitude for his splendid work in juvenile court reform, asserts:

"*For the past few years I have been actively engaged in the interests of better laws for the protection of the home and children. In this behalf I have visited some twenty States. I have found wonderful progress, and scarcely without exception it has been the members of the women's clubs who have championed every good law and secured the passage of nearly all the advanced legislation upon the statute books for the protection of the home and the children.*"

WOMEN WAGE-EARNERS.

It may be well to consider the several aspects of woman's life and of her work and condition in society separately. The first employment of women as wage-earners in industries in the United States of which we have a definite record, took place about 1820. In 1850, 225, 922 women were wage-earners. According to the census of 1910, out of a total number of women of ten years and over of 34,552,712, there were 8,075,772 women employed in gainful occupations,—that is, a little less than one-fourth of all the women in U. S. A. are wage-earners. In 1900 these women were scheduled in 295 out of 303 listed occupations, but 86 of them were to be found in only 18 occupations. It is thus seen that certain types of work attract the greatest number of women workers. About 65 per cent of these women are over twenty-one years of age. In the November number of the Annals of the American Academy of Political and Social Science, a list is given of the occupations mostly entered into by women. Each occupation given contains one per cent. or more of the women gainfully employed:

NAME OF OCCUPANTS:		NUMBER OF WOMEN ENGAGED:
Farmers	...	2,557,706
Farm Laborers (home farm)	...	1,176,585
Dressmakers and seamstresses	...	447,760
Millinery	...	122,477
Textile	...	352,639
Weavers in textile industries	...	99,434
Sewing	...	231,206
Tailoresses	...	163,795
Telephone operators	...	88,262
Clerks in stores	...	111,594
Saleswomen	...	257,720
Teachers	...	478,027
Teachers of music	...	84,478
Boarding and lodging house keepers		142,400
Housekeepers	...	173,333
Laundresses	...	520,004
Midwives and untrained nurses	...	117,117
Servants and waitresses	...	1,309,549
Book-keepers and accountants	...	187,155
Clerks (not in stores)	...	122,165
Stenographers and typewriters	...	263,315
	TOTAL	6,707,191

Women are in many industries considered "better adapted, cheaper, neater, and more reliable" than male workers, according to many employers; in spite of this, they receive uniformly lower wages. This is considered an injustice by many women and also men, and a strong agitation is going on against such discrimination. Aside from the occupations listed, the following may be of interest:

Women lawyers	1343
Women physicians	9015

Women Physicians.

When half a century ago, women first took up the study of medicine, they were met with bitter antagonism and ridicule, and at times had to leave the colleges on account of the unbearable persecution persistently followed up by their male fellow-students. In practice, also, women physicians met, and to a certain extent still meet, with a great deal of suspicion on the side of the public and with slights from their male colleagues. But by now the woman physician is rapidly becoming an accepted and welcomed factor and women patients begin to count it a real blessing to have the privilege of being examined by a woman instead of by a man, and the work of obstetrics and gynecology bids fair to be transferred to the hands of women physicians. In the treatment of women's and children's diseases lies the greatest field for women physicians. A good many hospitals and sanatoriums are established and conducted solely by women physicians throughout the States. They are lending indefatigable aid in the sanitation of the slums of large cities and in the care of the poor.

Women in Education.

Out of a total of 619,285 teachers and professors in colleges listed in the census of 1910, 484,115 are female. It can thus be seen that more than three times as many women as men are engaged in teaching the youth of the United States in both primary and intermediate as well as academic education. Among these women, some hold very high positions in the educational world. The Superintendent of the Chicago schools is a woman, very famous for her innovations and splendid discharge of her duty. She recieves $2400 a year (7200 Rupees). In cities of over 5000 population, 936 high school principals are women (six of who receive 2500 dollars a year), likewise 285 high school assistant principals. There we find also 824 women superintendents of schools. Women teachers have been most active in bringing about the playground work of the schools, insisting on the need for children of play, air and sunshine.

Prostitution.

"The double standard of morals" as applied to men and women, is one of the most hotly debated questions of the day. The tremenduous prevalence of venerial disease among men; the "privilege of men" who insist that their present and future wives should be blameless in their moral character, while they reserve for themselves almost unrestrained freedom and never hesitate to stain the lives and bodies of their wives and children with disease; the ruthless economic exploitation in industries, which forces so many women down into a life of shame;

all these questions agitate deeply the woman of America to-day. Organized womanhood and single workers are trying their best to stem the tide of degeneration and to ameliorate or eradicate the outer and preventible causes which in the ultimate lead fellow-women into the underworld. The day is long since past when the average woman considered every prostitute as innately bad, and the day has dawned when they are beginning to resent the fact of any fellow-woman being pushed down a victim to mere passion. America does not publish its deepest shame in tangible numbers and it is not possible to know how many women lead degenerate lives. But the reports of the Vice Commission, which has extensively investigated the conditions of prostitution in Chicago, give ample proof of the crying need for immediate attention to this problem from the side of the American women. Chicago alone is reported to require yearly 5000 new girls to satisfy the demands of prostitution in refilling the places of such as dropped out through death and disease. About fifty per cent. of these girls are under seventeen, hardly more than children. The fact that the age-long cover is being ruthlessly torn from the face of vice, is one of the pregnant signs of a rejuvenation of moral conceptions in America. The ballot is being used effectively to bring about legislation to ameliorate such conditions.

WOMAN-SUFFRAGE.

In the States, where woman suffrage obtains, many beneficial protective laws have been enacted in this and other matters in which women, girls and children are concerned.

To-day, the women of the East of the U. S. A. are waging a determined and hard struggle for the recognition of their economic and political rights, while the women of the West enjoy full equality with men. The sweep of the westward-movement, broad and democratic in the very esssence of its spirit, instead of burying the Western woman under the Eastern and old-world burden of political inequality, has swept her on to the crest of its wave, has gladly recognized her domestic, social and political equality. Wyoming had granted suffrage to its women even before it joined the Union as a State in 1860. In California, where the question of equal suffrage came to a decision in 1911, the result was probably the most significant among all testimonies of the attitude of real American men towards their women. San Francisco and the other large citics, where the liquor interests and other large industrial interests unfavorable to woman suffrage were strong, went against it, and on the eve of election day it seemed as if the day was lost. The next day, however, the returns came in from the outlying country districts, where the memory of woman's heroic share in pioneer work was freshest and most revered, and turned the tide in favor of woman suffrage. Here, in the West of the United States, we find a clear-eyed, free-limbed, fearless type of woman, which promises fair to rear the most distinctive type of Americans. It is to her that her Eastern sisters are looking for assistance and inspiration. During the present International

Votes for Women a Success

The Map Proves It

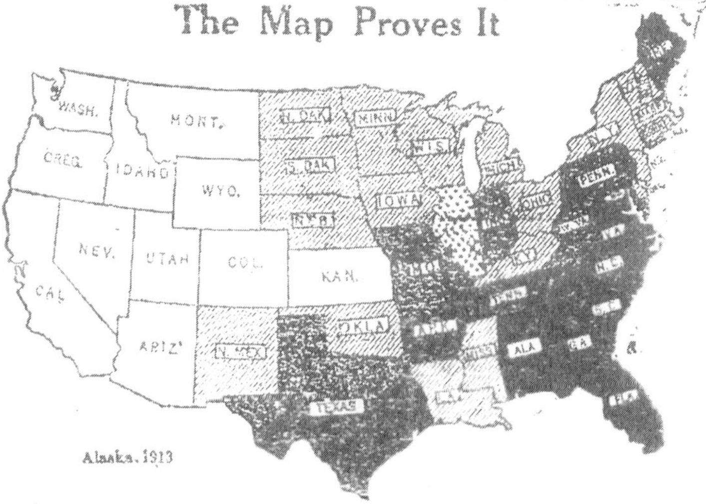

WHITE STATES: Full Suffrage SHADED STATES: Taxation, Bond or School Suffrage
DOTTED STATE: Presidential, Partial County and State, Municipal Suffrage BLACK STATES: No Suffrage

SUFFRAGE GRANTED

1869—WYOMING
1893—COLORADO
1896—UTAH
1896—IDAHO
1910—WASHINGTON
1911—CALIFORNIA
1912—OREGON
1912—ARIZONA
1912—KANSAS
1913—ILLINOIS
1913—ALASKA
1914—MONTANA
1914—NEVADA

Would any of these States have adopted EQUAL SUFFRAGE if it had been a failure just across the Border?

NATIONAL WOMAN SUFFRAGE PUBLISHING COMPANY, Inc.
PUBLISHERS FOR THE
NATIONAL AMERICAN WOMAN SUFFRAGE ASSOCIATION
505 Fifth Avenue New York City

Panama-Pacific Exposition, the women of the East have specially petitioned the aid of the Western sisters, nearly 4,000,000 of whom have vote in national elections, to help them in securing an amendment to the constitution granting nation-wide suffrage.

The day does not seem far distant when the American woman will be on a par with the American man in every respect.

Marriage.

Probably no other country on earth has ever offered a richer field of observation of the relations between the sexes than the United States. The great free mixture of nationalities and to some extent even the mixture of races, the new conditions of life, the economic and social freedom of women, the comparative ease with which homes can be founded, the continual migration of the population from one end of the continent to the other, all have tended to develop new aspects of the eternal sex question.

The freedom of American social life permits the girl from her earliest childhood to mix with the boys in play and work. The public schools are co-educational, so are most of the high schools and colleges. Throughout her whole period of education, the American girl therefore is closely thrown into touch with the other sex. Those girls who do not pursue higher schooling find ample chances in social life or in working conditions to associate with comrades of both sexes and of their own age. This, and the further fact that the greater chances which a young man without fortune have in the United States to provide for a family, has brought about a condition in which most girls freely choose their own husbands after more or less prolonged personal acquaintance, and choose them for love's sake. It is true that the fiercely competitive industrial system, under which great numbers of young girls pine, has somewhat affected the choice and motives of its victims. There are many girls in the rank of the laboring class whose main motive in marrying is that of securing a good home and release from the struggle of bread-winning, not that of love.

But it is fair to say that the greater part of American marriages are love-marriages, in which economic and other considerations play only a secondary part.

As a rule, the newly married couple repair to a home of their own, where they live alone instead of living with parents or relatives. It is the generally accepted fact that this is the best arrangement under which to start their new life. Each woman therefore becomes sole mistress over her little kingdom at the time of her marriage, be this in a mansion with a retinue of servants, or in the tiniest two-room apartment in a city, or a ten by twelve foot shack in the country.

Owing to the freedom of choice and the economic independence of the women, the standard of qualifications for marriage is steadily rising. The demand for an equal standard of morals for both men and women is growing year by year. Women are less and less willing to marry men unable to provide a clean mental and physical inheritance to their children. Eugenics is growing in adherence. Ellen Key called this the Century of the Child, and American women are truly endeavoring to make it such. Along with the raised standard in home and child life goes an increasing unwillingness to retain a marriage bond that has proved itself to be built upon destructive and inharmonious foundations, and has lost its love and life.

The brilliant French writer, Montaigne, remarks: "Is not marriage an open question, when it is alleged from the beginning of the world that such as are in the institution wish to get out, and such as are out wish to get in?" From all sides, from within and without, severe criticism has been directed against the "looseness" of the marriage relation in the States, and such looseness, if it exists, is attributed by the critics to the greater freedom and economic independence of the American woman. It may be well however, to investigate carefully before leaping to conclusions.

With the exception of the polygamous marriages of the Mormons in Utah, against which popular sentiment all over the States was very bitter and which have lately been suppressed by law, monogamous marriages have always been the only legally recognized marriages in the United States. Several forms of monogamous marriage, however, obtain or have obtained. Up to 1902, in the State of New York, marriage was treated merely as a civil contract not requiring legal forms, religious ceremonies, nor any special mode of proof; and strict proof of marriage was only required in prosecutions for bigamy and in actions for criminal conversation. Such a marriage was known as "common law" marriage.

This form of marriage, however, did not prevail to any extent. The most usual form is that of a legal marriage contract, followed by a religious ceremony, performed by the ministers of the church to which the applicants belong or by a justice of the peace. The contract must be signed by two witnesses and filed with the town clerk within six months from the date ot marriage. There are differing laws concerning marriage in the different States, but some general requisitions hold good. For instance, fourteen in a male, and twelve in a female, are everywhere the lowest ages of legal consent. Some States have raised the age of legal consent to 18 in a male and 16 in a female, and other States have raised it as high as 21 and 18. Throughout the United States, there is a movement on foot that aims to raise the age of marriage. At present, the average age of marriage falls between the years of 18 and 23.

The variance between the different State laws has led to interesting phenomena. A very common occurrence was and still is for affianced parties whose plans are interdicted at the place of domicile, to go to some district whose jurisdiction will permit their marriage. A little hamlet in Ohio is thus cited. This hamlet, called Aberdeen, turned a regular place of pilgrimage for eloping parties because of the ease with which the marriage knot could be tied there. There was a blacksmith in Aberdeen, who was also a justice of the peace. When couples came to him from Virginia, Kentucky and Ohio, he would lay down his hammer or release a horse's hoof at any time during the day, or get up in the middle of the night to give his legal sanction to their marriage. He required no license, made no inquiries, and gladly accepted any fee that was offered him, from 25 cents to 10 dollars. This blacksmith married all in all over 5000 couples before changes in laws put a stop to his practice.

The same confusion obtained until lately with regard to divorce because of the differing State laws. Reno, Nevada, required only a six months' residence before anyone might go into the courts and apply for a divorce, who had been unable to obtain such a divorce at the place of his permanent domicile. Like Aberdeen, Reno became a veritable place of pilgrimage for people dissatisfied with their marriage bonds.

The question of color has created a certain amount of confusion. Some States forbid marriage between members of the white and the black race, and hold such marriages null and void, even when contracted outside their boundaries.

No man or woman can be married against his or her will in any part of the United States. If the nominal or putative assent of either or both is obtained by force or fraud, such marriage may at any time be annulled by the aggrieved party.

In most states a woman may not marry persons held by Canonical and Levitical laws to be incapable of entering matrimonial relations. This excludes marriages between near relatives.

Many States forbid re-marriage to persons convicted of adultery in a divorce suit, and in Lousiana the defendant may not marry the co-respondent.

Mormon Polygamy.

The marriage code of the Mormon church, mentioned above and now rendered legally invalid, was the only institution in the United States which recognized polygamy. With it, it recognized two kinds of marriage as, the "temporal" and the "spiritual"—the former for this world only, the latter for eternity,—the first was a "joining," the second a "sealing" process. A woman could be "sealed" to only one man, but that same man might be "sealed" for eternity to as many women as he desired and the church would allow. The consent of the first wife to a later marriage had to be asked, but if she refused, the husband was at iberty to proceed against her will. The first wife was expected to present the succeeding brides to her husband at the marriage ceremonies.

The Book of Mormon, upon which the Mormon church is based, forbids plural marriages, but their Prophet, Joseph Smith, instituted polygamy in obedience to a "divine revelation." To these men, living in a mostly agricultural community, many wives and children meant cheap labor and wealth in addition to easy pleasure and ample satisfaction of carnal desire. They instituted a regular recruiting system all through the United States to obtain more brides, and when opposition grew at home, they even started sending their "missionaries" to Europe.

In countries abroad, stringent government measures were soon enacted against this Mormon recruiting system. In the United States, women especially sympathized with the suffering in which they pictured the Mormon women passing their days, and in 1905 the head of the Mormon church was forced by the pressure of anti-polygamy enactments of Congress to make public another "revelation" prohibiting polygamy. The United States women are fully alive to the fact and smile at it, that "divine revelations" on this subject given to men always granted plurality of wives, but never plurality of husbands.

Breach of Promise.

One of the fertile grounds for sensational journalism, which never fails to be exploited by the perverted taste of the American press, is the breach of promise suit. When a man and a woman have promised to marry each other and one of them refuses to carry out the agreement, the other may bring a suit for damages in the courts, as in case of other contracts. Thus we have the unique spectacle of people coming forward in public and rating their love and hurt feelings in dollars and cents. Such suits are by no means infrequent, most often against rich men by women claimants, but at times we even find men coming forward and demanding that a woman should drop sweet balm on their bruised love in the form of big sums of money. The San Francisco Examiner, June 1915, brings on its front page the following item :

PLASTERER SUES WIDOW FOR 50,000 dollars.

Breach of Promise Action Filed Against Mrs. Edith Amos, Who Adopted 27-Year-Old Son.

Contractor Declares He Gave Up His Business on Promise of Woman to Become His Wife.

Widow Denies Friendship for Cabaret Singer Caused Her to Jilt Man Seeking Heart Balm.

BY INTERNATIONAL NEWS SERVICE.

Los Angeles, June 24.—Mrs. Edith Amos, a wealthy widow, who legally adopted a 27-year-old son several weeks ago, became the defenand to-day in a 50,000 dollar breach of promise suit, adding another eventful chapter to a romantic career.

The complainant in the case is Louis A. Sullivan, formerly a plastering contractor of Oakland, who alleges that on the widow's promise to marry him he gave up his business at Oakland.

Mrs. Amos admits there had been an engagement. She declared that she broke it because Sullivan was not the kind of man she thought he was. She denied that her adoption of Alois Maiter, the cabaret singer whose voice and presence charmed her into making him her heir, was the cause of the break between her and her former fiance.

NEVER HAD BUSINESS.

"It is a lie," she declared vehemently, "that Sullivan gave up his business at Oakland. He never had any business. He was nothing but a plasterer. He came here with me as my secretary. I provided him with money and he squandered it. Alois, my adopted son, had nothing to do with the matter. I had fired Sullivan before the adoption."

Attorneys Ford and Hammond filed the suit in behalf of Sullivan.

The history of the eventful life of Mrs. Amos was unrolled in a deposition which she made several days ago before Attorney W. J. Ford in connection with a suit which she had brought for the recovery of property said to have been deeded to the man she was to have married.

Whist parties and divorce courts figure prominently in the story.

It was at a whist party in Oakland that she met Sullivan two years ago. Both were ardent devotees of the game.

She had Husband.

A mutual admiration for the other's expertness in the game became successively a warm friendship and then love. Each admits that. But marriage was impossible at the time, as Mrs. Amos was not free of a certain incumbrance in the form of a partially divorced husband.

On June 13, 1914, Mrs. Amos, who was then Mrs. Edith Davis, wife of Charles Davis of West Berkeley, was granted an interlocutory decree of divorce and given the right to resume her former name of Edith Amos, acquired through marriage in Australia nearly twenty years ago.

At the time she first met Sullivan, according to the deposition, Mrs. Amos was not wealthy. A week after she obtained her divorce from Davis her mother died, leaving her a large fortune. Her mother was the widow of Frank Burke of San Francisco, at one time one of the leading realty operators in the West.

Mrs. Amos received her final decree from Davis ten days ago. June 20 had been set as the date of her marriage to Sullivan, but when he appeared for the happy event, she spurned him.

The deposition made by Mrs. Amos also sets forth

that she came to Los Angeles, accompanied by Sulivan, last August, and they occupied a home which she purchased on West Vernon avenue and which she is said to have deeded to him.

In the complaint Sullivan alleges that he had received on June 15 last Mrs. Amos' definite promise to wed him five days later, and that she immediately thereafter changed her mind. The damages of 50,000 dollars are asked because of the loss of his business and the humiliation suffered by him.

These breach of promise suits are only one of many proofs that marriage is regarded as a trade by many, a condition brought about by the tremenduous social and industrial revolutions of the last centuries. Women have come to have a definite value as saleable goods subject to damage and therefore a lessening of value as a desirable ware in the marriage market.

Divorce.

Divorce is a well defined and firmly established institutiou of the 19th century,—as firmly established as that of marriage. Henry C. Whitney, Counselor of the Supreme Court of the United States, in "Marriage and Divorce" says:

"While it has always been known and practiced since the era of organized society, it has attained its highest development in this age of the greatest enlightenment, and in this land of the utmost freedom of conscience and action."

"The names of people from every rank and grade of society appear on our divorce dockets; and if divorce be a necessary evil (which we do not believe), it is one for which general society is responsible, and indicated either the progress of humanity, or the demoralization of the age."

There are only two institutions in the United States which do not recognize divorce: the Roman

Catholic Church and the State of South Carolina. The law of the State of South Carolina, however, permits a man "to give or settle for the use and benefit of said woman with whom he lives in adultery, or of his bastard child or children . . . . . one fourth part" of the clear value of his estate,—thereby making legal the institution of concubinage, but denying redress and freedom to the husband or wife injured.

The cry has risen that divorces are of an alarming, ever-increasing frequency, and pessimists foretell the disruption of all family life. As a fact, according to statistics, there is no calling or vocation listed which human beings enter into which shows so small a percentage of complete failures as marriage. Of all marriages contracted, only one per cent. are dissolved in the divorce court.

It would seem that the proper field for reformers would be in the social world, and not in the legislative, in which latter are always to be found those who would do away completely with the institution of divorce. If the causes for divorce are eliminated in society, divorce as a result will diminish of itself. The greatest cause for divorce mentioned by authorities is that of the economic instability of homes provided by the men. Only a very small percentage of Americans own their own homes; by far the greater part live in rented, crowded, shifting dwellings, rarely knowing where they will be a few years hence. Another great cause for divorce is the modern business conditions which take the husband away for the greatest part of the day and the greater number of evenings and often for long periods at a time, leaving a young wife at home alone and often with insufficient interests to occupy her mind and abilities in the little home. Henry C. Whitney, quoted above, remarks: "However great may be the evil of so many divorces, a much greater social evil would supply its place if the causes for divorce were suffered to continue, and the remedy of divorce were withheld."

It is interesting to note that in the eyes of that curious demi-god, law, a quiet and sane agreement between husband and wife to be divorced constitutes a complete bar to obtaining such divorce, when discovered. The law forces them to drag every pitiful detail of their private disagreements into public light, and the newspapers rejoice over the good copy which furnishes the greedy readers with another day's sensationalism. Below is a summary of the main causes for which women may obtain divorce in courts.

Adultery,
natural impotence,
bigamy,
failure or neglect of husband to provide for family,
imprisonment for crime,
force or fraud,
marriage under age,
concealment of loathsome disease at marriage or contraction of such after marriage,
incompatibility of temper,
desertion,
drunkenness,
disappearance,
insanity,
joining of religious sects during marriage,

living apart,
husband notoriously licentious before marriage.

The most frequent causes for divorce alleged by women are cruelty, drunkenness, and desertion, while the cause pleaded mostly by males is adultery.

Alimony.

A divorce naturally involves the settlement of property matters and the question of the future surport of the children, who are generally awarded to the innocent party. As a rule, a woman obtaining a divorce, asks for "alimony", that is, a monthly allowance to defray her living expenses. The condition and station in life of the husband decide the amount he is to pay her; she is considered within her right in asking to live in a style befitting the husband's income and rank. There is no settled rule as to how much or how little this amount is to constitute. Most states grant what is generally known as an "interlocutory decree of divorce," ranging from six to twelve months, which is then followed by a final decree, if so desired by the complaining party. This time is generally allowed in favor of possible reconciliation. Alimony is payable during this intervening time also.

Property rights of women.

An unmarried woman may hold property and carry on a business under the same conditions as a man, with the difference that in some states she is excluded in voting on questions which concern her property interests, such as taxation, for instance.

A married woman may make a pre-nuptial contract and by so doing, remain a separate-property holder during her married life. If she fails to conclude such a contract, then her property at marriage becomes "community property" over which the husband has main control and which becomes liable for all his obligations. A woman's separate property is not subject to her husband's control. She may use it as she chooses without joining with or receiving the consent of her husband. She may make separate contracts which are considered as binding on her separate property. She may bequeath such property by an ordinary will without the husband's consent. The number of pre-nuptial contracts arranging for separate property seems to be on the increase.

In conclusion, let me say that through all the effort towards obtaining greater economic, social and political rights for women, there runs a newer, higher valuation of motherhood and a deeper sense of personal responsibility towards children. Equal opportunity for physical, mental and spiritual growth for every child before and after birth—that is the highest goal of the present women's movement.

Child Wage-earners.

It is impossible to write of woman's work in the United States without special reference to the aspect relating itself to the children of the nation. The day is rapidly passing when the type of motherhood is admired which concerns itself only with the most tender care, protection, and nursing of its own physical offspring, and knows nothing of and cares still less about the conditions in which other women's children live.

Just as the stigma of "old maid," embittering so many lives in Europe, is rapidly being lifted oft the shoulders of single women in America, a prize is being set upon not necessarily physical, but essentially spiritual motherhood. The woman who looks after the welfare of the greatest number of children is considered the realest and best type of mother, whether married or not. A woman like Miss Addams of Hull House, Chicago, who has brought air and sunshine into the dark lives of thousands of children, is known and loved as a mother everywhere.

The tide of immigration, the industrial development, and the economic conditions in America have forced not less than 1,990,225 children between 10 and 15 years of age, (according to the census of 1910) into the wage-earning ranks. 637,086 of these are girls, whose future potentiality of motherhood and citizenship is seriously affected and lowered by the warping effects of unwholesome forced labor. In the cotton mills of the south, where the most unwholesome labor conditions exist, according to the census of 1910, children under the age of ten are found working for long hours each day. The age of the youngest worker is reported as seven. The suffering of such a childhood can only be imagined, not told, and the ultimate loss to the nation can not be calculated. Since the women of the nation have begun to realize the terrible pity and haunting shame of such child labor in a country where untold wealth exists and where thousands of grown men and women live idle, luxurious lives, they have not rested in their endeavor to ameliorate and ultimately abolish this condition. They are trying all avenues open to them to bring about the end in view. They work through charity organizations, churches, by influencing public opinion and public men, and through the ballot, where they have the use of it. In the States where woman's suffrage has not yet been granted, the hope of more successful work in combating child labor through the ballot forms one of the strongest incentives in their effort to obtain the vote. The women feel that the men have been too busy in their struggle of opening up and developing a new country to properly attend to this phase of protection of the children of the nation, and that it remains with the mothers of the race to see to it that the children of the race retain their uninfringed birthright to a happy, wholesome childhood. They have been largely instrumental in creating the nation-wide movement which has culminated in The National Child Labor Committee.

This committee has at present a membership of 8300 men and women. It is carrying on a most active propaganda through the press and by lecturing and aims mostly at the reform of laws. The following "Vicious Circle" and the "Making of Human Junk" are taken out of their Panama Pacific International Exposition Handbook and are intended to illustrate their methods.

"THE VICIOUS CIRCLE."

"You all know how the circle goes: child labor, illiteracy, industrial inefficiency, low wages, long hours, low standards of living, bad housing, poor food, unemployment, intemperance, disease, poverty, child labor, illiteracy, industrial enefficiency, low wages—but we are repeating. Where does it start

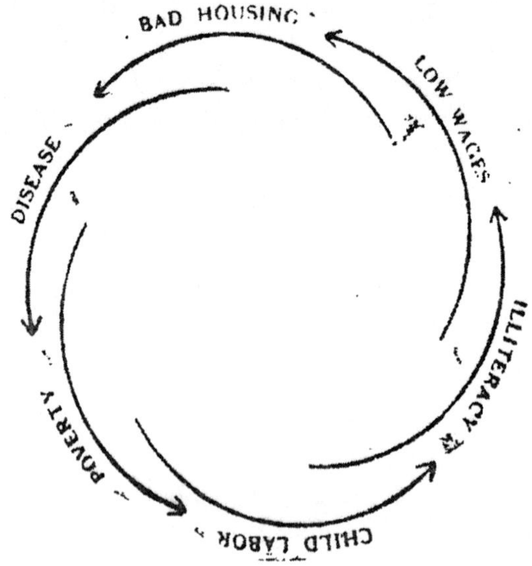

and where does is end? It is a vicious circle indeed. If you put an American citizen at any point in this circle it is likely to lead him to all the rest. The little child working at the manufacturer's machine is the one who becomes industrially inefficient."

The objects of the National Child Labor Committee are:

To promote the welfare of society with respect to the unemployment of children in gainful occupations.

To investigate and report the facts concerning child labor.

To raise the standard of public opinion and parental responsibility with respect to the employment of children.

AN ILLUSTRATION TAKEN OUT OF A PAMPHLET ISSUED BY THE NATIONAL CHILD LABOR COMMITTEE FOR THE P. P. I. E., 1915.

To assist in protecting children by suitable legislation against premature or otherwise injurious employment, and thus to aid in securing for them an opportunity for elementary education and physical development sufficient for the demands of citizenship and the requirements of industrial efficiency.

To aid in promoting the enforcement of laws relating to child labor.

To co-ordinate, unify and supplement the work of state or local child labor committees, and encourage the formation of such committees where they do not exist.

The committee has drafted a uniform child labor law which was adopted by the National Conference of Commissioners on Uniform State Laws in 1911, and is now under consideration. They well illustrate the attempts to legally regulate the emplyment of children:

SECTION I. No child under fourteen years of age shall be employed, permitted or suffered to work in, about or in connection with any (1) mill, (2) factory, (3) workshop, (4) mercantile or mechanical establishment, (5) tenement-house, manufactory or workshop, (6) store, (7) office, (8) office building, (9) restaurant, (10) boarding-house, (11) bakery, (12) barber shop, (13) hotel, (14) apartment house, (15) bootblack stand or establishment, (16) public stable, (17) garage, (18) laundry, (19) place of amusement, (20) club, (21) or as driver, (22) or in any brick or lumber yard, (23) or in the construction or repair of buildings, (24) or in the distribution, transmission or sale of merchandise, (25) or in the transmission of messages.

This section, with some modifications, is now in force in twenty-two States.

SECTION 2. It shall be unlawful for any person, firm or corporation to employ, permit or suffer to work any child under fourteen years of age in any business or service whatever during any of the hours when the public schools of the district in which the child resides are in session.

This law is applied in slightly altered form in 14 States.

SECTION 23. No boy under the age of sixteen and no girl under the age of eighteen years shall be employed, permitted or suffered to work in, about or in connection with any establishment or occupation named in section 1 (1) for more than six days in any one week, (2) nor more than forty-eight hours in any week, (3) nor more than eight hours in any one day; (4) or before the hour of seven o'clock in the morning or after the hour of six o'clock in the evening.

This section is enforced in 14 States.

The desire on the part of the best and most active women not only to create the best home and social conditions for their own children, but for all children with whom their own may come into contact, is one of the most broadening and promising movements of the present time, and the best proof that the modern woman of America is not losing her "feminity" in the attempt to get "equal rights with men", but is in reality only deepening and widening her motherhood to embrace and protect and cheer all that come into contact with her.

CASTE IN AMERICA

In India we are led to think that caste distinctions are a peculiarity of Hinduism and are to be found nowhere else in the world. It is true that the caste system, as developed by Hinduism, is perhaps unique. Nowhere has it been organized on such a scale and to such an extent as in Hindu India. But the principles and the reasons on which caste is based in Hinduism are by no means entirely peculiar to that system.

It is remarkable that the original Sanskrit term denoting caste should be an equivalent of the English word "color." The English word Caste means "jat," which is not to be found in any authoritative exposition of Hindu Law or Hindu religion. These latter talk of "varna," but never of "jat" or "jat dharma."

Similarly, speaking of what are practically caste distinctions in America, American writers of all classes and creeds speak of "color line" or "color prejudice." The word caste also occurs frequently in their writings, in fact more frequently than it occurs either in ancient or in classical Sanskrit, but not so markedly or so often as the "color line." This leads one to think that the caste system in India owed its origin to probably the same considerations and causes as are to be found at the bottom of the caste feeling in the United States of America.

In his chapter on "the color line," Mr. Haworth,

an American writer, remarks that if the subject be considered in all its aspects, "it is hardly too much to say that the problem of the color line is one of the biggest problems of the ages."* That gifted Negro writer, Dr. Du Bois, so often referred to in my articles on the Negro problem in America, also remarks in rather striking language that the color question is the problem of the twentieth century. His book, "The Souls of Black Folk," is a most forcible, pathetic and masterly exposition of the iniquity of the color distinctions in this country. The best American writers are agreed that in beauty of composition, grandeur of style and artistic expression, the book stands unsurpassed in the whole range of American literature. Yet such is the strength of the color prejudice in this country that this great writer (although fair in color) would not be admitted into any restaurant, hotel, or theater, in the capital of the Union Government. A Harvard professor of economics told me how once, on the occasion of a conference of the sociologists of the United States, after the sitting of the conference was over, he with other American (white) professors expressed a desire that they should in a body go to an eating place and continue their talk, in reply to which Dr. Du Bois remarked that the only eating place open to him was the refreshment room of the railway station, and how eventually all of them had to go there in order to have the pleasure of Dr. Du Bois' company.

Yet even a superficial observer of American life

* "America in Ferment," page 116.

takes no time to find out that "color" plays a very subordinate part in the prejudice. The prejudice is not even racial or political. There are thousands, possibly hundreds of thousands of colored men in the United States, having "white" blood in their veins, who are as fair (if not even fairer in some cases) as the purest blooded white American, to whom the bar of color applies as rigidly as to the blackest black, having no white blood at all. The same may be said about the Chinese and the Japanese. I am disposed to think that the prejudice is even less racial than economic and political. Most Americans know that the Hindus come from the same stock as the Europeans ; yet they exclude them from America even more rigorously than the blacks of Africa. Again, it is not right to say the white American hates the Negro for his color or for his race. There are millions of white people in the United States who place the most implicit faith in the loyalty and reliability of the blacks ; millions of them employ them in the closest relations of life as cooks, as general servants, as gate-keepers, as attendants, even as guards. There are millions of them who would prefer them over white servants and would entrust them not only with the care of their property, but even with the care and honor of their women.

The same may be said of the Chinese and the Japanese on the Pacific Coast, though possibly not to the same extent and with the same force. The prejudice only enters when the Negro begins to claim political or civil equality.

It is again remarkable that, as in India, so in America, the discrimination against people of different colòr (between the *Varnas* of the Hindus) should be manifested in almost identical ways, i.e. over and above the political distinctions, color should be a bar to interdining and inter-marriage. Color also stands for different standards of justice and education. The worst features of the code of Manu find their parallel in American life. So far as the former is concerned, perhaps they were the ideals set up by a highly jealous and exclusive priesthood to guard against the mixing and intermingling of the different *Varnas* and against the possible lowering of their own status in society, but in America they are actual facts observed in everyday life and for which the whole body politic is responsible.

Now let us see how it works. Of the political and educational disqualifications of the Negro we have already spoken in two previous chapters. The Asiatics also partially share those disqualifications, more particularly on the Pacific Coast. Conditions of justice and interdining, too, I have incidentially mentioned. There are no Negro Judges. The punishments meted out to Negroes are different, severer, and more exacting than those ordinarily administered to the white man for the same offences. It hundreds of cases the Negro is judged by the mob rather than by courts of justice. He is burnt alive or hanged for suspected offences for which the white would only receive a sentence of imprisonment, or in some cases only of fine.

Will Mr. Farquahar, who is so hard on Hinduism, tell us in what respect this is different from the punishments prescribed in the current code of Manu for Sudras offending against the Brahmin?

Then, as regards interdining, no white would sit on the same table with the colored man. On the Pacific Coast they would not sit on the same table with the Asiatic; and this even if the Negro and the Asiatic are Christians. (A Christian Negro is not admitted into the churches of Christ maintained by white congregations). Nay, they are not admitted into the white man's restaurants, cafes, lunchrooms and hotels. Then, once a Negro, always a Negro. The disqualification can never cease, even if the Negro becomes a minister of the Church of Christ or obtains the doctor's degree of the most exacting of American seats of learning. The worst is that even the fusion of the white blood does not improve the social position of the Negro. In India, the issue of a Sudra woman by a Brahmin father achieves a higher social position than that of his mother. In fact, there are some authorities on Hindu Law who hold that the son of a Brahmin from a Sudra woman is a Brahmin. The Hindu epics are full of such instances. The great Veda Vyas, the compiler of the Vedas, one of the greatest names in Hindu literature, was treated as a Brahmin of the highest order, though his mother was a Sudra woman. That is by no means a solitary instance. Dr. Du Bois, however, continues to be a Negro and is being treated as a Negro. I know of another gentleman, Dr. Hope, President of the Morehouse College at Atlanta, who, like his wife, is as fair-colored as any white man or woman can be. Both are the children of white fathers. Both are highly educated. Dr. Hope's father had to bequeath his property to his children by name. The law forbade his mentioning them as his sons or daughters. Yet Dr. Hope has to occupy a back seat in a street car and give up the front seats to the most ignorant, dark-colored, white scoundrel. Neither the fact of their fathers being white people, nor that their own color is fair, nor their education and learning is of the slightest help to them so far as their social and political status is concerned. It is a standing comment on the doctrine of the equality of men and of universal brotherhood preached by Christianity.

Christian laws forbid the Negro loving a white girl and having issue by her, but they give a free license to a white man having negro concubines. We are told by Mr. Haworth (p. 138, *America in Ferment*) that illicit relations are "decidedly more common between the male Caucasian and the female Negro" and that "race prejudice does not prevent illicit unions." "It is a strange paradox of human nature", continues Mr. Haworth, "that men who declaim most loudy against race equality will sometimes stoop to the most intimate relations with colored women possible between human beings." He illustrates this by a quotation from another writer, Mr. Ray Staunard Baker, who has related the following story in one of his books. "In one town I visited," says Mr. Baker, "I heard a white man expressing with great bitterness his feeling against the Negro race, arguing that the Negro must be kept down, else it would lead to the mongrelization of the white race. The next morning, as chance would have it, another white man with whom I was walking, pointed out to me a neat cottage, the home of the Negro family of the white man who had talked with me on the previous evening. And I saw this man's colored children in the yard." According to the census figures of 1910 no less than 29 per cent. of the Negro population were mulattoes,* *i.e.*, over two millions.

To me it seems that the Hindu Aryans of India never applied the color bar so rigidly as the Christian whites of the United States of America are doing today, in the 20th century of the Christian era. Yet Christian writers who dare not raise their voice against the color line in the U. S. A., have no hesitation in sitting in judgment on Hindus and denouncing them and their religious system for the institution of caste. Of course, there are noble exceptions among the white Americans, who are ashamed of the color prejudice and there are some states in the Union which have made some attempts to give them equal treatment, but the very fact of these exceptions proves the intensity and the rigidity of the general rule.

Some time ago I had occasion to go to a moving picture show where they were showing the play of "Ku Klux Clansman," also called the Birth of a

* A term used for half breeds.

Nation. This is a play in which the Negro is shown in the worst possible colors. It professes to show life in the South in the years immediately following the abolition of slavery. Every episode in the play makes the most irresistible appeal to the passions of the white people. The audience at times reaches the highest pitch of race hatred. Wherever it is produced, the show attracts the most crowded houses. Seats are booked several days in advance. To me, this is a better and surer index of Christian feeling in this country than any number of books written by Christian missionaries. Some of the best and the wisest of American writers of fame deplore this feeling, but they are helpless in the face of the universal hold which the feeling has over the country.

The subject has had a great fascination for me, and wherever I have been in the course of my ramblings in this country, I have tried to probe the best minds on the point. At New York, I put a direct question to the greatest sociologist of the Columbia University as to how, in his opinion, the problem was going to be solved. The reply was very discouraging and depressing. The amalgamation of the two races was, in his opinion, impossible. The intensity of the race prejudice might or perhaps will lessen in course of time. In some cases, the mention of the subject at the table or in conversation at a social function was declared to be bad taste. In two cases, my charming hostesses, very kind to me personally and expressing a great admiration for Hindus and Hinduism, flew into a sort of temper at my even remotely suggesting that the Negro was not having a fair and square deal in this country. "Oh, Mr. Rai", said one of them, "you do not know how wicked the modern Negroes in this country are. The old generation was very good, even lovable. They knew their place and were very faithful servants. My father had a Negro gardener, and he was a dear. We used to love him; but the new generation are so wicked that every time I went out for a ride in Virginia, my father armed me with a revolver lest a Negro might assault me." The wife of a University professor in one of the mid-Western states expressed similar sentiments. All this is evidence of the deep-rooted prejudice that defies all education and enlightenment. To me the prospect of the disappearance of the caste feeling in America, in the near future at least, seems to be very meagre. And this in spite of the fact that the best mind of the nation is engaged in disproving the theory of inherent intellectual or social inferiority in any race of men merely by reason of their physical differences. One of the most advanced and respected thinkers of America, Professor Royce of the Harvard University, had examined the subject in a masterly essay, wherein, after summarizing the scientific evidence on the question, he says: "In brief, there is hardly any one thing that our actual knowledge of the human mind enables us to assert with any scientific exactness, regarding the permanent, the hereditary, the unchangeable mental characteristics which distinguish even the most widely sundered physical varieties of mankind."* Later on he concludes that "our so-called race problems are merely the problems caused by our antipathies." These antipathies he considers to be "extremely capricious and extremely suggestive mental phenomena" which on closer examination are nothing but "illusions." We all have illusions, says he, but let us not hug them. Let us not sanctify them by the name of science.

The color line, however, is not the only caste line in the Western world, though that is the most obvious and one that obtrudes itself rather too prominently and too frequently. A century ago there were four well known and well recognized castes in Europe, viz., that of the serf, who had no freedom of action, that of the ordinary labourer, who had some freedom, that of the trader, and that of the feudal lord. The fifth was that of the priest. The priest and the feudal lord were almost above the law. They were the law-makers and they were the judges. The social interchange between them was extremely circumscribed and the chances of one's rising higher than the caste in which he was born were only few and far between, though there was no such bar as was till lately to be found in the Hindu system. Under modern conditions, however, that has been considerably changed; but the workmen, whether skilled or unskilled, still constitute a caste, and so do the hereditary nobility in England and Germany. The liberal and the social writers often speak of the governing class or classes. The most celebrated

* "Race Questions and other American Problems," page 45.

writers of the West speak of the submerged caste. The so-called labor unions are nothing more than closed castes based on contract and mutual understanding, but not on birth. There are no rigid bars to interdining and inter-marriage between these castes, but the prejudice is so strong, paramount, well established and widespread that it works as a practical bar. The love marriage of a noble lord with a common girl is considered to be romantic.

America is a ready market for financially embarrassed lords and barons of Europe, who readily exchange their titles for a substantial bank account and a wife into the bargain. Marriages between parties of unequal social position are still looked at askance. Fallen women are the outcasts of society and are denied all chances of regaining their lost caste. The position of the factory-laborer is only a bit different from that of the old time serf. The feudal system is gone, but the modern industrial system is almost as cruel and crushing and demoralizing as the former. It is hard to distinguish the modern industrial magnates from the old time feudal lords except that a feudal lord could never set aside his serfs and was bound to maintain them and give them protection even when disabled either by age or by accident, which the modern industrial lord is not bound to do unless forced by law under certain circumstances.

My readers will thus see that America is doubly caste-ridden. It is ridiculous, therefore, to talk of the existence of the caste system as a bar to political advancement on the lines of the West ; nor does it lie in the mouth of the American missionary in India to talk disparagingly of Hinduism for that reason. This, however, does not justify caste. The rigid caste system we have in India is, without doubt, a social curse and cannot but be denounced in the most unmeasured terms. The Indian social reformer is quite justified in attacking the absurd and inhuman rigidity of the Hindu caste system without necessarily attacking Hinduism. The current ideas on caste are not a necessary part of Hinduism or of the Hindu religion. The ancient division was well suited to the times and based on fundamentally right ideas. The world has yet to produce a class of high-minded, noble-spirited, self-denying and unselfish leaders of society such as the ancient Brahmins of India were. The democracies of the West know it to their cost how hard it is to get laws made which would secure them justice and protection against the blood-sucking and soul-killing devices of the capitalist. They have yet to discover that the legislators of a nation should be men who have no interest in property, in business, in trade, in capitalism, or in industries. No comparison can be instituted between the Brahmin legislators of ancient India and the capitalist legislators of the modern world. Both are liable to fall. After centuries of disinterested and pure legislation, the Brahmins fell and misused their power and influence in forging chains of intellectual bondage for the bulk of the nation. They gave themselves divine honors and pretended to save the souls of men in exchange for pecuniary offerings, *i.e.*, like the Popes of Rome, but they did not establish a soul-killing industrial system such as the modern industrial Brahmins of the West have done. I would at any time rather be ruled by a Rabindranath Tagore than by a magnate of Wall Street.

Yes, this is all true, but that does not in any way lessen the paramount duty we educated Hindus owe to our society and to our country of removing the obnoxious caste barriers that stand in the way of social consolidation, intellectual progress and political advancement. We must do away with them as soon as we can. Hence all honour to those who are engaged in the work, particularly that department of it which concerns the uplift of the depressed classes and the untouchables. America has its own untouchables, but their condition is in some respects even better than that of the best educated and the most enlightened among the Indian castes. This for reasons which I need not state.

INDIA IN AMERICA

For long I had cherished a desire to visit all those parts of the world where there were a large number of Indians either settled or temporarily congregated for purposes of study or labor. When I actually left my home in April 1914, I had no intention of staying out longer than six months. England and parts of Europe were the only places I proposed to visit. On reaching England, however, and after the Komagata Maru incident, the desire to visit the British dominions and colonies grew stronger. When I met Mr. Henry Baurassa, the Canadian statesman, in London, on the suggestion of Mr. Charles Roberts, the Under Secretary of State for India, I spoke to him of my desire to visit Canada and received encouraging promises of help from him. About the same time I received an invitation from one of the Sikh leaders in Canada. My desire and intentions were beginning to take more definite shape when the war broke out and I considered it expedient to postpone my visit to Canada and other parts of the British Empire.

In November, however, after I had finished my book on the Arya Samaj, I decided to pay my second visit to the United States. The object was to know more of that fascinating land, to study the social and political conditions that prevail there, to cultivate acquaintance with a few at least of its intellectual leaders, to get first-hand knowledge of its system of education and to find out what opportunities we had of training our young men there. Along with it went a strong desire of knowing as intimately as possible the conditions of Indians that had settled in America, and also why the American prejudice against Hindu immigration had developed so strongly in recent years.

The very first day I landed at New York, I saw several Indian faces. They were Bengalee gentlemen who had come to receive our distinguished countryman Prof. J. C. Bose and his wife. During my stay in New York I came across about two scores or more of my countrymen, Bengalees, Panjabee, Mahrattas, belonging to almost all the great communities of India. I also had the pleasure of meeting two of my countrywomen, one a Baroda State scholar studying at one of the women's colleges, and the other a Parsi lady. Then at Boston I met about a dozen Indians coming from different provinces and belonging to different religions. Most of them were studying at Harvard. Here also I met a Parsi lady who had been there for several years with her husband. At Chicago I met about a dozen or more Indian students coming from all provinces and belonging to all communities. At the Illinois University, Champaine, there were about fourteen or fifteen students, mostly from Bengal and the Panjab, including one Mahommedan gentleman. There are a number of Indians at the Universities of Michigan, Wisconsin, Ohio, Cornell, from whom I received invitations which for want of time and for other reasons I could not accept.

More or less, Indians are spread over all the United States—or for the matter of that, all over the continent of America. They are to be found as far North as Alaska and as far South as Brazil, Argentine, and Chili. There are large numbers of them in Mexico, in Central America, and in British Guiana. In North America, the area where they are located in largest numbers, is the Pacific Coast from Vancouver in British Columbia, Canada, in the North, to Panama in the South. The bulk of them are Panjabees and Sikhs ; there are a few U. P. men and a few Bombayites, a few Bengalee students and a very few Madrasi students. It is impossible to fix their exact numerical strength, but it runs into thousands and in all probability their number exceeds ten thousand on the Pacific Coast alone. By religion, they are Hindus or Sikhs, with a fair sprinkling of Mahommedans. Our readers will thus see that so far as numbers are concerned, India is better represented in America than in Europe.

Now I will classify them :

(1) Intellectually or educationally at the top, among those who are not actually studying at some university, are the religious preachers, most of whom belong to the Ramakrishna-Vivekananda Mission. They are called Swamis. There are some Swamis, however, who are not connected with the Vivekanand Mission. There are some religious preachers who are neither connected with the Vivekanand Mission, nor are they Swamis, but their number is

exceedingly small. Vedanta centres are connected with the Vivekananda Mission in almost all the most important cities of America. I know of such centres in New York, Boston, Washington, Chicago, Los Angeles, San Diego, San Francisco. I think there are some at other places also. At New York, Boston, and San Francisco they have buildings of their own. Every centre has its own organisation and its own funds. With the exception that they are all Vedanta centres, there is apparently no other link connecting them with one another. The great majority of their constituents are women. Except at New York, all the centres are reputed to be well off financially. The centre at New York is financially in straightened circumstances, due to no fault of the Swami who is just now in charge of the centre. The Swamis do not form a large class, but inspite of their limited numbers they are a very important group.

(2) The class next in importance, though larger in size, is that of the students. The students may be divided into three classes :

(a) those who receive money from home or from some public organisation or from some State. This number is exceedingly small ;

(b) those who receive some help from home and are partially supporting themselves by work. They also are few ;

(c) those who depend entirely upon their own work. Their number is the largest.

The Indian student in America is a prodigy of enterprise and industry and resourcefulness. The story of his struggle against adverse circumstances reads like romance. It makes one proud of the coming generation of one's countrymen. A good many of these students left their homes without the permission or against the will of their parents. Some of them perhaps had no parents or other relatives to advise them. Some had no funds in their pockets when they left home, or just sufficient to bring them to some seaport out of India, where they could find work and earn enough to take them to the next seaport, until they reached one of the American ports with at least 150 or more Rupees in their pockets.

I know of one young man, a Panjabee, who walked on foot from New York to Chicago (a distance of 1200 miles) without a single penny in his pocket. He slept on roadsides and earned his food by whatever work he could pick up in the course of his journey. This young man had studied in an Anglo-Sanskrit School in the Panjab up to the Entrance Standard. I know another young man, also a Panjabee, who did not know a word of English when he reached this country about eight years ago and who is now in the highest class at the University of California in the Engineering Department. His knowledge of English is still very poor, but in his class he is among the best students and the University honors him by appointing him to mark the answer papers of the Junior students in mathematics.

Some of those who left their homes with the object of prosecuting their studies in America, gave up all idea of university education when they reached here, and joined the ranks of their countrymen to work on farms or ranches or wherever they could get work. I found one such (an old student of the High Department of the Anglo-Sanskrit School Hushiarpur) working in an asparagus field in the State of California. · I found another (a vernacular middle passed) doing the same work in another neighborhood. I know of two Aggarwal youths of fairly well-to-do families of a Panjab District, who left their homes with very little money in their pockets, worked their way to America and are now in a fairly good position from a financial point of view. One of them has graduated from a business college; the other is a domestic servant in an American family near Los Angeles and hopes to join a university after he has saved sufficient to put him through the university. In the Panama Pacific Exposition there are a number of Indians rolling wheel chairs. In some cases the stories of their struggles are heartrending. Picture to yourself an Aggarwal young man of U. P., coming from a respectable family, working on a railroad track under construction, either cutting stones or doing other hard work, sleeping on the ground at night and cooking his food in tin cans thrown on the road by wayfarers. Some of the most brilliant university students have to work as waiters or domestic servants or fruit pickers or farm hands, or otherwise to earn money in order to follow their course when the university is in session. Others work for a year and then read for a year and so on.

Among them, of course, are some black sheep who

occasionally cheat or defraud their own countrymen or earn money in ways not quite honorable. For example some give lectures under Christian auspices and draw revolting pictures of the conditions of things in their own country. They caricature their people and thus win the sympathy of the public for the various missions that employ them. Some pose in photoplays and thus help the companies living on sensational shows to caricature conditions in their country. A few become the tools of that army of adventurers who trade under the name of spiritualists, clairvoyants, mind readers, professors of psychic knowledge, astrologers, palmists, and so on. I have heard that some even go to the length of fomenting quarrels among their own countrymen so as to get the chance of serving as interpreters when their cases go to court. It is possible that some of these stories are exaggerated or are the outcome of malice or jealousy, but in any case the number of such black sheep is very small and the motherland has every reason to be proud of the hundreds of Indians who have within the last fifteen years been educated in America.

What pleases me most is their spirit of enterprise and their industry. Here they are in a country thousands of miles distant from their home, amid strange people, with strange customs and manners, with absolutely no organisation* to encourage them,

* It is true that the Hindu students in America have organised themselves into the Hindusthanee Students' Association of America, but as it is, for lack of financial support the Association cannot be of much practical use to them. The

to help them, in case of need, to watch their interests, or to befriend them in any way whatsoever. Add to this the volume of prejudice against which they have to battle to get work. First, there is the color prejudice; secondly, there is the race prejudice; thirdly, there is the prejudice of religion; fourthly, they have the powerful force of organized white labor against them. Last but not least they are absolutely new to the work. At home they could not even think of ever doing such work. In school, they received no training for it. What little education they received in Indian schools was purely literary and had unfitted them to use their hands in manual labor. Yet they struggle against all these forces and in the majority of cases come out successful. At times perhaps they have to starve or to live only on bread and water; at times some among them have to pass a night under the shadow of a tree or by concealing themselves in a railway car. They do all this and cultivate a spirit of self-reliance and self-confidence which they lacked so much when they were at home.

In the university centers I have visited, I heard university professors praising their industry and

Association keeps clear of politics and can be very useful if properly financed. I think it is only due to the younger generation of Indians struggling for education against heavy odds in this country, that some philanthropist should come to their rescue and make some provision for the proper support of this Association and for enabling the latter to help students in crises. At times, as I have said above, our students get stranded and find themselves in an awful situation.

sobriety. For some, the professors have genuine praise, and as a class they have nothing against them. At every university I found some in the professorial staff who take special interest in Hindu students, who welcome them to their homes and take pleasure in befriending them in such ways as they can. At every center there are some women either among the wives of the professors or outside the university who take motherly or sisterly interest in Hindu students and give them every kind of encouragement. Now this could not be if the "Hindu"* students in America were as a class undesirable.

On the whole I am proud of the "Hindu" students in America and the country of their birth has no reason to be ashamed of them. My complaint against them is that on their return home they do not display that spirit or that respect for labor which pulled them through in this country.

(3) The third and the largest class of Indians to be found in America are the laborers who have been attracted by the high rates of wages that prevail in this country. This is not the place to discuss or to give a detailed account of the economic values of the country, but this much may be stated that the wages for unskilled labor range from one dollar (three rupees) to three dollars a day. Two dollars a day, i.e. six rupees, may be considered to be a fair average for a working day of nine to ten hours. Consequently the cost of living, too, is very high, but the Indian coolie, or peasant or farmer, is a proverbially

* The word "Hindu" is synonymous with Indian in America.

frugal person and can live on very little. As a rule the Hindu laborer on the Pacific Coast cooks his own food. Those who work in the fields or on farms or on ranches can get any amount of vegetables or fruits in the fruit season for nothing. For the rest, wheat flour does not cost more here than in India. Milk, butter, and oils are as cheap or as dear as at home. Meat no doubt costs more, but not so eggs. The Indian laborer cares little for meat ; he does not smoke ; nor does he spend much money on coffee or tea. He however drinks liquor and many a hard earned dollar goes into the cash register of the saloon keeper. Yet every one does not drink and those who do not drink save considerable. Even those who indulge in strong drinks save something for the rainy day.

As a worker, the Indian laborer is very conscientious and efficient ; particularly on farms and ranches. Judged from the output or from the standard of efficiency, he is very much sought after, particularly by the employers of agricultural labor. But for his race and color, he would never be out of employment and there would be room enough for hundreds and thousands more. Ten or fifteen years ago, there was no prejudice against him, but during this period the volume of prejudice has grown thick and fast. The reasons for this are various. I propose to examine them one by one.

First, he is in most cases illiterate ; but so are a fair proportion of immigrants from Europe. On page 81 of his book "America in Ferment", Paul Leland Haworth says :

"Most of the immigrants are poor and, much more serious, most of them are ignorant. Of the 838,172 who came in 1912, over 177,000 were unable either to read or write and comparatively few were well educated."

Secondly, he can live very cheaply and his surroundings are unclean, and his moral and civic standards are low. Now so far as moral standards are concerned, it is ridiculous to say that the moral standard of the Indian is in any way inferior to that of an average American or European of the same class. It is in no way worse, if not better. As for cheap living and unclean habits here again I do not think there is much difference between the poor European immigrant and the Hindu laborer. Speaking of the Slovaks from Hungary, Mr. Haworth, an American writer already quoted, remarks that

"Their (i.e., the Slovaks') standard of living is almost as low as that of the Chinese. They herd promiscuously in any room, shed or cellar, with little regard to sex or sanitation. Their demand for water is but very limited for the use of the outer body as well as the inner. They drink 'Slivovitz,' a sort of brandy made from potatoes or prunes. They wear sandals and caps and clothes of sheepskin, which latter also serve as their bed. They are excessively ignorant."

With a view to having a first-hand knowledge about these matters, I have been to a few places where the Sikh laborer on the Pacific Coast works and lives. I have also been to places where the European laborer works and lives. To me there seems to be very little difference between the two, except that the Sikh on account of his head dress and color can be easily distinguished from the rest of the laboring population, whether American or foreign, while the different nationalities among the white foreign laborer cannot be so easily made out. In the matter of living and personal habits of cleanliness, I am afriad, there is hardly anything to choose between the two; but if at all, the contrast would be favourable to the Sikh in fifty cases out of a hundred. The non-American white laborer cannot be easily made out from his American fellow laborer and he mixes with the latter on terms of equality. The Sikhs who have removed their hair and put on hats can easily pass as Spaniards or Mexicans or South Americans. Similarly, in the matter of drinking and kicking up rows when drunk, the Sikh has the disadvantage of being immediately identified as such —a disadvantage which the white laborer does not share with him even if he is not American.

It would be thus easily seen that these objections have nothing serious in them. The real objection lies in a prejudice which has been accentuated by economic considerations. The Hindu is a formidable rival in the field of labor as well as trade. So is the Jew. The Jew, however, has a white skin and has adopted the habits and manners of the European. He has been accepted to be as good as a European. So neither the racial nor the color prejudice stands in his way. The Hindu is also Caucasian by race, it is true, but then his color and his habits and manners are so different that the Europeans are not prepared to acknowledge that his racial origin is the same as theirs. So the consideration shown to the Jew is not extended to the Hindu. More or less all

Asiatics share the prejudice which is shown against the Hindu, but the political status of the Japanese and the Chinese being higher at home gives them advantage over the Hindu. The Jap has to be tolerated because he is "a citizen of a country which recently whipped one of the great powers."* Against the Chinese, the Americans do not feel the same bitterness as they display against the Jap or the Hindu. The former they hate; the latter they hold in scorn; but the Chinese they pity. China is America's protege and the Chinaman in the United States, though dreaded as a competitor in the labor market and therefore now absolutely shut out by law, is otherwise petted. The Sikh has intensified the prejudice against him by his pagri (turban) and by his long hair.

Personally I have nothing but praise for this trait of his character. Go wherever he may, he maintains his Indian character; he keeps his distinctive dress and cooks his own food. A vast majority of them preserve their national prejudices and sentiments. The uneducated Hindu and Sikh laborer does not eat beef. I met a Brahmin of Hushiarpur at Los Angeles, who, during the five years he has been in this country, has never tasted the American bread and has never even for once eaten at any of the American restaurants. He is a strict vegetarian as many others are. On the other hand it is hard to come across a Hindu student who does not take beef. I have so far met only two Mahommedan students. One of them was strict in his religious

* "America in Ferment," by Haworth, page 116.

prejudices; the other partook as freely of pork as the Hindus do of beef. The uneducated Mahommedans, however, are strict in the matter of diet. They do not take pork nor do they touch fat. I had the honor of being entertained by them at a strictly Indian dinner cooked by themselves.* Those Mahommedans who can pass as Persians or Turks or even as Egyptians, are better treated. The Indians (called Hindus regardless of their creed) are however universally despised in other than learned or cultured circles, but from what I have seen of my Hindu, Sikh, or Mahommedan countrymen of this coast, I have nothing but respect for them. They are as a rule warm and generous patriots, hospitable and courteous.

Among the Sikhs and Hindus liquor creates havoc. The reason is obvious; they have no other diversion. In the absence of female society, in the absence of leaders to whom to look for guidance or example or precept, in the absence of a superior social strata to mix with even occasionally, in the absence of any real recreation and amusement to forget the hard toil of the day, they see no harm in burying their fatigue and in purchasing temporary forgetfulness of the cares of the world in a draught of beer or in a peg of whisky. Once in a saloon and once having started, some of them forget where to leave oft and have to be carried away to their rooms by their comrades or shut up in the lock-up by the police.

* Some people are not disposed to attach much importance to the question of what they eat, but I do. In my view the question is one of stamina and character.

The Sikh in America, whether in Canada or in the United States, must have donated hundreds of thousands of dollars for the *Panth*, but the *Panth* has done precious little for them. There are Sikh Gurdwaras in both countries, where Sikh Scriptures are kept and where Granthis are stationed and maintained, but no class of human beings can live on credal religion alone. Religion cannot fill all their life outside work. The religious leaders have by overzeal added to their difficulties. For example, they brought nothing but ridicule on themselves by insisting on singing *Bhajans* and doing *Kirtans* to the accompaniment of Sikh instruments of music, like the *Kartal*, *Dholki*, etc., in the streets of Stockton. I have not so far heard of any attempts having been made to educate them, to create and encourage a habit of reading among them, to establish social and recreative centres for them and otherwise to cater to their social and physical desires on wholesome lines.

The Sikh and the Hindu laborer on this coast have been exploited in turns by the religious and the political fanatic, but neither of them has done anything for him in the way of supplying him intellectual or social food or creating for him a healthy social and mental atmosphere.

Oh how I wish that some worthy Indians were to consecrate their lives to the service of these men, cater to their intellectual and social wants and guide them out of harm's way. Any one attempting to do that, will have a tough battle to fight and can only succeed if in addition to disinterested devotion to duty and love of his countrymen, he gives not only his time free, but also finds funds for his cause outside of America, for these people have become extermely suspicious of those who ask them to contribute. They have so often been cheated and imposed upon, that they now strongly resent being asked to pay either in the name of patriotism or philanthropy or religion; yet both the religious and the political movements are financed by them.

Besides, for want of an organization to look after their material interests, in the absence of intellectual and business leaders, with none of their class in the banking or trading circles, they do not get the full value of their labour and are oftener than not deceived and defrauded. Both Indian and American sharpers victimize them. They are a fine, good-looking, hard-working, simple-minded, honest, warmhearted set of people, these "Hindu" laborers (including Sikhs and Mahommedans) on the Pacific Coast, and my heart goes forth to them in love and sympathy. Except in one or two instances, I have seen and studied them without disclosing my identity. I have partaken of their prasada (their bread and vegetable and meat) without their knowing exactly who I was and whence I had come and why I was there. Of course they have their own hotels and eating places as the American hotels and restaurants would not receive them. The Chinese and some of the Japanese hotels and restaurants are, however, open to them and such of them as wear hats may even go to American hotels and restaurants. In the South and in the West of America, the position of the Hindu is rather curious. In the South he is confounded with the Negro and the only way to escape the indignities, that are heaped on the Negro there, is to put on a turban. In the West, a turban has to be scrupulously tabooed, because with a turban you stand the chance of being excluded from hotels, restaurants and theaters and of being looked down upon.

I am of opinion that public bodies in India should find out some means of improving the lot of the Hindu laborers on this coast. The immigration department admits no more Hindus into the United States. There is no law forbidding their entrance as such, but the laws and regulations are so administered as to shut out and effectively exclude the Hindu from entering America, unless he comes on a short visit or for purposes of trade with plenty of money in his pockets, or as a student with sufficient evidence that he would be supported from home. Those however, who are already here, have no intentions of leaving the country soon. It would be a good thing if some way could be found to let them send for their womenfolk.

THE SWAMIS.

The orthodox Christians of America and the churches do not like the Hindu Swami or the Hindu lecturer. They not only encroach upon their preserves, and are considered as poachers, but they help in disillusioning the people of America as to the civil and religious conditions of that "heathen" country. With the exception of a few high class Hindu teachers of the class of Swami Vivekananda and Swami Ram Tirtha, the general run of Swamis that come to this country are not above criticism. Their youth, their style of living, their lack of experience of the world and other things create enemies for them. I am afraid they are by no means the best representatives of Hinduism. Inspite of misrepresentation and misstatements made by missionaries, Hinduism in the best circles of this country stands for high spirituality, high ethics, mysticism, purity of life and high morality. I have no reason to say that the Swamis that come to this country are anything but good men, but surely they are not the best representatives of Hinduism. Oftener than not, their knowledge of their own scriptures is poor ; their age subjects them to temptations which are fatal to their mission ; their pretensions to high spirituality or yogic or psychic powers place them on a level with American dabblers in occultism and with professional clairvoyants. The fact that they depend for their maintenance and wants and also for the maintenance of their organization upon the support of Americans, also brings in a spirit of greed and commercialism which is alien to the true spirit of Hinduism and tends to bring discredit sometimes. In fixing prices for admission to lectures or classes and in asking for offerings at the end of lectures, they adopt the American spirit of commercialism which jars on Hindu ears and drags them down to the level of professional men. At times in their eagerness to manage their affairs well, and efficiently, they take lodgers in their buildings and deal with them on strictly business lines. All this takes away from their character of places of worship or places of "Dharma" and stamps upon them the trade mark of American commercialism. To me it seems absurd and quite opposed to the spirit of the Hindu Shastras that a young man of 20 or 25 or 30 years of age should assume the position of a religious teacher or preacher, especially when he has not passed through the first three Ashramas and has not undergone the discipline that is necessary for the conquest of the senses and without which one does not acquire the experience of human nature and human weaknesses which is so essential for a successful preacher. It is bad that modern religious movements in India should have to act in opposition to the spirit of the Hindu Shastras in this respect; but it is worse that we should send mere beardless youths to interpret Hinduism to the world at large. I am afraid poor Hinduism has to suffer a great deal from this mistake. Yet it is marvellous to what a great extent Hinduism has influenced the religious thought of America. Reincarnation and the previous and future lives of the soul are accepted almost as an axiomatic truth. "Karma" is a very common word in religious phraseology. The Bible is being very laboriously overhauled to bring it into conformity with modern religious thought, and many a Hindu idea is being given out to the world in Biblical language and Christian phraseology. A true Hindu has reason to be mighty glad of it without cavilling at the use which the Christian world is making of Hindu thought without acknowledging the debt. In the learned circles there is nothing but respect for India's past and India's culture. Tagore also has helped India considerably in that line. Among the modern writers widely read and appreciated in really cultured circles in this country, Rabindranath Tagore is always to be found.

With all this, I think, India needs to be better represented in the United States than it is at present. The Ramakrishna Mission should depute some of its senior men to interpret Vedanta to the Americans. The men who come out as teachers should have nothing to do with the business side of the mission. The Vedanta centres should, moreover, be open to poor Hindus or to new arrivals from India in the country from twenty-four to forty-eight hours without any charge. It is un-Hindu to insist on the payment of rent by everyone, even if he cannot afford to pay it and does not know where else to go for shelter. The teaching of religion should be absolutely separated from the financial or the business side of the organisation. I am of opinion that wealthy Indian potentates like the Maharajas of India should endow lectureships for foreign countries. Competent Hindu lecturers should be sent abroad to give lectures on Indian subjects.

Of India, Americans generally know very little; perhaps not more than what they read in Kipling's books or in the writings of their own missionaries. A Hindu girl told me a story. She is a high school pupil and the course of history prescribed for her class includes Indian history. One day she asked her teacher why the latter ignored that part of the subject. The teacher's reply was, because the Indians had done nothing to have a history; they were a backward people having nothing to their credit. The Hindu girl, of course, did not accept the reason given by the teacher and gave a bit of her mind in reply ; but such is the colossal ignorance of educated foreigners about India. My readers would laugh if I were to recount the stories that I know of the ignorance of even Englishmen about the geography and history of India.

Here again, the Indians themselves are responsible for this ignorance and if they and their country suffer thereby in the estimation of the world, the fault is theirs. How many Indians are there who feel that they owe a duty to their country to bring it into the open forum of the world, so that it may find its due recognition there by learning other people's point of view and giving its own for the benefit of others?

Some friends connected with the University of California have constituted themselves into an India Society for the purpose of studying Indian literature and Indian questions and creating interest in India among Americans. Professsor Pope of the University of California has been clected its first President and Dr. David Starr Jordan, the great scientist and scholar, Chancellor of Stanford University, Mr. Edwin Markham, the poet, Mr. Winston Churchill, the great novelist, have consented to be its Vice-Presidents. It is hoped that the society may stimulate interest in Indian matters in America and be a source of friendly exchange of ideas between these two great countries of the East and the West. Indian publishers and Indian publicists would do well to send them their publications for notice and study.

THE END